RUMBA UNDER FIRE

D1563347

RUMBA

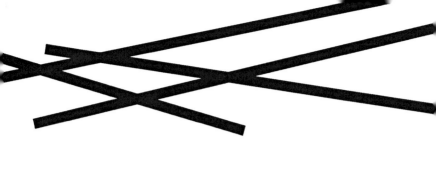

UNDER FIRE

THE ARTS OF SURVIVAL
FROM WEST POINT TO DELHI

EDITED BY IRINA DUMITRESCU

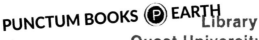

PUNCTUM BOOKS Ⓟ EARTH

RUMBA UNDER FIRE:
THE ARTS OF SURVIVAL FROM WEST POINT TO DELHI
© 2016 Irina Dumitrescu

First published in 2016 by
punctum books
Printed on Earth
http://punctumbooks.com

punctum books is an independent, open-access publisher
dedicated to radically creative modes of intellectual inquiry
and writing across a whimsical para-humanties assemblage.
We solicit and pimp quixotic, sagely mad engagements with
textual thought-bodies. We provide shelters for intellectual
vagabonds.

ISBN-13: 978-0692655832
ISBN-10: 0692655832

Cover and book design: Chris Piuma.
Cover photo: Private Walter Koch of Ohio of the Sixth United
States Army takes a break during torrential rain in northern
New Guinea in 1944. Photo used with permission of the Aus-
tralian War Memorial.

Before you start to read this book,
take this moment to think about making a donation
to punctum books, an independent non-profit press,

@ http://punctumbooks.com/about/

If you're reading the e-book, click on the image below
to go directly to our donations site.
Any amount, no matter the size, is appreciated
and will help us to keep our ship of fools afloat.
Contributions from dedicated readers will also help us
to keep our commons open and to cultivate new work
that can't find a welcoming port elsewhere.

Our adventure is not possible without your support.
Vive la open-access!

Fig. 1. Hieronymus Bosch,
Ship of Fools (detail; 1490-1500).

TABLE OF CONTENTS

for Mircea Trifu
who fought with a rapier wit

INTRODUCTION

Irina Dumitrescu

> Death could drop from the dark
> As easily as song—
> But song only dropped,
> Like a blind man's dreams on the sand
> By dangerous tides
> —Isaac Rosenberg, "Returning, We Hear the Larks"

It is popular these days to bemoan the "crisis in the humanities," or even triumphantly to declare their death.[1] Enrollments in liberal arts majors have fallen dramatically, students having realized that studying art history or philosophy will consign them to a lifetime of flipping burgers and pouring coffee.[2] The humanities have lost their way: in abandoning the

[1]   Tamar Lewin, "As Interest Fades in the Humanities, Colleges Worry," *New York Times*, October 31, 2013, http://www.nytimes.com/2013/10/31/education/as-interest-fades-in-the-humanities-colleges-worry.html; Ella Delany, "Humanities Studies Under Strain Around the Globe," *New York Times*, December 2, 2013, http://www.nytimes.com/2013/12/02/us/humanities-studies-under-strain-around-the-globe.html.

[2]   Jennifer Levitz and Douglas Belkin, "Humanities Fall From Favor," *Wall Street Journal*, June 6, 2013, http://www.wsj.com/news/articles/SB10001424127887324069104578527642373232184.

tried-and-true classics of the Western canon, they have also abandoned any claim to authority, tradition, or lasting and objective values.[3] The humanities have lost their edge: by failing to reflect the experiences of increasingly diverse student bodies, they have become at best irrelevant, at worst oppressive.[4] The humanities take place in the wrong media: print is outmoded, and the failure of scholars to adopt the new modes of thought and communication offered by the digital age will leave them behind. But the Internet is rendering universities obsolete anyway, as online courses offer a more flexible and democratic educational format. Besides which, nobody reads long books anymore. The post-digital world simply does not have the attention span for traditional humanistic work.

   It has, naturally, become just as popular to argue against any crisis in the humanities. Enrollments are not really falling—rather, more students are studying more subjects, thus rendering the humanities less dominant in universities.[5] The perceived "crisis in the humanities" is nothing new, having been around since the 1970s, or the 1930s, or the 1620s, depending on your perspective.[6] Employers still value the

---

3   Diana E. Sheets, "The Crisis in the Humanities: Why Today's Educational and Cultural Experts Can't and Won't Resolve the Failings of the Liberal Arts," *Huffington Post*, July 15, 2013, http://www.huffingtonpost.com/dr-diana-e-sheets/the-crisis-in-the-humanit_b_3588171.html.

4   Chad Orzel, "This Is Not What I Want As a Defense of 'The Humanities,'" *ScienceBlogs*, February 27, 2015, http://scienceblogs.com/principles/2015/02/27/this-is-not-what-i-want-as-a-defense-of-the-humanities/.

5   David Silbey, "A Crisis in the Humanities?," *Chronicle of Higher Education*, June 10, 2013, http://chronicle.com/blognetwork/edgeofthewest/2013/06/10/the-humanities-crisis/.

6   Gideon Rosen, "Notes on a Crisis," *Princeton Alumni Weekly*, July 9, 2014, http://paw.princeton.edu/issues/2014/07/09/pages/0635/index.xml; Blaine Greteman, "It's the End of the Humanities as We Know It: And I Feel Fine," *New Republic*, June 13, 2014, http://www.newrepublic.com/article/118139/crisis-humanities-has-long-history; Alan Ryan, "Humanities Crisis? Which Humanities Crisis?," *Times Higher Education*, August 1, 2013, https://www.timeshighereducation.co.uk/comment/opinion/humanities-crisis-which-humanities-crisis/2006072.article; Heidi Tworek, "The Real Reason the

critical thinking and communication skills honed by the liberal arts. Digital humanists have changed the way scholarship is done and disseminated, making it fairer, more accessible, and intellectually innovative.[7] If there is a crisis in the
humanities, it is wholly the result of neoliberal austerity policies that promote their anti-intellectual agenda by defunding
higher education.[8]

What both of these positions have in common is an
unquestioned belief in two basic propositions: first, that
"crisis" is a state of exception for the humanities, and second, that the definition of "crisis" is a weakening or failure
of the university. This book takes a radically different starting
point, suggesting we think differently about what it means
for the humanities to be "in crisis." To begin with, the liberal
arts have a history beyond the university, whether that is in
other institutions (schools, churches, courts, monasteries)
or in the private sphere. We also need to consider a broader
variety of crises: while decreasing liberal arts majors and the
adjunctification of the university are deeply threatening to
humanistic study, so are war, incarceration, censorship, exile,
and oppression. Intellectuals have been at the mercy of direct
persecution or general political turmoil at least since Socrates
was executed in 399 BC for his impiety, considered a corrup-
tion of the young men of Athens.[9]

Humanities Are 'in Crisis'," *The Atlantic*, December 18, 2013,
http://www.theatlantic.com/education/archive/2013/12/the-real-
reason-the-humanities-are-in-crisis/282441/.

7   Carl Straumsheim, "Digital Humanities Bubble," *Inside Higher Ed*,
        May 8, 2014, https://www.insidehighered.com/news/2014/05/08/
        digital-humanities-wont-save-humanities-digital-humanists-say.

8   Andrew Hartman, "How Austerity Killed the Humanities," *In These
        Times*, May 19, 2015, http://inthesetimes.com/article/17962/how-
        austerity-killed-the-humanities. For another perspective, see Gary
        Gutting, "The Real Humanities Crisis," *New York Times*, November 30,
        2013, http://opinionator.blogs.nytimes.com/2013/11/30/the-real-
        humanities-crisis/.

9   Debra Nails, "The Trial and Death of Socrates," in *A Companion
        to Socrates*, ed. Sara Ahbel-Rappe and Rachana Kamtekar (Malden,
        MA and Oxford: Blackwell Publishing, 2006): 5–20, at 5.

Nor is the relationship of crisis to the work of the mind a straightforward one. The liberal arts—and more broadly, the arts—are at the mercy of political turmoil, economic collapse, and religious persecution, but they also respond to these calamities. If they survive, scholars and artists can continue their work *within* crisis, perhaps even *because* of crisis. Political trouble can be a boon for intellectual and artistic creation in those cases where rulers or governments attempt to gain prestige through patronage. To take one example, it has been argued that literary and scientific production in medieval Spain, or Al-Andalus, reached its peak not during the "golden age" under a unified Umayyad caliphate, but during the subsequent, politically unstable period of the Taifas, petty kingdoms whose rulers competed with each other by funding poets and scholars.[10] To turn to another case, during the Cold War, the CIA used the Congress for Cultural Freedom to fund cultural programs that would improve the image of the United States among writers and intellectuals around the world and serve as a bulwark against communism; Eric Bennett has argued that among the beneficiaries of this strategic largesse was the Iowa Writers' Workshop.[11]

In these comparatively happy situations, general political turmoil and the threat of war led to remarkably comfortable working conditions for artists and scholars. The list of intellectuals who continued their work despite great personal danger and physical discomfort is, unfortunately, longer. A variety

10   "A century of political stability provided the economic and cultural framework for a literary golden era during the Taifa period. Ironically, it can be argued that the sudden political disintegration and process of governmental decentralization of that period sparked cultural efflorescence." Peter Heath, "Knowledge," in *The Literature of Al-Andalus*, ed. María Rosa Menocal, Raymond P. Scheindlin, and Michael Sells (Cambridge: Cambridge University Press, 2000): 96–125, at 113–14.

11   Eric Bennett, "How Iowa Flattened Literature," *Chronicle of Higher Education*, February 10, 2014, http://chronicle.com/article/How-Iowa-Flattened-Literature/144531/. Bennett's book, *Workshops of Empire: Stegner, Engle, and American Creative Writing during the Cold War*, is forthcoming from the University of Iowa Press.

of stories can be told here, most of them familiar. There are
the exiles: Ovid, who composed the *Tristia* and the *Epistulae ex
Ponto* while banished to Tomis; Dante, who penned both the
Commedia and his essay *De vulgari eloquentia* while exiled from
Florence;[12] Voltaire, whose expulsion to England resulted in
his *Letters Concerning the English Nation;*[13] Erich Auerbach, who
wrote *Mimesis* while living in Istanbul, having been forced to
leave Germany. Along with him, the entire body of German-
language *Exilliteratur* that resulted from the oppression of
dissident or Jewish writers in Nazi Germany and occupied
territories.[14] Then there are the prisoners: Saint Perpetua, a
Christian martyr who seems to have written an account of
her captivity;[15] Boethius, whose masterwork *The Consolation of
Philosophy* was a result of his imprisonment by Theodoric the
Great; the *Travels of Marco Polo* was, according to its prologue,
written by Rustichello da Pisa based on accounts Polo related
to him while both were in a Genovese prison;[16] Miguel de
Cervantes' five-year imprisonment in Algiers and his later
jail term in Seville served as inspiration for two plays and,
if we are to believe him, for *Don Quixote.*[17] The series could
continue through Antonio Gramsci's *Prison Notebooks*, Martin Luther King Jr.'s *Letter from Birmingham Jail*, and through a
host of other creative and intellectual texts either written in

12   Steven Botterill, ed. *Dante. De vulgari eloquentia* (Cambridge: Cam-
      bridge University Press, 1996), xiv.

13   Nicholas Cronk, ed. *The Cambridge Companion to Voltaire* (Cam-
      bridge: Cambridge University Press, 2009), xi.

14   Dirk Wiemann, *Exilliteratur in Großbritannien 1933–1945* (Opladen:
      Westdeutscher Verlag, 1998); Woflgang Elfe, James Hardin, and
      Gunther Holst, eds., *The Fortunes of German Writers in America: Stud-
      ies in Literary Reception* (Columbia, SC: University of South Carolina
      Press, 1992).

15   Vincent Hunink, "Did Perpetua Write Her Prison Account?," *Listy
      filologické* 1–2 (2010), 147–155.

16   Peter Jackson, "Marco Polo and his 'Travels'," *Bulletin of the School
      of Oriental and African Studies* 61.1 (1998): 82–101, at 84.

17   Anthony J. Cascardi, "Introduction," in *The Cambridge Companion to
      Cervantes*, ed. Anthony J. Cascardi (Cambridge: Cambridge Univer-
      sity Press, 2002): 1–10, at 5–6.

prison or reflecting on the experience of incarceration. Finally, we might consider the rich body of works composed during war or as a reaction to it. These would include Xenophon's *Anabasis*, Ernest Hemingway's *A Farewell to Arms*, Erich Maria Remarque's *All Quiet on the Western Front*, George Orwell's *Homage to Catalonia*, Joseph Heller's *Catch-22*, and the lyrics of Siegfried Sassoon and the other poets of World War I.

To catalogue such successes in the face of hardship or tragedy is to risk romanticizing catastrophe. The immediacy of the work before us threatens to blot out the suffering experienced by its author, real to them if not to us. This suffering they might well have preferred to avoid, even if it did eventually result in transcendent work. There is no way to compose the list of books not written, scholarship not done, and ideas left undeveloped because of poverty, oppression, or slaughter. What might have Marc Bloch or Walter Benjamin or Jean Prévost or Irène Némirovsky or Antal Szerb or Bruno Schulz given the world had they evaded Nazi violence and survived World War II?

We might speak, then, of a tension between the productive and destructive aspects of crisis. It is this tension that the essays and poems of this book explore. The questions we ask include: What does it mean to teach, create, study, and rehearse in situations of political crisis? How do people faced with catastrophe tell stories to sustain themselves? What strength do these stories offer, and when do they fail? What remains untellable, incomprehensible? Can art and intellectual work really function as resistance to power? What relationship do scholars, journalists, or even memoirists have to the crises they describe and explain? How do works created in crisis, especially at the extremes of human endurance, fit into our theories of knowledge and creativity?

▨ ▨ ▨

I have spoken of the "arts" and the "liberal arts" together, eliding the differences many people now perceive between these
categories of human endeavour. This is deliberate. There is, of
course, a tendency to think of art as primary, scholarship as
secondary; the wild-eyed figure of the Romantic artist seems
a fundamentally different creature from the bespectacled professor with patches on the elbows of his tweed jacket. But
we treat the two together, and for a number of reasons. The
first, and most central to this book, is that people facing crisis
have used fine arts and liberal arts to similar ends: to survive,
to maintain their humanity and identity, to interpret their
own experience, to pass the time. The second is that the lines
between these activities have been drawn more boldly in the
popular imagination than is warranted.

The liberal arts, or *artes liberales*, were so called because
they provided the general training appropriate to a free man.
Their roots are to be found in classical education, especially
in the Greek ideal of ἐγκύκλιος παιδεία, what one might
call "general culture" or a "well-rounded education."[18] The
Romans adopted and developed the Greek school system, and
by the early Middle Ages there was a set curriculum: students
began with the *trivium*, composed of grammar, logic, and
rhetoric, and continued on to study the *quadrivium*, compris-
ing music, arithmetic, geometry, and astronomy. However,
Roman lists of liberal arts also included other topics. Varro
included medicine and architecture in his encyclopedia on the
liberal arts; Vitruvius, in his book on architecture, included
optics, history, and law as well; Galen, who wrote for doctors, mentioned sculpture and drawing as optional subjects.[19]
Moreover, it is worth pointing out that "grammar" included
the study and composition of poetry, and "rhetoric," especially in the medieval period, was also applied to poetics. The

18   Henri-Irénée Marrou, *A History of Education in Antiquity*, trans.
      George Lamb (New York: Sheed and Ward, 1956), 303.

19   Aubrey Gwynn, *Roman Education from Cicero to Quintilian* (Oxford:
      Clarendon Press, 1926), 84–85.

liberal arts curricula from the ancient period to the Middle Ages combined analysis and creativity, and, for that matter, what we might call humanities, sciences, and professional training.

The liberatory potential of the arts lies in their twinned powers of understanding and creation: being free means both understanding how the world functions and shaping some bit of that world to your ends. One can, in fact, do both at the same time. Lucretius versified natural science in his *On the Nature of Things*, while Boethius explained Neoplatonic philosophy in both prose and verse in his *Consolation of Philosophy*. But there is another, less idealized way that art and scholarship resemble each other. They have often been practiced in the same institutions, their work funded by some of the same sponsors. Monasteries, courts, and universities have all taken their turn supporting both those who explain and interpret, and those who create and perform. The teaching of the arts is also often intertwined—a contemporary school of music will have practitioners and theoreticians, a contemporary department of English might offer both a PhD and an MFA.

Rumba Under Fire traces ways that people have turned to the arts, liberal or fine, for highly personal reasons, reasons often inimical to the workings of power. Anand Taneja considers traditions of local storytelling that run counter to official national histories; Judith Verweijen shows the ways soldiers find their sorrows reflected in song lyrics; Cara De Silva describes the "dream cooking" that allowed starving prisoners and POWs to hold on to their identities; Carla Baricz and I chronicle the efforts of political prisoners to maintain their sanity through writing and teaching; and Denis Ferhatović illuminates the ways the survival of books could signify the survival of a persecuted people. But the stories here are not simply uplifting. There are, after all, limits to the redemptive or even explicatory powers of the arts. Tim Albrecht traces the ways the "periods" of history fail to represent the experiences of individuals caught in the aftermath of war; Greg

Brownderville explores the inability to escape war through art; Sharon Portnoff writes of the exhaustion of art and dreams of silence; and Andrew Crabtree imagines the magical, civilizing potential of books ultimately left unread. Finally, while the arts can counteract powerful ideologies, they often exist in an uncomfortable balance of cooperation and subversion with established structures. William Coker and Susannah Hollister explore the ambivalent experiences of teaching the humanities inside universities dedicated either to neoliberal or to military training, and Prashant Keshavmurthy critiques the failure of defenses of the humanities to take into account postcolonial realities.

◼ ◼ ◼

There is a danger to describing the productive relationship between crisis, creativity, and scholarship. If intellectuals and artists can produce timeless work when imprisoned or exiled, why should they be funded, supported, given well-appointed offices in air-conditioned institutions of higher learning? If the humanities thrive in crisis, shouldn't politicians seek to destroy them even more completely?

The answer to this is twofold. One of the arguments of this book is that there is, indeed, a life of art and culture outside of schools and universities, and beyond official channels of power and patronage. Many people turn instinctively to art and study in moments of emotional and spiritual need, no matter the level of their formal learning. One does not need a university education to find solace in composing a rhyme, remembering a tune, or writing down a recipe. However, a survey of historical examples and of the stories in this book shows that formal education does make a difference to how individuals live in and with crisis. Education offers the prisoner, the exile, the refugee, the soldier, and the camp survivor greater cultural resources to draw on, more refined skills of analysis and interpretation, a treasury of texts, and most important of all, a perspective beyond the present. Yes, the arts and liberal arts can survive on their own, but they are better and stronger when institutions nourish and maintain them. Institutions preserve a repertoire of strategies and skills for dealing with crisis—the ancient term would be *wisdom*—and we are all poorer when this repertoire is attenuated.

The word "crisis" can be used in different ways. Sometimes it describes thousands of people fleeing a civil war in their homeland; sometimes it describes a lack of tenure-track jobs for graduates of doctoral programs. Although both conditions are distressing to the people caught up in them, they are, needless to say, not in any way comparable. Our focus on the latter kind of crisis has led us to neglect the former. It has also led us to overlook the relationship between the two. To wit: although one of the signs often cited for the general decline of civilization is that people go to university to improve their chances of a job rather than to widen their minds, formal education has, in fact, always been largely instrumental and career-oriented. The good old days in which learning was universally cherished for its own sake never existed. Over the ages, students have studied the liberal arts to achieve prominence as lawyers and politicians, to pursue careers in monastery or church, to become teachers and physicians and professors and clerks. The point is that their education gave them more than they sought. Those who later faced deep adversity were better equipped to understand, to reflect, and to endure because of their liberal arts training, whether or not they had ever aimed to acquire these inner resources. And herein lies the relationship between upheaval in institutions of higher learning and serious personal or political catastrophes. The tragedy is not that PhDs will be underemployed or that French departments will fold. The tragedy is not that philosophy majors will become baristas. The tragedy is that young people who either cannot afford university or are forced to study strictly vocational topics will be denied the training of mind and heart that will help them comprehend and survive the greater crises to come. The tragedy is that they may be trapped in the inexorable now.

The contributions to this volume, both poetic and essayistic, have taught me that there is a special relationship between crisis, time, and the arts. Crises name and give shape to time—one does "time" in prison or lives through wartime. Crises mark the points where eras flow into each other—historical periods are defined as post-war or pre-war. Time in crisis is paradoxical: during a catastrophe everything moves quickly, too fast to manage, but disastrous events also make people profoundly aware of the slow-moving, glacier-like movements of history. Crisis often creates a space apart from the regular flow of time, one in which individuals can practice art and scholarship, as when a group of women and men retire to a villa outside Florence to tell stories and sit out the Black Death. Practicing the arts and humanities during crisis means being able to live "out of time"—with a perspective beyond the mere present. Indeed, crises require this understanding of the connections between present and deep past and future, this turn to the *longue durée*. Sometimes art and scholarship done in crisis necessarily emphasize the big picture, because detailed work is not possible; one thinks of Auerbach in Istanbul, lacking a proper research library and thus focusing mainly on primary literature. Crises require us to keep time, and the arts teach us how to do it.

The essays and poems in this book do not propose clear-cut solutions, but do tell stories—analytical, emotional, historical, personal—about arts and humanities in times of crisis. They may be used to comfort or trouble, to reflect upon or fight with.

TRIPTYCH (THE LIBRARY)

Andrew Crabtree

Looking up I thought I saw
A spaceship out of an old book,
A hail of brilliant yellow lights like
Some pale wizard's holdfast: graceful
Constellation of a thousand stones
Enchanted in the semblance of a swan.

Looking back, I knew it was
A bulwark of poured concrete,
Arrow-slits and murder holes
For windows — narrow venues
Warding off barbarian advance.

I didn't guess that inside slept
A labyrinth of crayon-coloured metal,
Pages, brown and warm and crisp with age,
Bound in blue and shelved and seldom held,
Halls that echoed with the hush of hoarded words,
A treasury of dormant thoughts and study-nooks,
And children dreaming of the streets below.

WHAT BOOK WOULD YOU NEVER BURN (FOR FUEL)?

Denis Ferhatović

Cityscapes of Resilience and Beauty

I was in Sarajevo for the first time in the summer of 2003. I visited it again in 2007, and then again, in 2012. Sarajevo is a fabled place with real wounds. You may have a number of associations with the place: the fateful shot that started World War I; the 1984 Winter Olympics; the flowering of music and film in the eighties; the horrible 1425-day-long siege; the annual film festival attended by Brangelina; the serious problem with packs of stray dogs; ćevapi and pita and a variety of Ottoman and Austro-Hungarian sweets that you can buy at the Sweet Corner. As you walk the streets, admiring the fashions of youthful and middle-aged passers-by or dreaming of a freshly baked roll of pumpkin börek, your gaze may float downward where you can see a hole in the ground left by a grenade. These declivities are filled up now, sometimes with red paint, which means that someone was hit and killed on that spot. When they are marked with red paint, people call them "Sarajevo Roses." A horrible beauty permeates these words, as does a hope for renewal, for resurrection. Sarajevo is an example *par excellence* of elegant resilience or resilient elegance. It always reminds you of vulnerability and instability, of life's preciousness and aesthetic possession. "You know

3

Sarajevo has something strange" a sticker on an electric post that you run into proclaims in English. Foreign backpackers you run into in hostels, beer halls, and parks tend to agree: they have seen Vienna and Budapest, Belgrade and Zagreb, but Sarajevo has this energy, man. Where else could you still see—in a row—a half-destroyed building with cracked walls and open wiring; an almost intact building gray from years and socialist realism; and a restored building for which a jolly Scandinavian nation had given hard cash and chosen soft colors such as pink and turquoise. Wherever I look, I see proliferating reminders of ruin and promises of renascence. Wherever I look, along the main street, in the area demarcated as the flea market, or near small bridges over the miniature Miljacka, I see used-book vendors.

Used books have a particular meaning in the city with the terrible siege in its recent past. To keep warm in the harsh winters of the nineties, as well as to cook meals from their dwindling stocks or from hardly edible humanitarian aid, Sarajevans burned their private libraries in addition to anything they could lay their hands on. Need fuels imagination: hardwood floors, furniture, neighborhood trees chopped into wood, and old shoes burned. Of course, many of these used books now for sale in the open air of the Bosnian capital came from elsewhere, but some of them, I believe, are real survivors. They must have withstood the long siege and come through to the other side. They hold stories inside their pages in more than one sense, some so painful that you wish you could forget them. Some must hold inscriptions by those no longer here, dead in war. Some must have contributed comfort by candlelight to someone as the enemy from the surrounding hills pounded the city. They, too, like much in Sarajevo, are a living witness, contributing to the palpable, irresistible magnetism of the city. They do not call out to you from their piles to buy them. If you are lucky, you will get an uninterested salesperson who will be cracking hilarious—and untranslatable—jokes with a friend while you are browsing. More likely you will receive Eastern European customer service. The salesperson will act insulted if you ask too many questions. "Do you want the book or not?" These books do not need to be wanted. They seem to know they can carry us over into the future.

No Kindle™, Just Kindling

Several years back, an online literary journal that featured work by young writers from the region asked the authors, among other questions, frivolous and serious, "What book would you never burn (for fuel)?" I do not remember how they responded. A considerable portion of the journal is gone now, and I cannot find those answers anywhere. (E-mailing its editor in July of 2010 did not help.) We often forget that new digital forms are not eternal, that web pages vanish or are taken down, that technologies becomes obsolete with such speed that today I would be hard pressed to find a machine that can read a floppy disk from my college years. Could it be that in the future enemy hackers will erase online repositories of text with several clicks, and that in the dark, under siege, we will be able only to obtain whatever heat a MacBook on fire can provide? I looked through some forums in the local language, and indeed, some Bosnians with amusing monikers had pondered the same resonant question. I made a partial list of answers: Ray Bradbury's *Fahrenheit 451*, Rumi's *Masnavi*, Goethe's *Faust*. The books that *would* go into the blazing furnace include Paolo Coelho's *The Alchemist* (but, as someone quips, it would not provide much heat, being so slender), Meša Selimović's novel *The Fortress*, and the textbook *Geological Engineering*, along with a number of thick communist books with the exciting, now terribly ironic titles like

The Labor Union in Action and *The Guardians of Yugoslavia*.[1] This is literary criticism at its most immediate.

The usefulness of large ideologically suffused tomes for wartime kindling turns out to be a trope. Dubravka Ugrešić touches on the topic at hand in an essay from her 1994 collection, *The Culture of Lies*, which contains many sharp observations about war, nationalism, and memory in former Yugoslavia. In "The Tale of the Grenade Shell and the Book" (translated by Celia Hawkesworth as "The Tale of the Bomb and the Book"), she mentions a Sarajevan acquaintance, a survivor of one year of the siege, who tells her that communism's disappearance from Sarajevo was especially warm. The author is puzzled before she receives an explanation:

> It turned out that during the winter the inhabitants of Sarajevo had warmed themselves with their own collection of books. The people who did best were those who had kept among their books the works of the communist leaders. When books like that are tied tightly with wire, they burn slowly, with no rush, like the best coal. At first the people of Sarajevo warmed themselves with "communist" briquettes, and finally it was Shakespeare's turn. Radovan Karadžić—the supervisor of work on the project of the destruction of Sarajevo—had himself written a little volume of verse, of inferior calorific value, unfortunately.[2]

The exiled Croatian writer's summary of the situation is accurate and memorable. A curious individual could extrapolate

---

1   "Koju knjigu nikad ne bi naložili," accessed September 13, 2014, http://forum.djesi.ba/showthread.php?t=4163. *Forum Djesi.ba.* The thread was initiated by "Istaknuti Član" on 30 November 2003 (*Fahrenheit 461, The Alchemist*). The responses are by "Divlja Orhideja" (*Masnawi, The Fortress, Geological Engineering*), "Luna" (*The Labor Union in Action*), "Žešći Anonimac" (*The Guardians of Yugoslavia*), and "Lucky" (*Faust*). The site is currently down (April 26, 2015).

2   Dubravka Ugrešić, *The Culture of Lies*, trans. Celia Hawkesworth (University Park, PA: Pennsylvania State University Press, 1998), 152.

a person's education, taste, and attachments by reading a list of books in the order in which he or she sacrificed them, from communists at the beginning to Shakespeare at the end. Ugrešić's mention of Karadžić, a war criminal currently in the Hague, introduces a deep, bitter note of irony to our discussion. A poet was ordering the shelling of the city that nurtured him; a man who wrote books directly overlooked the destruction of Sarajevan libraries, such as the Oriental Institute and the National Library (the latter reopened only in 2014), and indirectly forced people to burn their own personal collections. While his own "little volume of verse" could in theory fuel the flames that warm, not destroy, the book was too slim to be any good. Dark humor out of the way, Ugrešić enters the terrain of melancholy:

> An object that has been destroyed, like a life, is not replaceable; it disappears for ever. Devastation is never solely material, it has multiple aspects, multiple meanings, but it is always final. We shall build new libraries, publish new books, announce the optimists, accustomed to a regular rhythm of destruction and rebuilding. But the idea of reconstruction contains the notion of future destruction.[3]

If the destruction is inevitable and final, what can we do in face of it? I would be inclined to qualify Ugrešić's pessimistic statement, because she is, after all, a polemical essayist. She herself says that she does not necessarily believe everything she writes in her essay. Is this essay of mine guilty of reckless optimisms? It is easy for me and her to talk about using books as kindling since we have never needed to do that. Turning from the anonymous young people on the Internet who are contemplating what they would and what they would not burn, and from Ugrešić's secondhand account, I wanted to find a firsthand account of the situation by a book lover under siege in Sarajevo.

---

3   Ugrešić, *The Culture of Lies*, 153.

Sarajevo Shahrazads

The Internet provided. I found a two-page-long text. It was a
brief essay by Sulejman Grozdanić titled "A Book, Ashes..."
from a collection by various hands called *A Hundred and One
Nights: Stories from Sarajevo*, published in 1993, after that many
nights of siege. The allusion to *The Thousand and One Nights* is
no coincidence. To describe survival in the wartime Sarajevo,
more than one person has reached for Shahrazad's brave, pro-
tracted storytelling, which saved her life and those of many
other young women from the tyrant Shahriyar who, stung
by his wife's adultery, wished to marry one every night and
execute her the following morning. Esad Duraković spent the
siege translating the entirety of *The Thousand and One Nights*
from Arabic into Bosnian, and in his preface draws a parallel
between his creative endeavor and Shahrazad's.[4] Duraković's
translation, in four big volumes, more than two thousand
pages in total, was among the books I took to college with me
in 1999; I had had it shipped from Sarajevo to Roanoke, VA,
and its sheer monumentality, all those words in my mother
tongue, assured me on my journey. Now that I think of it,
enormous, almost monumental books that were published
immediately after the war in Sarajevo, such as Duraković's
Nights or a series of anthologies of Bosniak (Bosnian-Muslim)
literature by Alef Publishing, did not only bespeak survival
of an ethnic group, often with the nationalist resonances of
a people who had lived through a genocide, but also survival

---

4   Esad Duraković, trans., *Hiljadu i jedna noć* (Sarajevo: Ljiljan, 1999).
       "[Our situation] was almost identical to Shahrazad's fantastical
       world, a competition between creation and death, creativity and
       cruel barbarism and cold, as well as the fear that our children
       will truly starve to death. That fantastical inversion still lives, but
       without doubt, having gone through almost unreally cruel Bosniak
       reality, resembling the darkest realms of Shahrazad's world, we
       are, in spite of everything, approaching our 'thousand and first
       night,' at the end of which fidelity and freedom burst with light,
       and at the conclusion of which Shahriyar's deadly sword returns
       irrevocably to its sheath" vol. 1, 42; the translation is mine.

of a book as a physical object. To get back to Grozdanić, these side comments do not seem as meandering when we realize that he was an Arabist and translator of Nagib Mahfouz, a writer also indebted to the *Nights*.

Grozdanić begins the story with a dedication to Danilo Kiš, a polyglot, bibliophile, world-famous Serbian-Jewish writer who self-consciously explored the writer's role in the time of twentieth-century totalitarianisms, Nazi and Stalinist. The title itself "A Book, Ashes..." is an explicit allusion to Kiš's semi-autobiographical work *Garden, Ashes*. I should not neglect to note that the writer of *Garden, Ashes* died in self-imposed exile in Paris in 1989, shortly before the murderous nationalisms ran unchecked in former Yugoslavia. Though Kiš did not live to see the siege of Sarajevo, his writings became more and more pressingly important in the nineties. "A Book, Ashes..." begins thus:

> I am a professor. My life depends on words. Spoken and written. On books. Perhaps this is how I survived the Sarajevo winter of 1992/93, that war-ravaged year. I used books as fuel, I burned the written word. Their flame warmed me, but it scorched me, too. Their pyre was also my pyre. As if I myself incinerated literary treasures. Of the Oriental Institute and the precious holdings of the National Library. Am I an accomplice of all the book-burning barbarians, from the Mongols sacking Baghdad, through the Inquision and German fascism in Europe, to those Balkan barbarians right here, on the hills surrounding Sarajevo?[5]

The fragments in that first paragraph slowly grow into a sentence, a long question with a chain of book-burners. The author then describes his method of selecting literary

5   Sulejman Grozdanić, "Knjiga, pepeo," *Književna Svaštarica* (blog), April 4, 2007, http://knjizevnasvastarica.blogger.ba/ arhiva/2007/04. All the subsequent quotations of Grozdanić come from this source. The translation is mine.

kindling. He compares the process to a religious ritual, to making an offering to a demonic force. Grozdanić says he does not burn books in order to appease the devil, but to survive and in surviving stand up to the diabolical power. He reports that he re-read many materials, including newspapers and journals, before setting them aside. He had three steps of selection before finally, when winter came, committing the texts to flames. "As far as quantity, I read an entire library of a university professor." War does not just force us into more urgent acts of literary criticism: it pushes us to pare down our library to the bare essentials, to read carefully, to see what is indispensable to have in hand and on the shelf, and what we can save only in our minds. We need to have all the evidence to make that dreadful decision. Still, the act does not come easy. "I need one of the books, the second one is important to me, the third dear to me, the fourth might come in handy to someone else, the fifth looks beautiful, the sixth..." Suddenly, we are faced with a multiplicity of attachments to these objects, at the moment when we might lose them forever. Grozdanić ends his brief essay by remarking that he wished to keep the ashes and either scatter them to the winds "so that the spirit of the book might float calmly to some distant valley of peace," or put them in urns with labels containing "the name of the author, title, publication date, and the date and place of burning: Sarajevo, winter 1992/93." In that final image, the author imagines the act of using books for fuel as cremation: they are put to rest and memorialized like people. Grozdanić died one year after the war ended.

Postscript #1

When I wrote the first version of this essay, I was newly teaching at Bilkent University in Ankara, Turkey. It was four years ago. A colleague of mine there, the most American person

I know (and ironically, I had had to come to Turkey to meet him; I do not know any very American people in America), wished to know what I was working on at the moment. When I explained the topic to him, he stopped, thought for a second, and then asked me the question. I answered that there was no book I would never burn. Was I recklessly putting my hope in the Internet or did I know that books can survive no matter what? Or maybe it was the experience of war—rather mild and limited in comparison to what many others have experienced, of course—that enabled me to practice Elizabeth Bishop's "One Art" so well. "The art of losing," I repeat to myself, "isn't hard to master." I brought only two books with me to Ankara, on account of their amenability to long airplane trips, Gamal al-Ghitani's book *Thousand Years of Cairo* in the Serbian translation of Dragana Đorđević and Marija Obrenović, and Tolstoy's *War and Peace* in the Pevear/Volokhonsky translation. (The latter, I am afraid, is still three-quarters unfinished. I got stuck in the part about the Freemasons.) I thought I would easily give up these books if I had to. All my college and graduate-school books were stored in the basement of my parents' house in Roanoke, VA. They stayed there until I moved back to the States in the late summer of 2012. For two years my parents would take their friends down to the basement, Americans and Bosnians alike, to show them my books. The guests invariably said that they had not seen that many books in one space before. My mother would go there alone, as well, to look at my collection whenever she felt she missed me more than usual.

My colleague at Bilkent revealed that he had formed attachments to particular copies of particular works. There was, he told me, one copy of *King Lear* that contains his marginalia from high school. "Is it humbling because you have changed so much, or because you have not changed at all?" I inquired. "Both," he admitted. The conference-paper version of this essay that I delivered over Skype to a panel and an audience in Austin, TX, that November day of 2010, concluded this way:

If I had such an artifact, a copy of Shakespearean play from high school with my critical juvenilia, I would throw it into fire with no regrets. Hell, I would burn it even if I did not live in a besieged city with a heating shortage. I would burn it right now in front of you. Okay, maybe I would not. Thank you.

What can I say? I was young, not yet thirty. I was trying to be provocative.

Postscript #2

Before I left Turkey, I sent off two large packages of books to my new institutional address in New London, CT. There were books in six languages in that shipment, which I had purchased in Ankara, Istanbul, Skopje, Paris, Berlin, Thessaloniki, and Podgorica. They arrived two months later in two torn, ungainly cardboard boxes, not the ones I had originally paid for them to be sent them in. Someone must have opened the boxes, taken out the books, bent and dirtied some of them, only bent others, and repackaged them. In the packages as they stood were things that did not belong to me: two pairs of worn-out women's shoes, a Turkish-German phrasebook, and a bundle of receipts from Ethiopian Mail. The only part of the original packaging that remained was my address label. Whoever handled my precious cargo did not find it precious. Almost everything was roughed up, but, luckily, no item was missing. What I experienced that time was not bad in comparison with Sarajevans who had to go through and then burn their books during the cold winters of the siege in addition to other hardships like crossing the streets in sniper fire and waiting in lines for water. It still felt like a violation. I had chosen those books carefully on two continents, touched them, smelled them, read them on planes, in metro trains, on park benches, in libraries, at friends' apartments, in my office, in my bed. Some were gifts and bear inscriptions by those I love; others had in them bus or plane ticket stubs as marks. They are eloquent witness to the story of two years of my life. I cannot imagine what went on through the mind of the official or officials who abused two big boxes of books. I suppose no empathy flashed across their bureaucratic hearts. Were they acting as literary critics, poring over the titles? How much could they understand? Did they have associations with any of them? Was there no work that tempted them?

In 2013, another, much smaller package from Ankara to New London, sent to me by my partner, underwent similar mishandling. This time, out of two books (and several post-cards and hand-written letters and souvenir refrigerator magnets) only one book arrived. Did some moustachioed, miserable middle-aged man take out Perihan Mağden's novel *Whom Were We Running From, Mother?*, look at it, and keep it, letting only the Turkish translation of Catherine Pinguet's historical account of dogs in Istanbul reach Connecticut? There is no way to know. What is certain is that this nameless book-thief, like his book-bending and dirtying pal(s), made me realize, once again, my attachment to my personal library. A book is a strange extension of ourselves, not merely its content but everything that happened to us surrounding it: when we bought or received it, when we read it, when we put it back on the shelf, when we lent it to someone, when we went to retrieve it from the person to whom we lent it. An attack on these possessions is an attack on our personal memory. The savage irony of books as fuel in Sarajevo became apparent to me as I was contemplating my own comparatively much less traumatizing situation: during war the enemy tries to destroy everything you hold dear, and then there is another horrible twist, in which they force you to participate in erasing traces of yourself, in order to survive.

POEMS IN PRISON
THE SURVIVAL STRATEGIES OF ROMANIAN POLITICAL PRISONERS

Irina Dumitrescu

In the region of Maramureș in northern Romania, close to the River Prut and the Ukrainian border, two monuments express the ways in which human beings struggle to hold on to beauty, art, and humour in the face of annihilation. The first of these is Cimitirul Vesel, the cheerful cemetery, where in 1935 the sculptor Stan Ioan Pătraș began to etch folksy poems into the town's tombstones. The result is the brightest graveyard imaginable, in which each oaken memorial includes a carving or two of the deceased in their natural element—at the plow or with a horse for the older graves, or sitting at a desk for the more modern ones — along with a rustic verse description of the individual's life and death, written in the first person. The whole is painted in vivid Crayola blue, red, yellow, and green. What emerges from this forest of colorful wooden steles is a chorus of voices, the departed citizenry of Săpânța claiming a right to their brief stories on this earth.

A twenty-minute drive away, in the same town where Elie Wiesel was born, the Memorial Museum of Sighetu Marmației tells a similar story, but in a much more sombre medium. Established in the notorious Sighet Penitentiary, the museum is dedicated to the memory of the victims of communism, including the prisoners who were there from 1948 to 1955 as part of a communist project to exterminate the cultural, political, and religious elites of Romania. Ironically, the first political prisoners in Sighet were not elites but a group of students, aged fifteen to twenty-four, held at the prison while awaiting sentencing for their supposed crimes. Two years later, in 1950, the prison began to be used for the slow killing of the Romanian political and intellectual class, including four former prime ministers of the country, along with a large number of priests and bishops from the Catholic Church and from the Romanian Church United with Rome.

I visited the Memorial Museum in 2006, and now, ten years later, the contents of two rooms are still vividly present in my memory. On the second floor, in room 51, the walls are covered with text—poetry composed in prison. Arranged in a nameless collage, the lines of verse depict the silent cacophony of prisoners' voices throughout the years. The inscription explains that prisoners taught each other Morse code and used it to transmit poetry from cell to cell. In fact, prisoners used a variety of tapping codes for communication, including an arduous alphabet code in which one tap stood for A, two for B, and so on, along with shortened codes of their own devising. The importance of these tapping alphabets only became clear to me later, as I read the memoirs of people condemned to solitary confinement. The tapping, which could be done without the guards' notice, provided the essential human contact solitary prisoners needed to hold on to their sanity.

Two doors down, room 53 is dedicated to the daily life of prisoners, and filled with the improvised tools and objects they made with stolen or hidden materials. I remember two things in particular: the first was a notebook filled with small, neat writing. Romanian officers imprisoned in Siberia had made ink from blackberries and used it to write down the French poems they could remember from school. The result was an improvised anthology, open the day I saw it to a poem by Verlaine. The second object looked, from a few feet away, like a plain piece of cloth. Only when I stepped closer did I see the writing. A prisoner with access to the infirmary had stolen scraps of gauze and, by pulling out a few threads, was able to sew near-invisible letters on the white cloth. In contrast to the lively paradox of the cheerful cemetery at Săpânța, where brightly-coloured letters carved in wood spoke for people who were already dead, here the living whispered in white threads.

The hidden poetry at Sighetu Marmatiei speaks not only to individual struggles to survive in the nightmare of the Romanian Gulag, but also to a form of cultural resistance that, in various, often isolated, forms, characterizes an important facet of the Romanian people's response to the destruction of their culture by their own dictator-state. The critic and translator Adam Sorkin has described how Romanian poets active during Ceaușescu's rule encoded messages critical of the government into their lyrics. In their dexterous attempts to evade the censor, so goes a story beloved by many Romanians, writers protected their lives by pushing their craft to ever-greater levels of allusive sophistication. Sorkin describes this favorite myth of Romanian literature as a "fortunate fall," in which "censorship led poetry to a complicated mixture of indirection, deviousness, obscurity, hermeticism, and sinewy, between-the-lines toughness."[1] I, like a number of Romanians who criticize this myth, am wary of romanticizing oppression too much, of idealizing a cold, dank prison cell because it was a space where language and literature really mattered.[2]

1   Adam J. Sorkin, "The Paradox of the Fortunate Fall: Censorship and Poetry in Communist Romania," *Literary Review* 45 (2002): 886–910, at 889.

2   The validity of "resistance through culture" is now debated in Romania. The Romanian television network TVR+ has produced a series called "Rezistența prin cultură," celebrating forms of cultural resistance such as the public singing of Christmas carols and contraband book circulation. The counterargument is that "resistance through culture" was an avoidance of real, political resistance, and by extension even a mode of collaboration. See, for example: George Damian, "Comunismul și rezistența la români," *Timpul*, February 25, 2011, http://www.timpul.md/articol/(comentai)-comunismul-si-rezistenta-la-romani-20927.html.

Still, it is a dark truth that totalitarian governments are profoundly conscious of the importance of the arts and humanities. The communist government of Romania demonstrated this first by destroying artists and intellectuals in a cultural genocide, and later by manipulating them through censorship, the threat of death or hard labour, and the lure of social and financial advantages. Both strategies met with resistance that at once hid itself, like the white threads on white gauze I saw in the Sighet Prison, and that affirmed the importance of recollection, creation, and meditation in moments of crisis.

Sighet was only one part of the broader undertaking the historian Dennis Deletant refers to as "the Romanian Gulag."[3] This consisted of imprisoning or sending to work camps anyone the illegitimate communist government considered a possible threat. Potential enemies of the revolution ranged from sixteen-year-olds to priests in their eighties, from former members of the fascist, nationalistic, anti-Semitic Legionary Movement to out-of-favour members of the communist party, and included a variety of religions and ethnicities: Greek Orthodox Christians and Jews joined Catholics in prisons, as did Yugoslavs, Saxon Germans, and the occasional Englishman or woman accused of espionage.[4] The level of political engagement of prisoners also ranged widely, but the government was not overly concerned with legal establishment of guilt. It cast a wide net, and trials, when held at all, followed Kafkaesque laws of the absurd, as when a man named Iţic Goldenberg wound up condemned as a "legionary courier."[5] The government held trials for prisoners known to be long dead, and, to balance the score, told concerned families that their still-living relatives had perished in prison.

3   Dennis Deletant, *Communist Terror in Romania: Gheorghiu-Dej and the Police State, 1948–1965* (New York: St. Martin's Press, 1999), 195–224.

4   Deletant, *Communist Terror in Romania*, 213.

5   Dan M. Brătianu, *Martor dintr-o ţară încătuşată* (Bucharest: Fundaţia Academia Civică, 1996), 68–69.

The communist government used the threat of imprisonment to inculcate widespread terror and self-policing, in which goal it succeeded, but it also became notable for its pointed attack on the country's cultural institutions and personalities. The persecutions reflect the Party's attempt to gain an ideological foothold in a country that before World War II had had the smallest communist presence, proportionally, in Eastern Europe. Katherine Vedery notes some of the Party's early moves: the abolition of the Romanian Academy and its replacement with a communist version; the expulsion of so-called bourgeois professors from their university posts; the replacement of the nation's history institutes with a single one, and of its historical journals with a single, controlled publication; the rewriting of Romanian history textbooks; and even the slavicization of Romanian orthography.[6] More tragically, individuals were persecuted: philosophers, jurists, theologians, economists, and artists found their way into political prisons or work camps. The most disturbing example of this process, the notorious Pitești experiment, encapsulates how imprisonment was not simply a way to deal with perceived political threats, but also an exercise in the destruction and "re-education" of humanists. The prisoners at Pitești were primarily university students, and they were subjected to a program of torture, physical, emotional, and spiritual degradation calculated to destroy their sense of self.[7] The final step of their journey was a demonic farce of the university: the victims were forced to become their friends' torturers and "re-educators" in turn.

Still, some writers of prison memoirs do describe the experience as a university: Stanciu Stroia titles his prison memoir

---

6   Katherine Vedery, *National Ideology Under Socialism: Identity and Cultural Politics in Ceaușescu's Romania* (Berkeley: University of California Press, 1991), 110–11.

7   Deletant, *Communist Terror in Romania*, 199–201. A useful short summary of the experiment is provided by Costin Merișca, *Tragedia Pitești* (Iași: Institutul European, 1997), 57–85.

My Second University, while Petre Pandrea, imprisoned at Aiud, calls the penitentiary "the last university I graduated from, as a vagabond and eternal student."[8] Aware of the cultural implications of their imprisonment—and noting, often, the lack of education of their jailers—the memoirists address the intellectual difficulties of their confinement as well as the physical ones. For they did not only have to contend with extreme cold and hunger, beatings, water boarding, enforced physical positioning (including during sleep), and constant supervision, but they faced intellectual challenges as well. Among these were: communicating with the outside world and with each other; ascertaining who else was imprisoned (those held at Sighet were particularly aware of the need to find out which dignitaries were also imprisoned there, and took special efforts to confirm their investigations); dealing with boredom, especially in extended solitary confinement; and, most of all, maintaining a sense of self in a system where truth and lies had lost all distinction.

The following are a few examples of the range of activities undertaken by prisoners as a response to these challenges. Like Prudentius' martyr Romanus, who kept speaking even after his tongue was cut out, prisoners found ways to speak despite prohibitions on communication, to write without pens or pencils or paper. The most accessible medium was, of course, memory. Thus Madeleine Cancicov, who after ten years of prison learned of her mother's death, worked through her trauma by "writing" her memoir, composed, memorized, and repeated paragraph by paragraph. In French.[9] There were physical media too. Lena Constante describes her attempt to write with "a splinter of wood" and her own blood, and how many times she had to bite between her thumb and forefinger

8   Stanciu Stroia, *My Second University: Memories from Romanian Communist Prisons*, trans. Dan L. Dușleag (New York: iUniverse, 2005). Petre Pandrea, *Reeducarea de la Aiud* (Bucharest: Editura Vremea, 2000), 36.

9   Madeleine Cancicov, *Le cachot des marionnettes: Quinze ans de prison: Roumanie 1949–1964* (Paris: Critérion, 1990).

to release this ink.[10] Petre Pandrea recollects George Manu's teaching methods: a professor of English language and culture, Manu wrote his lessons on string, tying knots for each letter.[11] Oana Orlea, imprisoned at the age of sixteen, had her first English lesson in the Jilava prison, scratching newly-learned words on stolen scraps of soap.[12] Prisoners created variations and adapations of Morse and other knocking codes. Orlea explains how prisoners could communicate without tapping the entire word, leaving the end to be understood contextually.[13] Ion Diaconescu describes the adaptations on Morse used when guards were paying attention: an engineer named Puiu wrecked his chair so that it would squeak when he moved while sitting on it, and used this function to transmit Morse signals. Later, the prisoners cough the code, an arduous process as Diaconescu points out: it took something like 250 coughs for a short message of ten words![14] Tapping, according to Lena Constante, offered a strange sort of immediacy:

> I realized that one's manner of tapping is just as expressive as the timbre of one's voice. As one's handwriting. Sometimes even more so. For it is unaffected by the unconscious censorship of the voice. Or the acquired control of gestures and facial expression.[15]

The most impressive invention of a writing medium, however, is described by Dan Brătianu. He and his fellow prisoners were

10   Lena Constante, *The Silent Escape: Three Thousand Days in Romanian Prisons*, trans. Franklin Philip (Berkeley: University of California Press, 1995), 21.

11   Pandrea, *Reeducarea de la Aiud*, 304.

12   Oana Orlea, *Les années volées: Dans le goulag roumain à 16 ans* (Paris: Éditions du Seuil, 1992), 45.

13   Orlea, *Les années volées*, 138.

14   Ion Diaconescu, *Temnița: destinul generației noastre* (Bucharest: Editura Nemira, 1998), 250–51.

15   Constante, *The Silent Escape*, 235.

supplied with DDT to deal with the lice that were tormenting them. They took small, leftover glass medicine bottles they had in their cells, covered them in spit, rubbed them with soap and sprinkled DDT on top. They could then scratch up to four hundred words on this surface with a sharp object, which they did particularly for foreign language training. Brătianu mentions that, after their release, some of the people who learned English from him in this manner passed the qualification exam for translators.[16]

Training in, and practice of, foreign languages was a favourite pursuit of prisoners. To some extent, this also served as demarcation of class: several memoirists mention using French to communicate secretly with their families as they were being arrested. The noted historian Constantin Giurescu learned Hungarian from another prisoner and taught it to another, and practiced his French, English, and German.[17] Egon Balas describes his time in solitary thus: "I had language sessions, in which I would conduct conversations in English, Russian, French, or German. Many words that I could not remember at first came to me upon repeated trials."[18] Arnold Schwefelberg also spent time recalling foreign languages he had learned, especially Hebrew, to the point where he could think in Hebrew fluently.[19] Prisoners describe the study of foreign languages as a way of exercising the brain. Language pedagogy joined prisoners in a common intellectual pursuit, but, though none of the memoirists I read say this explicitly, I suspect it also served as a reminder of spaces and lands outside of their own country.

---

16   Brătianu, *Martor dintr-o țară încătușată*, 83–84.

17   Constantin C. Giurescu, *Five Years and Two Months in the Sighet Penitentiary (May 7, 1950–July 5, 1955)*, trans. Mihai Farcaș and Stephanie Barton-Farcaș (Boulder, CO: East European Monographs, 1994), 108–9.

18   Egon Balas, *Will to Freedom: A Perilous Journey Through Fascism and Communism* (Syracuse: Syracuse University Press, 2000), 258.

19   Arnold Schwefelberg, *Amintirile unui intelectual evreu din România* (Bucharest: Editura Hasefer, 2000), 201.

Close attention to language is particularly evident in the prisoners' use of poetry, drama, and fiction. Oana Orlea's experience of prison was changed when she was transferred to a cell with older, more cultured women. She was amazed at their interior discipline, and the rigorous program they had devised to structure their time. Mornings were filled with lessons in German, English, and history, and with calisthenics. In the afternoons, they took turns telling stories, whether invented, from films, or recollections of what they had read; they sang or recited poetry; and they talked about recipes. Rarely did they tell personal anecdotes, or anything that might make them sad.[20] Lena Constante began by recollecting lines of French poetry; she scanned, analysed, and learned poetic technique from the snatches of verse she could recall, and then set upon writing her own poetry, in French, of course. Her happiest gift in prison was a book on prosody by Vladimir Mayakovsky. She writes:

> The reason I speak time and again of poetry is that my whole life in prison was infused with it. I had nothing. No paper or ink. The books lasted only a short while. But in this vacuum I had struck a rich vein. Words. The force of words. I had the words and I had the time. A huge amount of time. Enough time not to know what to do with it. Time lost. But lost or not, this time was mine. To allow it to become lost in vain was to lose a part of my life and I wanted to live my life. With this joining of words and time I lived. Survived. I even managed to be happy. Sometimes. I owe Mayakovsky a great debt of gratitude.[21]

In her eight and a half years of solitary, Constante also wrote eight plays, only three of which she wrote down after her release, and all of which succumbed to her "more objective

20 Orlea, *Les années volées*, 95.
21 Constante, *The Silent Escape*, 52.

assessment of my literary abilities."[22] While incarcerated next to an Englishwoman, Constante received English lessons—through taps on the wall, of course—and composed some short poetry in English as well. She would complete her verses by tapping the words she needed rhymes for on the wall, often with bizarre results.[23] Arnold Schwefelberg reports "writing" fifty to sixty lyric poems in prison, which he committed to paper upon release, as well as a play, *The Descendants of Manasse*, a two-act sequel to Moise Ronetti-Roman's *Manasse*.[24] Ioan Ploscaru, who spent what seemed like an endless amount of time in solitary confinement writing poems he dedicated to Christ, remarks that, "when they moved me with other prisoners, I almost regretted the loneliness and the space I inhabited in isolation."[25]

Poetry was meditation. Poetry was occupation. Poetry served as secret code. Ion Diaconescu describes how another prisoner communicated with him when he was in solitary. His neighbour recited the first stanza of a poem by Emil Gârleanu:

Afară ninge liniștit,
În casă arde focul,
Iar noi pe lângă mama stand
De mult uitarăm jocul.

Outside the snow falls softly,
At home the fire burns,
And we, beside our mother,
Had long forgotten play.

Thus Diaconescu, whose cell window was tiny, learned that it was snowing outside. Literature was also food. As Madeleine

---

22   Constante, *The Silent Escape*, 197.

23   Constante, *The Silent Escape*, 223–24.

24   Schwefelberg, *Amintirile unui intelectual evreu din România*, 202.

25   Ioan Ploscaru, *Lanțuri si teroare* (Timișoara: Editura Signata, 1993), 240.

Cancicov puts it, "Sometimes I recount books. The younger girl calls them cakes. The more captivating the books, the higher the cake becomes, it becomes a tiered cake with whipped cream. Dorothy Sayers and Agatha Christie will never know the joy Lord Peter and Poirot gave my companions over the years, allowing them to forget their misery for a few hours."[26]

Gheorghe Andreica, who was the first person to enter Sighet as a political prisoner and was a teenager at the time, describes how the only activity that helped him to deal with the interminable hunger was prayer. Hunger, he writes, diminishes the human personality, making the person like an animal without rationality.[27] Prayer, for him as for many of the memoirists I read, was what fed him, what helped him to remain human. For a medievalist, the prayer imagery is deeply evocative. I have long been fascinated with the way medieval poetry describes *tasting* the Lord's Prayer, and imagines people who do not know it as beasts.[28] Here, in the prison memoirs of Romanians, I found a practical explanation for this concatenation of images in the real effects of hunger. There were other distinctly medieval aspects to Romanian penitentiary life, and not only the ones one might expect. Ion Diaconescu describes how a priest, Father Balica, used Morse code to teach the other prisoners how to calculate the date of Easter in any given year.[29] Computus, in prison.[30]

---

26   Cancicov, *Le cachot des marionnettes*, 213.

27   Gheorghe Andreica, "Cu ghiozdanul la închisoare," in *Memoria închisorii Sighet*, ed. Romulus Rusan (Bucharest: Fundația Academia Civică, 1999): 7–104, at 32.

28   See the poem "Solomon and Saturn I," edited and translated in Daniel Anlezark, ed., *The Old English Dialogues of Solomon and Saturn* (Cambridge: D.S. Brewer, 2009), 60–71.

29   Diaconescu, *Temnița*, 255.

30   "Computus" was a medieval technique for calculating the date of Easter. For more information, see Arno Borst, *The Ordering of Time: From the Ancient Computus to the Modern Computer*, trans. Andrew Winnard (Chicago: University of Chicago Press, 1993).

As I noted earlier, memoirists, often following consciously in the steps of Maxim Gorky, repeatedly refer to the prison as their second, or lifelong, university. Schwefelberg writes:

> the downright febrile intellectual activity of the immense amount of "free" time I had then fixed much of my knowledge in my memory, clarified many ideas, helped me to form a well-articulated system of beliefs. So: a "university" all alone, in jail![31]

For the jailed professors at Sighet, this was not a metaphorical construction. Giurescu's memoir contains a lengthy list of seminars held by various faculty members on history, geography, and literature, filled out by the singing of Romanian songs and Italian canzonette. Some examples of the history lessons: "Foreign travelers in Romanian provinces" (twenty-five lectures), "Surcouf, the French Buccaneer," (one lecture) and "My biography" (twenty lectures). In literature, faculty lectured on *Le Roman de Tristan et Iseut*, "from the modern version by Bedier," a French version of Poe's *Descent into the Maelstrom*, and *Gone with the Wind*.[32] Most touchingly, and in rather Borgesian manner, Giurescu lists the "new scientific works" he planned and formulated, including:

> *The History of Bucharest, Fishing and Fish Hatcheries in Our Past*, a series of articles on History, Geography, Cartography, Archeology, Philology and Bibliography, about 260 articles, [and the] translation of *The History of Romanians* . . . in French, German, English, Italian, Spanish, Greek, Serbian, Bulgarian and Turkish, each translation having new information about the respective people. The titles will be something like *The History of Romanians with emphasis on their*

---

31   Schwefelberg, *Amintirile unui intelectual evreu din România*, 202.

32   Giurescu, *Five Years and Two Months in the Sighet Penitentiary*, 103–07.

relationship with the Greeks or *The History of Romanians with emphasis on their relationship with the Bulgarians.*[33]

Through language and scholarship, through prayer and poems, by teaching and composing, the prisoners of the Romanian Gulag brought the humanities into a space where humanity itself was under attack. A story from Dan Brătian illustrates how literature could be used as inspiration and secret code, a door to a place beyond the power of Party leaders and prison guards. During a search, a guard discovers a sentence written on the cell wall: "He who does not know how to die, does not deserve to live," signed "Seneca." Brătianu continues:

> We were immediately asked which one of us was Seneca. When we responded with total ignorance, the guard said to us, "Don't worry, you pigs, *we'll* find him!"[34]

▣ ▣ ▣

Many of the memoirists I read for this essay used the arts and humanities to maintain their spirit in conditions of extreme duress. Sometimes they also used the arts to affirm their identities as scholars, intellectuals, Christians or Jews. Some were aware that they were considered enemies of the state due to their elite status in pre-communist Romanian society, and they composed in French or quoted Seneca in stubborn defiance of the new, anti-class and by extension anti-intellectual order.

At the same time, there is something surprisingly egalitarian about their methods. Anyone could make up a story or describe a recipe. Anyone could write a poem, in Romanian if

---

33   Giurescu, *Five Years and Two Months in the Sighet Penitentiary*, 108.

34   Brătianu, *Martor dintr-o țară încătușată*, 64–65.

not in French. I learned the myth of the "fortunate fall" from my émigré Romanian parents, knowing that even if I read the books or plays they mentioned, I would never be able to grasp the hidden meanings they had thrilled to. But I was handed another cherished myth as well, that of Romanians as natural, organic poets, rhymes running in his peasant blood. In this sense, there is not such a large distance between the rustic verse carved into the tombstones of the Cheerful Cemetery and the Morse compositions of inmates at Sighet.

I am wary of this story even as I am charmed by it. I have studied and taught literature in countries where it is considered a frilly indulgence, not a matter of life and death. So I gather these old Romanian stories with unacknowledged longing, because they testify to a world where letters were as vital as I believe they are, and not only to a few, entitled people. A woman I know grew up in the western part of Romania, which had more connections to the outside world than Bucharest. When she was in high school, foreign novels would circulate in handwritten copies among the students, a precious contraband. Each student was allowed one night with a volume, so when she got her hands on a book she would tape dark paper over the window on her door and spend the night reading under the covers, with a flashlight. How am I not to be seduced by such tales, when my English majors consider just about everything more important than reading English literature? Would it be any help to tell them about a place where, after the 1989 revolution, people queued outside of bookstores and kiosks to buy words and ideas?[35] People desire things they do not have, and I cannot teach my students that hunger anymore than I can understand the literal hunger or pain or fear experienced by the memoirists I read.

---

35   "Polarizare şi tensiuni în presa din 1990," *Digi24*, January 31, 2015, http://www.digi24.ro/Stiri/Digi24/Special/1990+-+Anul+0/ Polarizare+si+tensiuni+in+presa+din+1990

The first Romanian prison story I learned is not in any book. In the summer of 2000 I worked at the Canadian embassy in Bucharest, translating interviews and doing background searches on visa applicants. I worked in a room with a group of vivacious, highly educated young women who had figured out that secretarial work for a foreign employer gave you an income five times as high as that of a senior university professor. One day, one of the women told me the story of her in-laws' marriage. Her father-in-law had studied literature and been imprisoned, like other university students, in Pitești. There, he was forced to eat his own excrement and subjected to all the other usual degradations. But he had one escape: he knew French, his cellmate knew English, so they passed the time teaching each other their languages.

Time passed, he was released, and sent to work, like many other intellectuals, in a factory. Under communism, educated people found their way to menial labour whether they wanted to or not. One day when he was leaving the factory he ran into a young woman, and they fell to talking. Like him, she had studied literature and gone to prison. She had also fallen in love with another factory worker, but was warned off from marrying him: due to her imprisonment she had a bad file, or *dosar*, with the government, while her fiancé's was clean. She was told that if she married him, she would ruin his file for life. So she called off the engagement. But now she had met another convict, and the way I heard the story she turned to him at one point and said, "Since you have a bad file and I have a bad file, why don't we marry each other?"

They married. He became a literary translator and used the English he had acquired in his cell at Pitești to render Byron into Romanian. Their apartment became a kind of salon, its doors open to artists and writers of all stripes. The forces that had attempted to destroy them brought them together.

It's a beautiful fairy tale, and like most modern fairy tales, this one veils its darker parts. But I think we can appreciate

its beauty even while looking directly at the ugliness, precisely because the ugliness is what makes it possible. I gather
prison tales because their authors have a laser-like focus on
what matters. They understand the power of stories and melodies not simply to move and entertain, but to sustain and
resist. The people who put them in prison understood this
too, thought that someone who lectured on Tristan and Isolde
posed a danger to their ideology. Tyrants can be such good
literary critics, censorship the best reading list.

We have been taught to think of art and scholarship as dec-
orative, unnecessary, wasteful. We have been taught to think
of it as optional. I do not want my students to understand
what these memoirists did; the price would be much too high.
But I also do not want them to fall prey to this new, more
insidious censorship, hard to fight because impossible to see.
Each of us will have a second university one day. I hope we
also have the reading list.

WRITING RESISTANCE
LENA CONSTANTE'S *THE SILENT ESCAPE* AND THE JOURNAL AS GENRE IN ROMANIA'S (POST)COMMUNIST LITERARY FIELD

Carla Baricz

In *Evadarea Tăcută: 3000 de zile singură în închisorile din România* or *The Silent Escape: 3000 Days Alone in Romanian's Prisons*, Lena Constante narrates the first seven years and seven months she spent in solitary detainment in the Romanian communist penal system. A playwright, artist, illustrator, and puppet-maker, Constante (1909–2005) was imprisoned as a result of one of the biggest Stalinist show-trials of the 1950s, the "Pătrășcanu lot," which auctioned off prison sentences to Lucrețiu Pătrășcanu[1] and his close friends and associates. Orchestrated by Gheorge Gheorgiu-Dej, the General Secretary of the Romanian Communist Party after 1947, and

---

1   Born in 1900, Pătrășcanu was a professor at the University of Bucharest, as well as a lawyer and economic expert who had helped found the Romanian Communist Party (he was one of its original supporters from 1921 onwards, helping the banned Party survive the Second World War). Pătrășcanu was Romania's representative at the Third International and rose to the position of Minister of Justice in the communist post-war government that was installed after the Soviet occupation and that had been made possible by the Paris Peace Treaties of 1947, in which Pătrășcanu participated. Arrested in 1948 and tried six years later with various friends and associates like Lena Constante, he was condemned to death for the crimes of espionage on behalf of foreign powers, a bourgeoisie mentality, and the propagation of Romanian nationalism. Pătrășcanu was shot by firing squad in the Jilava Prison on the night of 16 April 1954.

resembling the charges brought against prominent Party members like Ana Pauker, Vasile Luca, and Teohari Georgescu, the trial aimed at purging the upper echelons of the Party of dangerous political opponents, while simultaneously bringing Romania in line with directives from Moscow.

Lena Constante was drawn into the trial as a result of her friendship with Elena Pătrășcanu, Lucrețiu Pătrășcanu's wife, a friendship that had been strengthened through their collaboration on the first puppet theater in Bucharest, "The Țăndărică Theater," affectionately named after one of Constante's puppet characters. As Constante herself recounts, after having been charged as a minor collaborator,[2] she was

---

2   As Ioana Bot argues, Constante's accusers linked her both with Elena and with Lucrețiu Pătrășcanu, convicting her as Lucrețiu Pătrășcanu's mistress and arguing that she had facilitated meetings in her home between Pătrășcanu and his fellow conspirators. Constante passes over these accusations silently. Ioana Bot cites Lavinia Betea's study, *Lucrețiu Pătrășcanu. Moartea unui lider communist* [*Lucrețiu Pătrășcanu: The Death of a Communist Leader*], in which Betea quotes at great length from Lena Constante's own trial statement, while cautioning that all existing information regarding a supposed liaison between Constante and Pătrășcanu must be recognized having been obtained through various forms of psychological and physical torture: "Pătrășcanu was the only man whom I loved in this manner.... Three years of life with Pătrășcanu were three years of jealousy and waiting. In that nervous state of mind, I consistently never gave a damn about his political problems. I wanted one thing only: to know if he loves me, how much he loves me, if he, too, misses me.... I had nothing in common with Pătrășcanu except this constant desire to see him, to be with him, to at least touch his coat.... Sometimes I contentedly told myself that at least I hadn't lived never knowing what it means to love. Though now I no longer believe that this was love. It was a sick passion." Lavinia Betea, *Lucrețiu Pătrășcanu. Moartea unui lider communist* (Bucharest: Humanitas, 2001), 93. Ioana Bot adds: "the author of *The Silent Escape* [found] out during the trial that she (probably) had not been his [Pătrășcanu's] only lover in that period, that the possibility of using her home was the determining factor that had convinced him to make her amorous overtures, that he disdainfully told his intimate friends that she 'had the head of a horse, yellow skin, and is unbearably ugly in the morning.' She no longer had even the memory of a great love affair, shared with the man whom she had defended with all her power, to help her bear out the years of punishment. It is possible that many of the depositions that the trial documents record are false and were wrested [from the accused] during the investigation

sentenced to "twelve years of hard labor for high treason, [and] ten years for counterrevolutionary activity" (226).[3] Constante's *Silent Escape* chronicles the tortured, horrifying, brutal first three thousand days of this prison term, a period spent in full solitary confinement.[4]

The account that Constante eventually put together after her release in 1961 took the shape of a prison memoir that she would begin in 1973 and continue to write covertly over the next sixteen years in notebooks that she carefully kept hidden from the authorities. After the fall of the communist dictatorship in Romania on 22 December 1989, Constante was able to compile and publish the material that she had gathered in these notebooks in the form of a book she called *The Silent Escape*. The resulting text was released in France as *L'évasion silencieuse. Trois mille jours seule dans les prisons roumaines* (Paris: La Découverte, 1990). Subsequently, the author rewrote and

through methods similar to those recounted by Lena Constante (though never, I repeat, *never* would she write about this type of information offered to the investigators or discovered by them)." Lena Constante, *Evadarea Tăcută: 3000 de zile singură în închisorile din România*, ed. Ioana Bot (Bucharest: Humanitas, 2013), 13.

3   In the following pages, I will cite exclusively from the Romanian editions of the *Silent Escape* (Humanitas, 2013) and *The Impossible Escape* (Humanitas 2013). It seems to me that given that Romanian was the author's native language, the language in which she thought and kept her notebooks, and given that the Romanian editions were the author's final reworking and revision of the volumes she put together (in fact, a French edition of *The Impossible Escape* does not exist), one should follow her lead and give priority to the texts that she herself had considered authoritative.

4   Constante was released from prison on 14 July 1961, having spent a total of twelve years in detention—the first eight in solitary confinement and the last four in common detention. She would be politically rehabilitated in 1968, after Nicolae Ceaușescu became the de-facto leader of the Socialist Republic of Romania, having consolidated his 1965 ascendancy to the office of General Secretary of the Romanian Communist Party with election to the office of president of the State Council. Seeking to distance himself from his predecessor, Gheorge Gheorghiu-Dej, and to dictate a foreign policy independent of the Soviet Union, Ceaușescu condemned the Pătrășcanu trial as a malicious fabrication and launched a propaganda campaign to politically rehabilitate those who had been sentenced in 1954.

reedited the text in Romanian. Humanitas Press published
the first Romanian edition in 1992.[5] Over the course of the
next two years, Constante would add a second volume to
definitive edition, *The Impossible Escape* (1993),[6] penned—as
she claims—as a result of having received numerous entreat-
ies from French readers who desired to know more about the
last four years of Constante's prison sentence, an experience
that Constante had considered too banal to be worth recount-
ing, or at least not significantly different from that of any other
"political prisoner" who had been held in common detention.[7]

   While one can comfortably label *The Impossible Escape* a
post-communist memoir comprised of a series of sketches

---

5   A second Romanian edition of *The Silent Escape* came out in 1995 at
     Editura Florile Dalbe. A third edition, with a new introduction by
     Ioana Bot and an addendum that reprinted Lena Constante's "Self-
     Critique"—taken from the Pătrășcanu trial documents and signed
     by the author on 22 March 1950—was published by Humanitas
     Press in 2013.

6   In this second volume, Constante exchanged the journal form for
     a series of sketches that chronicled her removal from solitary eight
     and a half years after having been arrested and that outlined her
     time in common detention in the Miercurea-Ciuc Penitentiary for
     women. For more details regarding the publication history see:
     Lena Constante, *Evadarea Imposibilă*, ed. Ioana Bot (Bucharest:
     Humanitas, 2013), 13–16.

7   In the years following the Revolution, the Romanian market for
     communist memoirs grew steadily, as new publishing houses
     sprung up from the old, communist-run institutions. The author
     was able to publish this second volume directly in Romanian, at
     Editura Fundației Culturale Române, bypassing the Western
     European publishing houses that had often acted as cultural
     middlemen in the first months after the fall of the dictatorship.
     The *Impossible Escape* was meant to give Western readers—as well
     as a younger generation of Romanian readers who had not lived
     through communism—the wherewithal to understand what it
     had meant to be imprisoned in the communist penal system. As
     Constante herself put it: "I understood then that for the citizens of
     a free, non-communist country, everything that had seemed banal
     and lacking in interest to me, could take on a tragic and horrifying
     perspective. Did not Romania begin, in 1989, its long road towards
     freedom? [It was] a hard road, with stumbling blocks and sudden
     twists, though in a few years Romanian youth will live in a free
     country, and they too will have to know the tragic and horrifying
     lives of their parents." Constante, *Evadarea Imposibilă*, 20.

that detail Constante's experience of political detention in Romania's communist prisons, *The Silent Escape* is much more difficult to define. Its publication history and its composition history tell two very different stories. More specifically, before offering any kind of analysis of the text, one must decide what that text is. Should one call *The Silent Escape* a journal, looking solely at the original circumstances in which it was composed? Or, should one call it a memoir, examining the circumstances that in fact led to the work's publication? Or, should one take a different approach altogether and instead underscore the volume's formal characteristics that attempt a compromise between the author's original intentions — to keep a journal — and the subsequent memorialistic mode of composition that led to publication? In other words, one must decide how to delineate the relationship between what Raymond Williams called the "means and conditions of [a text's] production,"[8] and the formal structure envisioned by the author.

One approach to this dilemma might be to think of the relationship between formal characteristics and method of composition, and between generic form and publication history, as being dependent on inherited conceptions of the "literary." An author hoping to produce (and publish) a *literary* text will write in a certain manner, employing certain forms that signify as "literary"; he or she will use a certain style, diction, and vocabulary that he or she perceives to be "literary." Similarly, a publisher will decide to publish a text based on certain generic, stylistic, and lexical characteristics that in his or her mind signpost that text as being of a "literary" nature. One might say that, in order to be a literary work, a text must possess certain qualities that the author and the publisher deem to be inherent to "literary" texts. Such qualities are in large part determined by what Pierre Bourdieu famously called the "literary field." According to Bourdieu, the site of literary production is shaped by "the struggle between the two principles of hierarchization: the heteronomous principle, favourable to those who dominate the field economically and politically (e.g. "bourgeois art") and the autonomous principle (e.g. "art for art's sake"), which those of its advocates who are least endowed with specific capital tend to identify with a degree of independence from the economy, seeing temporal failure as a sign of election and success as a sign of compromise."[9] In other words, the literary work is the product of a writer, but it is also the product of the field of institutional, social, aesthetic, cultural, economic forces that shape the field into which it emerges. The field is in turn shaped by the struggle between conservatory and transformative principles, so that "the meaning of a work (artistic, literary, philosophical, etc.) changes automatically with each change in the field within which it is situated for the spectator or reader."[10]

Today, *The Silent Escape* signifies as a literary text with a great degree of merit. In 2002, Constante won the Romanian Academy's "Lucian Blaga" prize for the volume, a prize that stresses the felicitous quality of its winner's writing. Ioana Bot, the editor of the first Romanian edition speaks of the book's "literary" qualities and of its "literary dimension," arguing that "the fullness of the discourse gives it a body[;] by means of its specific processes literature fulfills the author's need to leave a recorded truth, as well as her readers' needs to know this truth."[11] The Romanian literary critic Dan Cristea-Enache similarly claims that *The Silent Escape* "was composed later, like a novel that is carefully delineated and composed.... The author traverses the matter of her own life behind bars with the calm of a great novelist, without the diaristic trepidations and oscillations that characterize *sur le vif* writing.... *The Silent Escape* [was] written with an eye towards the big picture, and it [was] written like a classical novel: one in which both

---

9   Pierre Bourdieu, *The Field of Cultural Production*, ed. Randal Johnson (New York: Columbia University Press, 1993), 40.

10   Bourdieu, *Cultural Production*, 30.

11   Constante, *Evadarea Tăcută*, 30.

the protagonist and the detailed history of her experiences
survive."[12]

Statements such as these tempt one to take as a given the
idea that Constante wrote a literary work, that she produced
a memoir that fully participated in the literary field of her day
and that placed her among the defenders of the autonomous
principle. Following this line of thought, one might say that
Constante wrote her literary work for its own sake, resisting
the official social-realist model that justified prisons as necessary centers of reeducation in which the former enemies of
the people could be converted to faithful communists. She
wrote her work knowing that it would never be appreciated
or read, refusing to adhere to the abstract, dogmatic "wooden"
language of Party publications.[13] She composed a novelistic
memoir that not only tells the truth about her imprisonment, but adapts some of the formal characteristics of "true
account" narratives in order to do so. Like the "advocates" of
Bourdieu's "autonomous principle," she composed *The Silent
Escape* for its own sake. Paradoxically, her time in prison gave
Constante the equivalent of a private income, the external

---

12   Daniel Cristea-Enache, "Singuratica (I)," review of *Evadarea Tăcută:
      3000 de zile singură în închisorile din România*, by Lena Constante,
      Observator Cultural, 26 April 2013, http://www.observatorcultural.
      ro/Singuratica-(I)*articleID_28556-articles_details.html.

13   Writers and academics alike often employ the term "wooden lan-
      guage" to refer to the impersonal, abstract, ideologically charged
      Romanian used by officials during the communist period. Though
      initially a term that simply meant something like "politically cor-
      rect," the adjective "wooden" increasingly took on pejorative con-
      notations, until individuals protesting the dictatorship came to
      use it as a way of marking the distance between free speech and
      political propaganda. To cite Norman Manea, "the one-Party sys-
      tem of the socialist dictatorship took over, gradually, any private
      ownership: land and banks, industry and schools, farms and hos-
      pitals and newspapers, apartments and kindergartens, stadiums
      and pharmacies and libraries, agriculture and culture—everything.
      We all were owned by the state, and the wooden official language
      of the Party dominated our daily life, sometimes our nightlife, too."
      Norman Manea, "Nomadic Language," in *Writer Uprooted: Contem-
      porary Jewish Exile Literature*, ed. Alvin H. Rosenfeld (Bloomington,
      IN: Indiana University Press, 2008), 5–6.

conditions necessary to write. By creating a voice that could speak for and represent herself, she gave a shape to the four hundred days of starvation,[14] the beatings, rape and torture, the bone-crushing cold, the tuberculosis, the fear, and the constant threat of madness that characterized life in Romania's communist prisons. She made use of what Bourdieu called "the mechanism which, here as elsewhere, leads people to make a virtue of necessity, in the constitution of the field of cultural production as a space radically independent of the economy and of politics and, as such, amenable to a sort of pure theory."[15] So the argument might unfold.

However, such arguments about literariness do not take into account the very premise that allows one to put them in motion. Statements such as these assume that the literary field of forty years ago was shaped by the same values that shape it today.[16] They treat the work of dissidents proleptically, overlooking the fact that, in totalitarian dictatorships, epithets such as "dissenting writer" were all too often rendered mere oxymorons by systematic censorship. Given the composition history and publication history of *The Silent Escape*, it is difficult to argue that Constante participated in any way in the literary field, or could be said to have influenced it or sought to change it by employing literary forms and adhering to certain literary standards that had been validated by the existing field of cultural production. It is true that, while serving out the term of her sentence, Constante

---

14   See Constante, *Evadarea Tăcută*, 89.

15   Bourdieu, *Cultural Production*, 62.

16   See Ruxandra Cesereanu on different values: "The Romanian reader especially, and the Eastern reader more generally, had to make up for an ethical-moral delay that can be explained in political terms; in 1990 [such a reader] suddenly transitioned from a *literature of hypocrisy* to a *literature of infernal truth*[s], which was later on followed by the "monotony of horror," by one's acclimation to the horrors of the gulag." Ruxandra Cesereanu, *Gulagul în conștiința românească. Memorialistica și literatura închisorilor și lagărelor communiste* (Bucharest: Polirom, 2005), 71.

wrote countless poems, eight full-length plays,[17] and kept the journal that would become the seed of *The Silent Escape*. However, it is also true that she wrote all of these works in her head, as mental exercises. As a writer, she cannot be said to have had a literary "output." The journal that would comprise *The Silent Escape* was not the result of her interest in success, be it economic, political, or cultural (the ability to define "literary" values). Nor was it written with any audience but herself in mind.[18] In fact, the journal was not written at all for a very long time. One might even say that it did not become a text until 1973 and not a *literary* text until Humanitas Press published it to great literary acclaim in 1990.

Rather, Constante's decision to write was the result of a desperate attempt to give each twenty-four hour cycle a meaningful shape, to reclaim the time of lived experience of which the penal system had sought to deprive her:

> I had words, and I had time. So much time that I didn't know how I could live it. Lost time. Nevertheless, lost or not, this time belonged to me. To allow myself to lose it pointlessly would have meant to lose a part of my life, and I for one wanted to live this single life that I had been given.

---

17   Only three plays survived intact in Constante's memory and were eventually committed to paper. For details regarding these plays see: Constante, *Evadarea Tăcută*, 293. It is unclear that Constante ever published these plays or staged them. The passage seems to indicate that they were transcribed merely so as to affectively recall the time that their author spent in prison.

18   Here one must differentiate between the original act of composition and the events that led to the book's publication after the fall of communism. Constante never envisioned having an audience and wrote simply to help herself survive incarceration. As she states a number of times in *The Silent Escape*, "I was neither a poet nor a composer. But I nevertheless composed poems. Songs too gave me contentment. I completely lacked a critical outlook. I only felt the passing miracle. I had found, at last, the key to escape. I had rid myself of the guilty obsession of lost time as well. I tried. I worked. I abolished the prison. Fear. Myself." Constante, *Evadarea Tăcută*, 105.

> Weaving words on the loom of time, I lived. I survived. I
> even succeeded in being content…sometimes.[19]

For Constante, the act of "weaving" words became a raison
d'être and a consolation. The mental inscription of passages
gave her a reason to keep living and allowed her to refashion
a self, to

> resist the temptation of giving up. Of relinquishing every-
> thing. Even yourself. The temptation to no longer want
> anything. Of abandoning yourself to fate.[20]

If the affirmations made in *The Silent Escape* and *The Impossible
Escape* are to be believed, the journal that she kept in her head
helped her reclaim the time that she had lost while imprisoned. In the case of *The Silent Escape* in particular, the account
of the composition of her plays and poems became an integral
part of the days she chronicled, the lived experience of the self
who endured and who told the story of her suffering in order
to go on writing, who remembered who it was, where it was,
and when it was because the day and the work had become
inexorably tied to each another, offering a silent escape.

Of course, the censorship of political prisoners made it
impossible to in fact *write* anything down—be it a poem, play,
or journal:

> My first thought? The calendar. Each morning for eight
> years I rip off a page from my mental calendar. I repeat
> the date multiple times. I fix it in my memory. Calendars
> are forbidden in communist prisons. As mirrors, watches,
> books, paper, and pencils are forbidden. Forbidden are
> forks and knives, sewing needles and scissors. Though for-
> bidden are also the trees and the grass and flowers and all

19   Constante, *Evadarea Tăcută*, 107–108.
20   Constante, *Evadarea Tăcută*, 61.

fruits and all vegetables, with the exception of potatoes, dried beans, carrots, and pickled cabbage.[21]

As this passage attests, the act of writing was itself "forbidden" to political prisoners. The condemned had no access to paper or writing implements.[22] They were not even allowed to know what day or week it was, much less to give this time meaning and shape by transforming it into literary production. Despite the affirmations that she makes in *The Silent Escape* and despite arguments such as those given above, in the end, Constante was not able to recount her experiences any more than she was able to set down the acts and scenes of her plays. Her mental efforts left no material traces. Though Constante's first thought in the morning was always the mental calendar, reckoned on fingers, remembered with discipline upon waking, that calendar and her mental annotation of it—the account of her days—did not survive. For all practical purposes, one might even say that the "journal" (if one can attribute a genre to an ideational text), the poems, and the plays not subsequently written down never existed. They were composed but never *produced*.[23]

---

21   Constante, *Evadarea Imposibilă*, 23.

22   Sometimes, there were exceptions to this rule. For example, Constante recounts that in August of 1952 she was given watercolors and drawing paper, and that in April of 1953 she was given paper and pencils, which allowed her both to write down her plays and to illustrate them. See: Constante, *Evadarea Tăcută*, 159–160, 170. These instances however were rare. Such gifts were one of the manipulatory techniques employed by Constante's interrogators, who hoped to convince her to give false testimony by promising her a certain degree of freedom. Once sentenced, Constante was never again granted such privileges.

23   It is equally difficult to claim that Constante's work—at least the work written after Constante was declared an enemy of the state—contributed to the cultural "thaw" of the 1960s or that it helped redefine the parameters of the dominant heteronomous principle, which in totalitarian systems "reign[s] unchallenged if, losing all autonomy,...writers and artists became [completely] subject to the ordinary laws prevailing in the field of power." Bourdieu, *Cultural Production*, 38. In fact, no work contributed to the cultural thaw of the 1960s. The censors' laxer stance was a result of Nicolae

This issue lies at the heart of all "literature" created under terror. The question of whether a text can have an impact in a literary field that is heavily skewed towards the heteronormous principle, which restricts the circulation of art that does not fall in line with the political and cultural norms established by the field of power, is first and foremost a question about whether such a restricted work that does not circulate or fully participate in the literary field and can be said to be "literary work." It is the dilemma that must be posed when discussing *samizdat* literature, the function of literary coteries in totalitarian dictatorships, or the role of state-run writers' unions in institutionalizing the parameters the literary field by constraining and defining the positions available within it.[24] One may describe such works as lexical forms of individual protest or as personal refusals to operate under the constraints imposed by the field of power, but can a work like

---

Ceaușescu's attempts to de-Stalinize Romanian communism and to ease the country from a Soviet to a nationalist model.

24   In a totalitarian dictatorship, the state determines whether an individual occupies a position in the cultural field of production. The difference between a "hooligan"—an individual who does not have a paid job—and a "writer" is that the hooligan can be arrested and imprisoned for unemployment, whereas the "writer" belongs to a state-sponsored union that "employs" him or her, thus providing legitimacy. A censured writer only becomes a "writer" if he or she succeeds in publishing his or her work in a different literary field, abroad, or if he or she restricts his or her audience to a group of close associates, operating in a sub-field with different parameters—that of the coterie. The union defines who can occupy a position in the larger literary field, giving the "writer" social and economic capital. Bourdieu explains how such system of sponsorship works: "the propensity to move towards the economically most risky positions [such as that of "pure writer"], and above all the capacity to persist in them..., even when they secure no short-term economic profit seem to depend to a large extent on possession of substantial economic and social capital. This is, first, because economic capital provides the conditions for freedom from economic necessity, a private income (*la rente*) being one of the best substitutes for sales (*la vente*)." Bourdieu, *Cultural Production*, 67–68. In this case, and the ability to secure any profit at all by publishing depends on the union, which provides both the economic and social capital.

The Silent Escape be thought of as resistance through literature if it does not participate in the field by making its resistance public?

We come across this problem in Orwell's *1984*. The diary that Winston Smith writes may be said to be a reaction to the field of power in which literary activity takes place. It embodies a personal form of resistance to both political and cultural norms. However, it is not a work in the same fashion that the treatise of the mysterious head of the Brotherhood, Emmanuel Goldstein, can be said to be a work. Winston's diary is never published and never disseminated. It never acquires a formal shape. No one but Winston and the Thought Police ever read it. On the other hand, Goldstein's book *is* published, widely disseminated, and read. It participates in the literary field. Winston hears of it long before he is given a chance to read it. However, as readers of Orwell's novel eventually find out, this dissenting treatise is in fact written by O'Brien, a powerful member of the Inner Party, who allows it to circulate widely in order to root out dissidents like Winston. Orwell ironically implies that the literature of resistance is itself a fiction created and employed by the system in power to keep itself in power.

If we cannot situate *The Silent Escape* in the literary field of 1960s and 1970s communist Romania, and thus call it a literary memoir that bears witness to atrocities or a true account, how then should we describe the relationship between its composition history, publication history, and its genre? Perhaps one way to do so might be to delineate and explain its *absence* from the field. Constante began writing her journal in prison. Though she was unable to give material form to her work, she did not give up. She attempted to recount her experiences a second time, after her release:

> September 1980. It's 9 AM. Sunlight. Warmth. A sense of calm. I am spending two weeks in Ouchy with my husband,

Harry Brauner. After the retrial in 1968, we were granted permission to travel quite easily. We travel to France, where Harry has a brother, and to Switzerland, to see his sister.

The weather is good. We still have our strength, and we're happy to be together and to be in Ouchy. Why is it that, all of a sudden, I've decided to continue writing down my memories? It's not easy to undertake a futile work. I know that these notebooks will remain hidden, and that I will never be able to publish them. Nevertheless, I would have liked to know people's opinions. I care all too little about what will happen after my death. When I began writing, I even thought of a kind of bizarre glory. Had I not been the only woman locked up alone for more than eight years?

This lone woman attempted to tell the story of how she succeeded in filling up these years, of how she managed to live. To escape thanks to thought, by means of a resolute will, if not through sheer stubbornness.[25]

Through a willful act of memory performed from 1973 onwards, Constante succeeded in rewriting the mental journal that her poems and plays helped motivate her to keep, if not the plays or poems themselves. However, the circumstances of composition had changed. As passage above makes clear, Constante was no longer writing from prison. She was no longer *in medias res*. At times, she was not even in Romania. Her years in prison had to be recollected now as a temporal whole— "the state of detention, as such"[26]—a period with a clear beginning and endpoint, "these years" that could be carefully marked out and set apart from the backwards looking duration of the past. However, Constante also needed to reconstruct the lost original journal, the authentic first account towards which all of her previous efforts had been directed. It

---

25   Constante, *Evadarea Tăcută*, 317–318.
26   Constante, *Evadarea Imposibilă*, 59.

is this composition history that gave her book its literariness. So, she chose to compromise.

The second journal, begun in 1973, attempted to recall the first by imitating its form. In it, Constante counts the days as she did in detention, though this time on paper. Each entry begins with a heading that tallies the days that Constante has spent in prison and makes a precise notation of the date: "The 1051st, 1052, 1053, 1054, 1055, 1056, 1057, 1058, 1059, 1060, 1061, 1062, 1063, 1064, 1065, 1066, 1067, 1068, 1069, 1070, 1071, 1072, 1073, 1074, 1075, 1076, 1077, 1078, 1079, the 1080th day of detention—31 December 1952."[27] Each entry follows this model, sometimes spanning scores of days, sometimes eliding whole months and passing over multiple seasons. The pattern never varies. The journal form is maintained at all costs because it embodies Constante's version of the truth. It is her way of negating the "truth" of her former interrogators by providing her own minute account of the trial and of her imprisonment. She insists on this form because

> I was no longer anything. My truth was no longer the truth. My truth was not their truth. . . . He [the interrogator] has permission to do anything. To impose "his" truth has become his idée fixe. For this lunatic the law doesn't exist, because he is the law. He is justice as well. And revenge. He is God.[28]

Maneuvering sudden and repeated shifts in tense that emphasize a continuing present that obscures the speaker's knowledge of events not yet been recounted while nevertheless acknowledging that she is writing many years after the fact, Constante asks herself the same question that Orwell's character would ask himself: "What can you do, thought Winston, against the lunatic who is more intelligent than yourself, who

---

27   Constante, *Evadarea Tăcută*, 46.
28   Constante, *Evadarea Tăcută*, 44–45.

gives your arguments a fair hearing and then simply persists in his lunacy?... 'We are priests of power,' [O'Brien] said. 'God is power.'"[29] Despite agreeing with O'Brien, Constante's answer is that one can nevertheless attempt to speak for one's self. One can state simultaneously one's own understanding of the facts and one's inability to deny the "truth" spoken by a Dickinsonian God-Inquisitor. For Constante, the best manner of preserving individual truth is not by arguing in political terms but by telling one's version of it the long way—as personal experience.

In *The Silent Return*, time is segmented and apportioned into days, so that by adding it up, one may come to the sum of its truth: a "human testimony."[30] Nevertheless, precisely because *The Silent Escape* is a subjective account, it can only provide a truth that is filtered through memory. As a reconstruction, the text falls pray to the same lapses, additions, compressions, and distortions that set apart the memoir and the autobiography from the journal or the epistolary collection.[31] Perhaps the clearest example of such compressions and distortions is given in the description of "the 1539th day of detention—4 April 1954." This entry comes in the wake of "the 1538th day of detention—3 April 1953," which is preceded by "the 1445th

---

29   George Orwell, *1984* (New York: Signet Classics, 1950), 262–264.

30   The passage is worth quoting in full: "Why should I write then? Simply to create a human testimony. As much as possible, to avoid speaking about the political aspects of my detention. I want to speak about the state of detention, as such. In full knowledge of the facts. The day to day life in a cell. I think that I have lived through a unique experience. A woman alone for many years. Years made up of hours, of minutes, of seconds. I would like to tell the story of these seconds, of these 3600 seconds in an hour, these 86400 seconds in a day, which drag on slowly along the body, slavering snakes rising in spirals from your feet to your neck, with no respite, no mercy, from morning till evening and during the nights of insomnia, too frequent, that continue to encircle you with no rest and no cessation, endlessly." Constante, *Evadarea Tăcută*, 59.

31   Constante adds an interspersed long passage to this journal format—the Fifth Chapter or The Second Part—which recalls her first detention (house arrest) between April and October of 1948. See *Evadarea Tăcută*, 193–224.

day of detention—31 December, 1953."[32] In three supposedly consecutive chronological entries, the author has jumped back and forth in time several times. Constante makes it clear that she has followed the first entry, 31 December 1953, with a return to April of that year in order to discuss the relationship between Stalin's death on the 5th of March, and the sudden dénouement of the Pătrășcanu trial.[33] However, Constante then jumps ahead from the 3rd of April 1953 to the 4th of April 1954. She acknowledges the change in year, but subjectively she can only recollect this span of time as a single twenty-four hour cycle—the 1538th to the 1539th day. Similarly, the 1538th day (3 April) signifies a jump *forward* from the 1445th day (31 December), but that 1445th day actually occurs *later* in the calendar year. There are a number of other instances when time seems to slow down, speed up, or halt completely as the writer stops to draw attention to certain individual or to a certain scenario. As Augustine would put it in the *Confessions*, for Constante "no time is wholly present.... All past and future are created and set on their course by that which is always present."[34] The present act of recalling the passage of time reshapes the time recalled.

As a memoir, the years chronicled in *The Silent Escape* came to stand for the incarceratory phase of Lena Constante's life, as well as for a set of experiences that according to official accounts never took place. However, as a textual object, the book that describes these years simultaneously embodies the period of silence from 1961 to 1989 when it existed only as another kind of journal, as a record kept for private use that,

32 Constante, *Evadarea Tăcută*, 173–175.

33 See Constante, *Evadarea Tăcută*, 175. "The Secretary of the Party was now afraid, rightfully so, of Lucrețiu Pătrășcanu, a possible rival. In order to maintain himself at the height of power—the only invulnerable place in the Party—he now had [to deal with] two major problems. To begin some sort of de-Stalinization and to get rid of Lucrețiu Pătrășcanu."

34 Augustine, *The Confessions*, trans. Henry Chadwick. (Oxford and New York: Oxford University Press, 1998), 229.

if discovered, would have sent Constante back to the deeper silence of a prison cell. Indeed, when it was published in 1990, the *The Silent Escape* came to denote a shorthand version of its own composition history, underscoring the absence of a certain kind of text in communist Romania's field of cultural production and symbolizing the systematic censorship of the penal literature of communism. The book was able to do so precisely because it acknowledged itself to be a *post-communist* construction, a historical document whose circulation was possible only now as a result of the transition that restructured the political field of power, which had led in turn to the restructuring of the literary field. Incorporating these various histories, the book's primary function became its ability to describe the "political aspects of my detention,"[35] the very thing Constante hoped to avoid discussing. Today, *The Silent Escape* is a text that is cited in works about the structure of the communist prisons and discussed in studies about political oppression, a volume that is used to generalize both about the experiences of women political prisoners and of writers, both male and female, silenced by the Romanian communist dictatorship.[36]

Here we have circled back to the question posed at the beginning of this essay. What is the relationship between authorial intention and available modes of representation? This is the problem that Foucault poses in *The Archeology of Knowledge*, a problem that cannot be swept aside by means of token phrases like "literature as resistance." As Foucault

---

35   Constante, *Evadarea Tăcută*, 60.

36   See, for example: Laura Anne Doyle, *Bodies of Resistance: New Phenomenologies of Politics, Agency, and Culture*, (Evanston, IL: Northwestern University Press, 2001); Vladimir Tismăneanu, *Stalinism For All Seasons: A Political History of Romanian Communism* (Berkeley, CA: University of California Press, 2003); Marius Oprea, *Bastionul cruzimii. O istorie a Securitații (1948–1964)* (Bucharest: Polirom, 2008); Dan C. Mihailescu, *Castelul, biblioteca, pușcăria: trei vămi ale feminității exemplare* (Bucharest: Humanitas, 2013); and Grațian Cormoș, *Femei în universul concentraționar din România (1945–1989)*, (Bucharest: Casa Cărții de Știință, 2005).

points out, no textual object can be brought into existence in a vacuum. Institutions have a role in producing our objects of discourse: "these relations [that enable an object of discourse to be embodied] are established between institutions, economic and social processes, behavioural patterns, systems of norms, techniques, types of classification, modes of characterization.... They do not define its internal constitution, but what enables it to appear, to juxtapose itself with other objects, to situate itself in relation to them, to define its difference, its irreducibility, and even perhaps its heterogeneity, in short, to be placed in a field of exteriority."[37] As is the case with the work of many other writers who were partially or completely silenced by the totalitarian systems in which they lived and created, the internal construction of Constante's work is shaped, at least partially, by censorship, by the means and conditions that allowed it—or rather failed to allow it—to be placed in a field of exteriority. It is in this difference, in the undefined tension between implicit form and its exteriorization that the question Orwell formulated in *1984* becomes pressing: can the humanities make a free, *meaningful* contribution in a time of terror if the ideological constraints placed upon the work predetermine its shape and/or prevent it from circulating?

Constante's memoir *qua* journal seems to provide a clear if disappointing answer to this question. The relationship between genre and material form suggests a reply in the negative. Constante never read her own trial documents, she was kept in solitary detainment, and most importantly, she had no hope of ever making her version of the truth public. If she had been allowed to keep and publish a journal she would have never written a memoir. Similarly, she would never have published a memoir thirty years later, in France, if, once freed from prison, she had been able to and criticize

---

37   Michel Foucault, *The Archeology of Knowledge and the Discourse on Language*, trans. A.M. Sheridan Smith (New York: Vintage Books, 2010), 45.

the system from within. This dispiriting publication history supports Robert Darnton's famous remark that a book is a product of the "communications circuit that runs from the author to the publisher (if the bookseller does not assume that role), the printer, the shipper, the bookseller, and the reader.... The construal of meaning [occurs] within a system of communication."[38] When this circuit is fully controlled by the encompassing field of power, it becomes difficult if not impossible to critique that field or to hope to change it by operating within it.

Perhaps then it is not by promoting active resistance that works such as Lena Constante's can aid individuals in challenging an encompassing totalitarian system. However, one should nevertheless insist that, even so, individuals who choose to *valorize* cultural contributions, as Lena Constante did by keeping her memoir-notebooks, nevertheless participate in a kind of passive resistance. "Resistance through culture," as many Romanian critics have called this model,[39] can make no political difference but it can provide a refuge to the individual who acknowledges that an autonomous principle can and should exist in the literary field. George Orwell knew this, which is why in *1984* it is not important what Winston

---

38   Robert Darnton, "What is the History of Books," *Daedalus* 111.3 (1982): 65–83, at 67, 78.

39   This controversial phrase refers to the refusal of Romania's intellectual elites to adopt the moral, ethical, or intellectual values of the political system whose ideology dictated their lives. As a 2009 study commissioned by the Romanian Academy's European Center for Ethnic Studies puts it, "resistance [through culture] ... is the expression of that movement and attitude that spontaneously turns against the fundamentals of the system, creating in its place a framework for the preservation and continuity of the spiritual traditions of Europe. The interwar generations, from whose ranks most of communism's political prisoners were recruited, also belong in the "resistance through culture" category; we will only mention Nichifor Crainic, Vasile Băncilă, Pan Vizirescu, Constantin Noica, Alexandru Paleologu, Edgar Papu, Brătienii etc." Radu Baltasiu et al., "Modernități fracturate: 1944–1989. 1990–2009. Elitele, România și 'Europa' (partea a II a)," *Etnosfera* 5 (2009): 1–20, at 2.

writes or that he has no audience. What matters is that he acknowledges that the situation in which he finds himself is aberrant, that it should not be the norm and that an alternative exists. For Orwell, the act of setting down words—even if only for one's self—is key because it displays a commitment to reason, to judgment, and to sanity. It refuses the premises of *goodthink*; it resists what Constante called "the temptation of giving up. Of relinquishing everything. Even yourself."[40]

> [Winston] wondered again for whom he was writing the diary. For the future, for the past—for an age that might be imaginary. And in front of him there lay not death but annihilation. The diary would be reduced to ashes and himself to vapor. Only the Thought Police would read what he had written, before they wiped it out of existence and out of memory. How could you make appeal to the future when not a trace of you, not even an anonymous word scribbled on a piece of paper, could physically survive? ... He was a lonely ghost uttering a truth that nobody would hear. But so long as he uttered it, in some obscure way the continuity was not broken. It was not by making yourself heard but by staying sane that you carried on the human heritage. He went back to the table, dipped his pen, and wrote.[41]

Though the comforts of keeping a diary, or of reciting nursery rhymes like "Oranges and Lemons," or of appreciating the beauty of a nineteenth century etching do not have the power to rescue Winston from the fate that awaits him, and that he anticipates from the very first pages of the novel, they nevertheless provide a temporary respite from the penal universe of Airstrip One and the means to keep sane. As Winston, Lena Constante, Constantin Noica, Nicolae Steinhardt, Ion Ioanid and so many other writers imprisoned and tortured

---

40   Constante, *Evadarea Tăcută*, 61.

41   Orwell, *1984*, 27.

by totalitarian dictatorships show us, literary creation consistently offers this form of silent escape, even as it fails to provide a more practical solution or to become literary production. As proof of free, uninhibited thought, it allows one to maintain one's humaneness, to endure a while longer, and to carry on the "human heritage" that all repressive political systems seek to abolish.

WAR AND THE FOOD OF DREAMS
AN INTERVIEW WITH CARA DE SILVA

Cara De Silva with Irina Dumitrescu

I discovered Cara De Silva's work on my own bookshelf, in the form of In Memory's Kitchen: A Legacy from the Women of Terezín, *her edition of a recipe collection written from memory in the Theresienstadt/Terezín concentration camp.[1] It is a moving document, listing instructions for deviled eggs, candied fruits, caramels, cherry-plum dumplings, and coffee cake, recalled and written down in the midst*

---

1   Cara De Silva, ed., *In Memory's Kitchen: A Legacy from the Women of Terezín* (Northvale, NJ and London: Jason Aronson, 1996). For reflections on the volume, see Charlotte Innes, "The Food of Memory," *Los Angeles Times*, July 23, 1997, http://articles.latimes.com/1997/jul/23/food/fo-15271; Judith Tydor Baumel, ""You Said the Words You Wanted Me to Hear but I Heard The Words You Couldn't Bring Yourself to Say": Women's First Person Accounts of the Holocaust," *Oral History Review* 27.1 (2000): 17–56; Rona Kaufman, "Testifying, Silencing, Monumentalizing, Swallowing: Coming to Terms with *In Memory's Kitchen*," *jac* 24.2 (2004): 427–45; Marlene Kadar, "Wounding Events and the Limits of Autobiography," in *Diaspora, Memory and Identity: A Search for Home*, ed. Vijay Agnew (Toronto: University of Toronto Press, 2005): 81–104; Marianne Hirsch and Leo Spitzer, "Testimonial Objects: Memory, Gender, and Transmission," *Poetics Today* 27.2 (2006): 353–83; Daniel E. Feinberg and Alice Crosetto, "Cookbooks: Preserving Jewish Tradition," *Judaica Librarianship* 16 (2011): 149–72; Marie I. Drews, "Cooking *In Memory's Kitchen*: Re-Presenting Recipes, Remembering the Holocaust," in *Edible Ideologies: Representing Food & Meaning*, ed. Kathleen LeBesco and Peter Naccarato (Albany, NY: State University of New York Press, 2008): 53–70.

of starvation. In one of her poems, Mina Pächter, one of the book's authors and the woman through whom it survived, describes the degradation to which Terezín's cultured, educated inmates were subjected:

Der Professor kommt täglich her
Früher las er den Homer
Und im Urtext: Herakles und Mark Aurel
Heute liest er nur Tagesbefehl
Und den Zettel der Menage.

The professor visits every day
He used to read the Odyssey
In Greek and Latin: Heracles
And works of Mark Aurelius
Now reads just daily proclamations
And chits that list starvation rations.[2]

In another poem, Pächter portrays two sisters in Terezín: "sie kochen zusammen oft nur platonisch" (they cook together, often only platonically),[3] *offering a darkly witty twist on what a classical education might achieve in times of extreme need. This platonic cooking, with only the imagination as ingredient, seems to describe the "cookbook" at the centre of* In Memory's Kitchen.

I asked Cara De Silva to speak with me about Pächter's book, how she came to edit it, and about the wider phenomenon of wartime cookbooks. In April of 2015 we met on Skype; the text below is an edited version of our interview, to which I have added footnotes. Despite the editing, we have chosen to preserve some of the oral nature of the text, in the hope that the emotion we both felt during our conversation would come across in writing.

---

2   De Silva, *In Memory's Kitchen: A Legacy from the Women of Terezín*, 81–82. Translated here by David Stern, Mina Pächter's grandson.

3   De Silva, *In Memory's Kitchen*, 86. My translation.

◨ ◨ ◨

IRINA: Tell me about Mina Pächter's cookbook. Where was it written down? How did it arrive in the United States?

CARA: The *kochbuch*, so haunting, so poignant, was set down in the concentration camp of Terezín, also known as Theresienstadt. Mina Pächter was one of what we think were four or five women who participated in its creation. I say that because Bianca Steiner Brown, who translated the recipes for publication (they were in German and Czech), thought she recognized that number of distinct hands in it. But it was through Mina herself that the cookbook survived.

I initially came to see the manuscript because I belonged to a group called the Culinary Historians of New York and knew somebody there, a great collector of cookbooks named Dalia Carmel. Dalia was friends with Mina Pächter's daughter, Anny Stern, and one day Anny suddenly said to her: "You are interested in cookbooks? I'll show you a cookbook!" And with that she pulled out of a drawer a fragile, hand-sewn group of pages covered with recipes in tremulous writing.

Let me supply a little context. During the Holocaust many prisoners talked about food a lot, not only about starving, which one might expect, but about particular dishes, about recipes, about where in their hometown they considered the best place to get an ingredient. They did what was sometimes called "Cooking with the Mouth." Much less common, although more common than I originally thought, was the creation of "cookbooks." When I first saw the Terezín manuscript I believed it was an anomaly, because who could imagine the setting down of recipes by people interned in camps or other places of imprisonment? After all, in general, there was no paper, there were no pencils. You had to be in a place where it was possible to do such a thing. Yes, there were what one might describe as "oral cookbooks," but the fact that the Terezín cookbook was written down is one of the things that make the *kochbuch* so important. Mina and four friends or bunk mates found bits of paper and a way to hold them together and inscribed recipes on them, about eighty in all.

That we have it involves an incredible story of mother-to-daughter transmission. I tell it here as it was recounted to me by the daughter, Anny Stern. On Yom Kippur 1944, as Mina Pächter, the mother, lay dying of starvation in the camp hospital, she gave a friend a package that contained the cookbook and asked him to deliver it to her daughter. Anny and her husband and son had left for Palestine in 1939, but Mina had refused to go with them, insisting that "no one will hurt an old woman." And now, because of the war, Mina couldn't give her friend the address. As a consequence, he simply kept the package with him in Teplice, a town in Czechoslovakia, where he had an antique store or an art store of some kind. Then one day a cousin of his came into the shop and announced plans for a forthcoming trip to Israel (formerly Palestine). Mina's friend handed the package to his cousin and asked that his deathbed promise be fulfilled. But by the time his cousin got word of Anny's whereabouts, it was only to discover that she and her family had recently moved to the United States. So now it was the cousin who kept the package with no way of delivering it.

A decade and a half later, a man from Ohio came to a meeting of Czech Jews in New York bearing the parcel. Nobody knows who he was or how he got the *kochbuch*, nor where it was in the meantime. But, at some point during the meeting he asked if anyone there knew Anny Stern. Someone raised their hand and said, "I think I do." Later that day, about twenty-five years after her mother had died in Terezín, Anny's telephone rang in a high-rise apartment in New York. And a stranger's voice said, "Is this Anny Stern?" "Yes," Anny responded. "Then," said the voice, "I have a package for you from your mother." When she first saw it, Anny told me, it was like her mother's hand was reaching out to her from the dead. She didn't open the package for a number of years, because it was too painful.

I: She didn't even open it?

C: No. She just kept it in the drawer. She saw the handwriting on the outside. She recognized it as her mother's, and she put the package away. It was a long time before she finally found the courage to take it out and open it, and there in front of her were all these recipes written down by starving women.

Eventually, she showed it to Dalia and the present part of this extraordinary tale began. Dalia asked Bianca Steiner Brown, also a member of the Culinary Historians of New York, to translate a few of the recipes simply to see what the manuscript held. What Dalia didn't know, however, was that Bianca herself had special knowledge of what those pages contained, not only because she had been born in Czechoslovakia, was a brilliant cook, and a food professional, but because she herself had been interned in Terezín and had heard the food and cooking conversations that took place among the women. She was a teenager at the time, too young to really understand, and told me she thought they were crazy to be talking about food while they were starving. It was only much later that, on reflection, she came to it with great awareness.

So Dalia first went to Bianca to translate a few of the recipes. And then Dalia came to me. I was on the staff of a major American newspaper called *Newsday / New York Newsday*, then one of the largest in the country, and I realized immediately this had to be a story. Fortunately, my editors agreed. It became a feature article that stunned readers. Went out on the wires. Grabbed everyone's attention. And calls started coming in from Holocaust Museums that wanted the *kochbuch* for their collections.

It is, by the way, in the United States Holocaust Memorial Museum in Washington.

I: That was what I was going to ask.

C: Yes. It's not on display but it is held and protected there, and people can request it. Anybody can see it.

In fact, it was in part because of the reaction of the Holocaust museums to the article that I ended up doing *In Memory's Kitchen*. When I started getting all these emails from the museums expressing a desire to have the manuscript (of course, it wasn't mine to give), it quickly became clear that the story of it needed to become a book. And that I was going to be the one who undertook it.

To be frank, I was really apprehensive. I am a very empathic person. I knew the process was going to be very painful. But I also knew that not doing it would be much worse. From the moral perspective, I really didn't have a choice. It was clearly of the greatest importance to memorialize its authors, to create in any way I could a vessel for their voices, to help people understand what food means beyond simple bodily nourishment, to contribute a new and heart-rending dimension to the burgeoning field of food studies.

More than that, I knew in my heart that I was the right person to do it. Even though the stories I heard growing up were about pogroms and I didn't have anybody that I knew of in the Holocaust itself, I grew up with it as I did with the older stories. Also, although I am a secular Jew, I'm very Jewish. The sense of obligation to these women, which I still carry with me as a daily part of life, was extremely strong. So I did it, and I cried every day for a year. There was no way to think about it and their circumstances as they set the recipes down, without my eyes brimming over. Sometimes I would fall into a friend's arms, emotionally exhausted, but, in general, I found that no matter how I felt, I couldn't complain without censoring myself. I discovered that once I had talked to survivors, undertaken work on their behalf, I could never freely complain about my own pain in response because no matter how much I hurt, it was so nothing in comparison to their suffering.

Ultimately, as editor, I asked Bianca to translate all the recipes in the manuscript, which she did with great pain and as homage to her fellow prisoners. I wrote the introduction and edited the text and the recipes, produced the other material for the book. On publication, *In Memory's Kitchen: A Legacy from the Women of Terezín* burst upon the scene. (The great response to my article had been just a prelude.) Magazine and newspaper stories appeared everywhere, both across the United States and in much of the world. The book became one of *The New York Times Book Review*'s most noteworthy books of the year. In time, it was included in a variety of critical studies, women's studies, food studies.

Not surprisingly artifacts such as the book, or rather the manuscript on which it was based, had been largely unheard of. It was extremely moving. It was startling. It was a new way to approach the Holocaust. A more straightforward connection. Everyone eats. And that was the primary reason for the phenomenal extent of the media coverage. But initially that coverage, though so wonderful, also came with a problem.

When I first began talking about *In Memory's Kitchen* to the press and lecturing to live audiences, I realized that despite what I had written in the introduction, many people were thinking of the published version as a real cookbook. A Holocaust cookbook. I felt profound dismay about that. And so I began to emphasize even more than I already had that it was not meant to be that, that its contents were dream recipes, a number of which didn't work because the authors were often dying of starvation as they were writing them down. Their recipes in some cases appeared to be compromised by protein deficiency and, in general, by the pitiful state they were in physically and mentally. In a sense, the condition of some of recipes bore witness. Of course, all of them could be cooked by an expert who knew the cuisine. Or by somebody who wanted to compare the recipes to versions in a Middle European or Czechoslovakian cookbook and then prepare them. However, essentially the manuscript is a memoir in recipes.

But women, even though they are usually the nourishers, don't always understand the larger meaning of recipes. And men understand perhaps even less. They don't see that food and cooking it go far beyond the pot, and far beyond taste, and far beyond dinner and the table. And so they don't understand that every recipe tells a story beyond the rules it sets out for a dish, and that recipes written in these circumstances tell an even bigger story. And in the case of the Terezín recipes, they didn't get the breadth of their meaning until I started being interviewed a great deal and until scholars got a hold of it, and until I began speaking and emphasizing that this was, in its way, even though written in food, a form of autobiography, a chronicle of life and culture before the Nazis.

I: I was going to tell you that I very deliberately avoided this book for a long time. This one year when my husband still lived in New York and I was living in Dallas, I would go to a bookstore called Half Price Books several times a week. Of course, I always went to the cookbooks and in the East European section of the cookbooks was *In Memory's Kitchen*. It wasn't in Judaica or history…

C: That's a whole other issue, why it was there.

I: It was Dallas. Somebody had to file the book and they filed it there. I was always looking for interesting Eastern European cookbooks because I don't actually cook too much in my tradition, and I would pick it up and I would open it and I would put it back. I think that the thought at the back of my mind was that I don't want to deal with this. And then at some point I finally bought it. I didn't necessarily want to deal with it but I couldn't leave it on the shelf either.

C: Ah, yes. I really understand that.

I: I also didn't look at it for a long time. It was in the context of *Rumba Under Fire* that I started to look at *In Memory's Kitchen*, and then it made sense to me in a different way. There is a little bit of a danger in getting too close. A lot of the recipes are from my childhood, and the language, German, is the language I live in now. And yet German carries with it the trauma of the past century. But you were talking about the book's genre.

C: Well, yes. The book went to thirty-two publishers before anyone would take it, and one of the central reasons for that was that the publishers who turned it down one after the other were saying things like, "How would we sell it? Where would it be in the bookstore? Where would it be filed? Would it be in the cookbook section? Would it be among Holocaust books? In the Jewish studies section?" And then, "This is a remarkable document. It should be published. But not by us."

Finally, the company that had the foresight to become the book's publisher bought it for very little, but since I was undertaking it as a mitzvah, or good deed, project, I would have done it even for a penny. (I should mention here that everybody, my agent, the publicist, the people closest in, were also doing it as a good deed. I referred to us as the Mitzvah Team.) Anyway, that is how the book began its life. And later, after it was in print, I began to see what the publishers had been talking about regarding categories, because mostly this powerful remnant of the Holocaust was filed among regular cookbooks, right along with Julia Child and *The Joy of Cooking*. Where you found it in Dallas, Irina, in the Eastern European section, was actually better than the usual filing here.

I also had a horrible and related experience with a well-known rabbi who thought that this really was "a Holocaust cookbook." He believed I was exploiting the Holocaust. And his protest appeared in a magazine. I thought I would die. I was so outraged, not only that somebody would think that of me, but also that he did not understand what this was at all. The organization he was part of went crazy with embarrassment because they didn't agree with him. But to him it was only a collection of recipes and, as I said, most people knew recipes largely as things you take to the stove and cook. It had no further meaning for him. I wrote in fury and explained.

I: Do you think it's because it's food? Because it's traditionally the province of women?

C: I think it is that, in part. I doubt that a woman rabbi would have had the same reaction. And I have heard other stories about men understanding in only limited terms what it is about the subject that might sometimes come to women more intuitively. And although men also collected recipes under duress, I doubt that it was in exactly the same way and out of the same need that drives women.

There was also a certain amount of conflict when all the articles about the book began to run in newspapers and magazines here and abroad. I felt that since this was not a cookbook as such, and since some of the recipes didn't work because of the condition the women were in, there should be no attempt to make any of them usable for publication. But everyone wanted exactly that. So I gave in, and Bianca, a superb cook who knew the cuisine so well, took about ten of the recipes she had worked on at the beginning as part of investigating the cookbook and wrote them up professionally. And then we had recipes that could be given to the press for people to make at home with the knowledge that the dish would be delicious. And that turned out to have its good side. There were people who told me that they pulled out one of those recipes, and that they were going to make it on Passover or Rosh Hashanah every year in memory of the women of the Holocaust. So very moving. Later, when, as I just mentioned, people told me that every year on a Jewish holy day, they were going to make one of those dishes in the book in memory of the women of the Holocaust, I found it so poetically just that they would do that.

I: I have a couple of questions based on that. I was reading Rona Kaufman's article on *In Memory's Kitchen*. She starts being uncomfortable with it, particularly with an article Laura Shapiro published about the book in which she had a recipe for Mina Pächter's chocolate torte.

C: Yes, that was in *Newsweek*.

I: And Kaufman wrote, "When I read that Shapiro was going to eat the cake that came from one of the recipes, I felt a little sick to my stomach. I imagined that she was eating not Pachter's torte but Pachter's body."[4]

C: My reaction is so different from that. For instance, when *In Memory's Kitchen* was published, I really wanted to have a book event around it. But how do you have a party for the publication of a book about the Holocaust? Well, a friend offered one of the rooms in her beautiful restaurant for it, and we had Yahrzeit (memorial) candles and a rabbi to preside. He spoke and I spoke and there were other events around it, but for me the biggest thing, and I will never forget it, was that the chef of the restaurant, Andrew D'Amico, along with Rozanne Gold, who is a well known cookbook author, undertook to make a number of recipes from the book. Some from Bianca's versions. Some not. They were both professionals and could bring their expertise to a recipe in the book if it did not work perfectly.

Well, when I walked over to that table and I saw the dishes they prepared laid out on it, but even more when I tasted them, I was overcome. I was so grateful to the chefs for what they had done. Not only was I tasting history, but in each dish I could feel the women's lives, their joy, their pain, their

---

4   Kaufman, "Testifying, Silencing, Monumentalizing, Swallowing," 427. Kaufman spells Pächter's name without umlaut.

longing! Even if the recipes were slightly modified, I was overwhelmed by this sense—I can't say it better than this—that I was eating the foods of their dreams. And I can still taste those dishes as they were realized that day and experience those dreams. It was a privilege. The opposite, I think, of what Kaufman said in her review. Rather a deep way to honor the women who created the book, to, for a few moments, live their fantasies.

I: It strikes me that recipes, especially in the whole context of the creation of the Terezín cookbook, imply a future, right?

C: Yes. But I think that whether the women who wrote the book had a future, whether they lived or died, and whether they were cognizant of their hope of a future or not, their spirits were driven at least in part by hope when they wrote these recipes down. But there were many other elements involved, too. Food is a powerful identity marker, much more so than most people realize. What we eat, and where we eat it, and who we cooked for, and the conversation at the table, the occasion, these are such intensely important parts of who we are and what we remember.

Writing those things down evokes a gentler time in the past, even when you are in the middle of hell. It expresses a hope not only that you might live, but that somehow, if someone makes those recipes again, if somebody carries on your heritage by doing it, that you are living on in those recipes in some way.

However, recipes in these circumstances are also a kind of weapon, not a bazooka or an Uzi, but a weapon of self defense, precisely because of the mightiness of food as a form of psychological reinforcement, as an identity marker, as a way of fighting back against someone who is trying to exterminate your heritage, your history, your birthright, and your deepest self. When you write or speak of or recollect the recipes that have marked your life, you are profoundly strengthening your sense of who you are.

I have heard that in Auschwitz—where, somebody said to me long ago, if they had had paper and could have made a cookbook it would have been thousands of pages long—women talked about food constantly. They would shout recipes to each other over the fences, so that if one of them didn't live, the other one might carry on and remember. That is just such a powerful image to me, knowing what else was going on in Auschwitz of course, but also knowing about the women's relationships in Auschwitz.

There are a lot of things I found out in further studies after I wrote the introduction to the book. One of them was how the older women taught the younger women to cook as part of carrying on their heritage. There was no food, but they taught them in words. I am not saying that people were aware of what they were doing. It was a cultural thing, perhaps also connected to the custom at that time of women creating a homemade cookbook for their children, so as to give it to their daughters when they got married, and maybe even to their sons and daughters-in-law. I think in a way that the authors of the manuscript, by writing down recipes in Terezín, were carrying on that tradition, doing something they would have done if they had not been in a concentration camp. Teaching cooking to younger women, shouting recipes to each other, and when possible, writing down recipes may have been part of that.

A few years ago I was speaking at the University of Wisconsin and a couple of weeks before I went, I heard about a poem whose subject was Auschwitz and food. I hadn't read it, but I felt instinctively that I absolutely had to make it part of my talk. But I couldn't find it. And it was making me crazy. As a lecturer, as a scholar, as great believer in the power of poetry, I really needed that poem. I knew it had been written by a woman named Ursula Duba and I bought her book. But it wasn't there. I searched through interviews with her trying to find a way to get to her. Nothing. But, then, finally, in desperation, at the very last minute, the night before I left for the conference, I made a final attempt. I searched for her on Facebook. And, thank you, social media, I found her at last. And within an hour I had the poem. It is called "How I Learned to Cook," and it recounts a conversation between two women, one, the poet, and the other her old friend who had survived this infamous *Lager*. "So what did you talk about all day in Auschwitz?" the poet asks her friend. "Did you talk about your fears of dying, about the fate of your family or relatives, how all this had come about, the insanity of it all?" And her friend answers, "Oh, No...None of that. We talked about food mostly. And recipes." And then she goes on to talk about what dishes and techniques she learned from the older women there. She describes recipe after recipe:

> in Auschwitz
> I learned how important it is
> to gently fold the flour into the beaten eggs
> for a successful pound cake
> and how you can't rush a yeast dough
> it needs time to rise[5]

I've never spoken since without that poem, or rather parts of it since it is so long, being the first thing that I mention. And then I talk about a little verse that was written in Terezín by a child (she soon died in a death camp), about how the women talked of food.

> Ten o'clock strikes suddenly,
> and the windows of Dresden's barracks darken.
> The women have a lot to talk about;
> they remember their homes,
> and dinners they made.[6]

---

5   Ursula Duba, "How I Learned to Cook," in *Tales from a Child of the Enemy* (New York: Penguin, 1997), 75–77, at 76.

6   Eva Schulzová, "An Evening in Terezín," in *I Never Saw Another Butterfly: Children's Drawings and Poems from Terezin Concentration Camp 1942–1944*, ed. Hana Volaková (New York: Schocken Books, 1993), 42–43.

It's very powerful to realize how common this talk of food was.

I: Could food do things poetry couldn't?

C: You have to tell me what you mean.

I: Well, for *Rumba Under Fire* I was reading memoirs of Romanian political prisoners from the fifties and sixties. A lot of them were intellectuals and professors, and they kept their spirit alive in prison by recollecting literature and movies, or by composing poetry. In one prison there were many scholars and they basically organized a seminar which they would take turns teaching from memory. I was reading your description of Terezín and the way it was set up as this model ghetto, where you could say there was an opportunity to keep Jewish culture alive. But that culture was also abused and instrumentalised for horrible ends. I don't know what it would mean to write poetry or put on a play or do this work of the spirit in a context where you were serving this Nazi ideology, or at least this lie that is being built up around you. Whereas recipes wouldn't do that, right?

C: I am not sure what you mean? That recipes couldn't be made to serve Nazi ideology? Or that you don't think writing down or confecting or reciting recipes is doing the work of the spirit? If the latter, I disagree. But no matter. As to the rest, even though Terezín, with all its horrors, was being used to promote the idea of a model ghetto, the Paradise Ghetto (as the Nazis called it, pitching it like ad men), to which early on, before deportations began, the Reich tried to coax the Jews to come voluntarily to wait out the war, and even though it was in that context that the Jews were allowed a certain amount of freedom, I think there would be pleasure and identity to be found in surviving in it. A friend of mine has reconstructed a powerful cabaret piece, a satire that came out of Terezín.[7] Remember that a lot of this was occulted. There were paintings hidden under the floorboards. In real life it was a camp and what you did in the daytime and what you did at nighttime were different. But I think the lectures in Terezín and the education which you'd go after so strongly, and which is part of the culture, would still have functioned in reaffirming identity. Even though you were surrounded by lies, even though you could be on your way to a death camp the next day, it would still have power. And yet they did this, and, aware or not aware, through their behavior they were saying "Fuck you!" They persisted in cultural and intellectual life. This satiric cabaret piece is an amazingly powerful thing. Works like that, or like the poetry that children were encouraged to write in Terezín to deal with their feelings, still served a purpose.

As for what you said before about the Romanian camps—"A lot of them were intellectuals and professors, and they kept their spirit alive in prison by recollecting literature and movies, or by composing poetry. In one prison there were many scholars and they basically organized a seminar which they would take turns teaching from memory"—well, the same kind of thing happened in Terezín, of which it has been said that the population there was the flower of Czechoslovakian Jewry. There, too, there were professors, scholars, artists, professionals. However, in Terezín it was at least in part both women and men who taught. Freidl Dicker-Brandeis, an artist, designer, and teacher who had been at the Weimar Bauhaus was a very significant figure in the camp. Mina Pächter herself used to lecture on the Prague Baroque, a style of architecture, but she also wrote down recipes. I would be curious to know though whether the Romanians you quoted were mostly men.

---

7   *The Last Cyclist*, based on a cabaret written in the Terezín Ghetto by Karel Švenk in 1944, reconstructed and reimagined by Naomi Patz. See http://www.thelastcyclist.com/ for more information on the play's textual history.

I: They were mostly men.

C: Not that men didn't ever gather recipes. Some did. And very actively so. However, the purpose of gathering for them may not have been identical to that which drove women. Food and its preparation, the setting of a fine table, was a large part of who women were. Women nourished people, creating "blood and bone" with their recipes. I think talking and writing about food is one aspect of that act of remembering and recreating life. What each of these categories brings is different and I think poetry can be extremely powerful, but what food brings is powerful, too. Very.

I: One of the women prisoners whose memoir I read talked about being young among a group of older women. Like Bianca Steiner Brown, she thought the older women were silly too when she first arrived and they started telling her their stories. If I remember correctly in her memoir she writes about building a cake in her mind. The cake would become more and more elaborate, and she worked on it until she could taste it. She fed on this imaginary cake while she was in prison.

C: I think the ability to do that is central to what we are discussing. There are many stories about how food functioned in such situations. To me, one of the most compelling of the realizations I have come to about this is how people managed, how they helped themselves survive with imaginary food. Not food in their mouths, just food in their minds, in their hearts, in their memories. I often quote a Chinese writer, Zhang Xianliang, who was in a labor camp, and who speaks very powerfully in his book, *Grass Soup*, about how two extra grains of rice could make a difference to whether a man survived another day or two.[8] It was obviously not because of the

8   Zhang Xianliang, *Grass Soup*, trans. Martha Avery (London: Secker & Warburg, 1994).

protein or the nutritive value of two grains of rice, he writes, but because of the hope they gave a man. It provided him with the strength to keep going. Though these two grains of rice were meaningless nutritionally, they were powerful encouragement psychologically.

There are many things that I have come across in this vein, showing how food and fantasy and memory worked in these circumstances. One of them is in a memoir called *Childhood in Times of War*, written by Andrew Salamon, himself a child during the Holocaust, who was hidden, with others, in the pit of a sawmill. The children spent the days underneath the piles of sawdust and would come out at night. In his book, he refers so beautifully to them, to the degree that anything could be beautiful about this, as a "band of starving dreamers."[9] He describes their games, which involved food and imagining. The point was to make the other person drop with desire by talking about foods you remembered. The winner was the person who brought everybody to their knees with longing. That image stays with me of these little eight- and nine-year-olds feasting on their memory, a band of starving dreamers.

I: They were remembering their childhood because their childhood was over earlier than it should have been.

C: Possibly. Boys and girls, still children, remembering their lost childhoods. How pitiful that would be. But though that might have been the case, I have come to suspect that that isn't necessarily what was happening. This phenomenon is too universal. It seems to occur wherever people are starving, under great duress, and they are literate and can find a pencil, or they have a mouth with which to tell someone else. They fantasize. And not only adults. Children, too. During the Siege of Leningrad, one sixteen-year-old kept a diary

---

9   Andrew Salamon, "Food Fantasies," *Childhood in Times of War* (Remember.org, 1995), http://remember.org/jean/chap4/part2/ fantasies.

and wrote the day before her seventeenth birthday about
how "when things are back to normal, she and her mother
will eat fried potatoes, 'golden and sizzling, straight from the
pan', salami 'thick enough to really sink your teeth into' and
hot, buttery blinis with jam'—'Dear God, we're going to eat
so much we'll frighten ourselves.'"[10]

Because of the work I engaged in after *In Memory's Kitchen*
it absolutely became plain to me that this happened continu-
ally. One of my concentrations is the meaning of food and the
power of food far beyond physical nourishment.

I already knew from doing *In Memory's Kitchen* that a cookbook written by prisoners of war in a camp in the Philippines
had been published in 1946. It was happening exactly at the
same time as the events in *In Memory's Kitchen* were going
on. And the recipe collection of these prisoners of war was
also written down. It is called *Recipes out of Bilibid*.[11] I didn't
know until much later to what degree this happened in other
prisoner-of-war camps, but I was to find out that it was
very much the same. However, it was largely men doing the
obsessing, probably because they outnumbered the women.
This happened not only during World War II, but also during
World War I, an obsession with food and recipes and cooking
as the POWs starved, and too often ate garbage or slop.

Filmmaker Jan Thompson, who was presenting at the
Oxford Symposium on Food and Cookery at the same time
I was years ago, was talking about how her father was a psychiatrist who had dealt with soldiers in World War II and
many of them recalled food memories. Among the things she
mentioned, and has mentioned in other work since, was a
soldier mentally laying out an entire farm while he was in
a POW camp. I remember, too, hearing that soldiers put up

10   Anna Reid, "Ration Book," review of *The Diary of Lena Mukhina:*
      A Girl's Life in the Siege of Leningrad, ed. Valentin Kovalchuk, Alek-
      sandr Rupasov, and Aleksandr Chistikov, *Literary Review* 433 (2015),
      https://literaryreview.co.uk/ration-book.

11   H.C. Fowler and Dorothy Wagner, eds., *Recipes out of Bilibid* (New
      York: George W. Stewart, 1946).

pinups of bread instead of Betty Grable or other movie stars. Subsequent to that, when I began to read more, I began to discover much more about what soldiers did. One woman walked around in a prisoner of war camp collecting recipes for her bridge parties! Can you imagine? There was in particular an important Italian cookbook created during WWI. It was put together by an officer named Giuseppe Chioni, who went through the camp collecting recipes.[12] There were soldiers there from all over Italy, so he ended up creating a regional cookbook of Italian food out of prisoner-of-war memories. One of Chioni's most memorable observations is expressed in a comment he makes. He says he doesn't know where or how these "warriors became cooks." What a powerful perception about the obsession with food that results from extreme deprivation. It really stayed with me.

But then I started reading about starvation more generally and the phenomena it creates. On one of Sir Ernest Shackleton's expeditions to Antartica, the emaciated men could not stop talking about foods they remembered from the past and meals they would prepare for each other in the future, when (and if) they got back to civilization. Their endless marches were also spent inventing imaginary dishes and cooking them in their heads. "No French chef ever devoted more thought to the invention of new dishes than we did," wrote Shackleton.[13] Creativity born of starvation again made men, in this case, explorers, into cooks.

I was particularly struck, too, by a starvation study that was done after the war in Minneapolis, at the University of Minnesota. It was a study to find out how to re-feed people who had starved, so that they wouldn't die. The person who did that study was Ancel Keys, who first talked about the

---

12   Giuseppe Chioni and Giosuè Fiorentino, *La fame e la memoria, ricettari della grande guerra. Cellelagher 1917–1918* (Feltre: Libreria Agorà, 2008).

13   Ernest Henry Shackleton, *The Heart of the Atlantic and South* (Ware, Hertfordshire: Wordsworth Editions, 2007), 246.

Mediterranean diet.[14] They used conscientious objectors who did their service by starving. Half-starving. They were given bits of food, as in the concentration camps, but basically they were starved. What was so striking to me when I was reading this was that here were people who could allegedly leave, they could do their service in some way other than staying, and yet their response to starving was the same as in a concentration camp. They obsessed about food. They obsessed about cookbooks. They read cookbooks constantly. There is an expression that was apparently used in the study to describe boys lying on their stomachs and turning pages of cookbooks: it was called "stomach masturbation."[15] And, again, as a result of this experience with starvation, a number of them said that they wanted to change professions and become cooks.

I: Wow...

C: All of this has illustrated to me, almost beyond anything I could have imagined before, the importance of food to identity, to who you are. I keep repeating it, but it merits repeating. Its value to the spirit as well as to the body is almost indescribable. So its worth for maintaining your identity, your culture, in the face of someone like Hitler, who was trying to exterminate everything about you and your heritage is immeasurable. More broadly, it has shown me how imagination and memory functioned in these circumstances and how they sustained people. Obviously not everyone in the Holocaust, not every POW, not every person who is starving, or *in extremis*, engaged in food-related talk and activities, in writing if they could, or

14   Ancel Keys, Josef Brožek, Austin Henschel, Olaf Mickelsen, and Henry Longstreet Taylor, *The Biology of Human Starvation*, 2 vols. (Minneapolis: University of Minnesota Press, 1950).

15   Hilde O. Bluhm, "How Did They Survive? Mechanisms of Defense in Nazi Concentration Camps," *American Journal of Psychotherapy* 53.1 (1999): 96–122, at 112. Originally published in *American Journal of Psychotherapy*, 2.1 (1948): 3–32.

just in fantasizing. There were some to whom the thought of focusing on food while starving was incomprehensible, but others, aware or not, used the fantasizing and remembering an aid to psychological and emotional survival.

As I began to discover more and more about the subject, I found an article in the *New York Times* about a diet that involved imaginary eating to sustain you. The dieter actually goes through the motions of eating, of cutting pretend food and eating if off a real, but empty plate. Almost unimaginable that it would succeed. But the person who wrote that article said it worked for him. It really makes you wonder if this, too, was part of the reason for the concentration on imaginary food and cooking in the camps.

I: You know, this brings up a question I had. I was thinking about who we are when we receive these recipe collections, how we can read them, to what extent can we empathize with them or understand them. I suspect that people who are likely to have access to these books and the leisure to read them probably also have enough food in their fridge. If you are spending money to buy the edited version of *In Memory's Kitchen*, for example, you probably also have money for lunch that day. I don't even know if we can understand hunger from descriptions of hunger. I suspect not.

C: I suspect not, too.

I: Is it important that we understand the hunger?

C: Well, I think that it can bring you closer to read what people wrote when they were starving to death, when they were dying or about to be sent to the camps in the East, and really had nothing except disgusting slop in front of them. It can bring you closer to see people fantasize and call up from memory wonderful meals. I think the question is where in your being you understand it. Most intelligent people could probably understand it in their heads, but whether it means understanding it in the very deepest sense, I doubt. I work on this all the time and I can imagine what they went through, it moves me beyond words and even to tears. Yet, of course, I don't really know what it means to starve. What we say when we say the word "hunger" is not what this is about. People say all the time, "I'm starving!"

I: "I'm starving to death."

C: Yes, and it's just meaningless. Because it's not starving. It's not what happens to your body or what happens to your mind as you waste away, or as you are denied those foods that encapsulate your identity. You can't understand what it means to suffer from protein deficiency and from absolute starvation, to watch your body turn skeletal, to see that your mind can't function anymore. To not recognize yourself. How could we know that? I can think about what it would be like. I can talk to you about it. I can feel about it very deeply, as you do. But I think the most that people can learn from it, even if its only intellectual, though for some people probably it goes deeper, is, again, the power of food to sustain us mentally and spiritually. Even as your body is wasting away and being destroyed, you can turn to food for the power to survive another day, another month.

I: I've read critiques of this kind of work we are doing on poetry in prison, or on art in prison, claiming that it presents a version of the past that is too positive, or too uplifting.

C: I've read similar things.

I: I have to say, I personally am pretty firmly on the side of being astounded at the ability of human beings to draw on these practices, especially when they are fighting for their humanity, when everything around them conspires to make them into animals or less than animals.

C: Yes, they were fighting for their humanity and people also fight this way for their heritage, their cultural patrimony, all as a way of sustaining their deepest selves. I've also read those critiques, and to me these practices and the examination of them don't take away from the darkness. I talked to many people beyond the book, and my belief, and I can't express it often enough, is that doing these things helped them to hold on in the most dire and dreadful circumstances. It was not just what was happening to them, but what they were witnessing. The entire idea of genocide, of trying to wipe out an entire people, is such an inconceivable thing. They had to face the disappearance of friends or even family suddenly gone from the camp, and know that they themselves might be on a transport the next day. I feel it's an incredible expression of the power of the human spirit to survive.

Once, for another purpose, I interviewed a group of survivors who got together regularly in London, England. As you know, survivors deal with this material very differently. Some never talk about it, some always want to talk about it. Some don't even tell their children. Bianca told me that until we spoke together at the Holocaust Museum in Washington right after *In Memory's Kitchen* was published, her children had not known a lot of what had happened to her and her husband. I've heard many such stories.

Well, when I first came into the room with all those survivors in London and said that I wanted to talk to them about their thoughts about food and cooking during the Holocaust, and their memories, and what it had been like, they reacted to a person, men and women, as though I must be crazy to want to talk about a subject like that. It was trifling. It was not important when they had suffered so long and gone through so much. Initially, I thought they were going to ignore me completely.

But once the first person considered a little longer and decided to talk to me about his food recollections, the room lit up. It was amazing how it changed. They had been taught to think of food as trivial, unlike the two of us, who know that it is such a huge subject that it is now acceptable on a scholarly level. And in their minds, especially trivial given the enormity of the Holocaust. But once they gave in to the profound pull of the subject and started to discuss their memories and dreams of food during the Holocaust, a line actually formed of people who wanted to tell me what they remembered. They had received the world's message that cooking is not important, not a serious topic, and certainly was not one in the context of their suffering and the Nazi horror, but then life took over. And the stories came pouring forth.

Eventually, what at first had seemed so unlikely to me when I began to work on *In Memory's Kitchen*, the talking about and even recording of recipes in time of great jeopardy and suffering, came not to seem unusual at all. In fact, I now believe that wherever people are literate and can find a pencil and a sheet of paper (one cooking manuscript I know of was written on propaganda leaflets for the Third Reich), foodways, cooking traditions, recipes, are likely to be called up and remembered. Indeed, I am sure that somewhere in this too often barbarous world, they are being talked about, and even recorded, right now.

ATEMPAUSE AND ATEMSCHAUKEL
THE POST-WAR PERIODS OF
PRIMO LEVI AND HERTA MÜLLER

Tim Albrecht

I.

When we speak of historical periods, we imagine stretches of linear time, separated by significant historical events. Yet the term "period" implied a circular structure when Thrasymachus introduced it into rhetoric in the fifth century BC, long before it became a heuristic tool for historiography.[1] In rhetoric, the period is a stylistic device, a particular type of sentence with a hypotactic structure characterized by a rhythm of tension and release: the first part of the period (*protasis*) builds anticipation, the second part (*apodosis*) offers resolution. Thrasymachus coined the term in analogy to athletics: *Peri-hódos* ("circular course") signifies the racetrack of the ancient *stadion*. The circular syntactic structure creates the impression of wholeness and completion. Just as the athlete in the stadium strives for physical perfection, the periodic sentence strives for linguistic perfection, marked by the perfect union of rhetoric and logic:

> The period is a circular construction...such that at the beginning of the period incomplete idea elements occur

1   Hartmut Krones, "Periode," in *Historisches Wörterbuch der Rhetorik*, ed. Gert Ueding (Tübingen: Niemeyer, 2003): 750–64, at 750.

which are in need of integration, and which are only integrated into a complete idea at the end of the period, while
the middle parts are embraced and oriented towards the
whole by this procedure. The end is thus expected and "in
sight," as Aristotle says.[2]

There are various possible explanations of how exactly the
term "period" disseminated from athletics via rhetoric into
historiography. One explanation is based on the fact that
some authors recommended particular subtypes of periods
for the writing of history. In this view, the meaning of the
phrase "historical period" underwent a metonymic shift from
signifying a stylistic device in historiography to denoting certain segments of history itself. A second explanation takes
into consideration a meaning the concept took on since late
antiquity in grammar and that is still familiar to us: the period
in the sense of "full stop" signifies not the sentence or its
structure but its end. By analogy, a historical period would be
a stretch of historical time defined by a historical watershed.
A third explanation bypasses rhetoric and grammar altogether
and takes into account that the term period was not only used
to designate the racetrack but also the four-year cycle of the
Pan-Hellenic Olympic games. This stretch between two athletic festivals may be understood as the first model for marking historical time in periods. A fourth explanation departs
from a more intimate relation of the term "history" itself to
the athletic circularity of the period: in the ancient *stadion*,
the *histos* is the post that marks the turning point between
the two legs of the race. For Michel Foucault, the referee
who observes the turn at the post represents an archetype
of the historian.[3] No matter which narrative about the nexus

---

2   Heinrich Lausberg, *Handbook of Literary Rhetoric: A Foundation for
     Literary Studies*, trans. Mathew T. Bliss, Annemiek Jansen, and
     David. E. Orton (Leiden and Boston: Brill, 1998), 414.

3   Cf. Michel Foucault, *Die Wahrheit und die juristischen Formen*, trans.
     Michael Bischoff (Frankfurt am Main: Suhrkamp, 2003), 31.

of "period" and "history" appeals most, the period—and by extension history as periodic history—is at once characterized by poetry and logic. The poetry lies in the rhythm of back and forth, flow and pause, departure and return; the logic lies in the fact that it offers the clarity of ends and conclusions.[4] The period leaves no remainders, nothing to be desired.

II.

In what follows, I discuss two autobiographical novels, both accounts, at once comparable and irreducible, of what it meant to live through the historical watershed of 1945. The two books arose out of the two dark shadows of the twentieth century, the concentration camp and the gulag, and they both extend, as I will argue, the scope of personal stories and narratives to the larger problem of historiography. By doing so, they call into question the idea of a clear-cut historical watershed as such. Each novel does so on its own by insisting that for dehumanized and brutalized individuals there is nothing but the *longue durée*. Yet they yield even more in comparison, because when considered together it becomes clear that one man's liberation may mean another man's imprisonment. World histories and their turning points can never be severed from specific local events and their particular impact on individual bodies. This is why the stories of these bodies matter.

The two books are Primo Levi's *The Truce* (*La Tregua*), first published in 1963 and Herta Müller's *The Hunger Angel* (*Die Atemschaukel*) from 2009.[5] Both novels expand the historical

---

4   *Protasis* (from *proteinein*, "to stretch forward") in Latin became *propositio*—if-clause (grammar), premise (logic), introduction of characters (drama). *Apodosis* (from Gr. *apodidonei*, "to give back") is the consequent in a conditional statement.

5   Primo Levi, *If This is a Man and The Truce*, trans. Stuart Woolf (London: Abacus, 2010); Herta Müller, *The Hunger Angel*, trans. Philip Boehm (London: Portobello Books, 2012). In the course of thinking

turning point of 1945 to claim a narrative space for telling their stories of survival and return. In doing so they describe "post-war periods" characterized by a paradoxical temporality: neither do they simply start after the war nor is it evident when or whether they will come to an end. Originally, the idea of reading these two novels alongside each other derived from the (at first sight) rather coincidental fact that the novels' German titles both make reference to the act of breathing: *La Tregua* was translated into German as *Die Atempause* ("the breathing pause"), while *Die Atemschaukel* is a neologism that literally means "the breath-swing." Both titles refer to the passing of time—suspended in Levi's case, symbolized as a pendulum-like movement in Müller's case. Indeed, the "period," logocentric in the way its rhythm of protasis and apodosis provides a structure of premise and conclusion, is closely tied to the breath in rhetoric. Aristotle states: "The period of several members is a portion of speech (1) complete in itself, (2) divided into parts, and (3) easily delivered at a single breath — as a whole, that is; not by fresh breath being taken at the division."[6] Quintilian cites Cicero's view that "[the period's] length should be restricted to the equivalent of four *senarii* [usually: iambic trimeters], or to the compass of a single breath."[7] The period is thus equally defined by *Atempausen* and *Atemschaukeln*, by the stretch of time between two breaths and the filling of that stretch of time with the regular pendulum motion of tension and release.

The Italian philosopher Benedetto Croce linked precisely these characteristics of the period to historiographical *logos*:

---

and writing about *The Truce*, another text of Levi's, his Auschwitz memoir *If This is a Man* more and more became the center of attention. This is not coincidental but in many ways supports the argument I am making here. The two memoirs were published in the same volume.

6   Aristotle, *The Works of Aristotle*, trans. W. Rhys Roberts, vol. 11 (Oxford: Clarendon Press, 1971), 133.

7   Quintilian, *The Institutio Oratoria*, trans. H.E. Butler, vol. 3, The Loeb Classical Library (London: William Heinemann, 1922), 577.

To think history is certainly to divide it into periods, because thought is organism, dialectic, drama, and as such has its periods, its beginning, its middle, and its end, and all the other ideal pauses that a drama implies and demands. But those pauses are ideal and therefore inseparable from thought, with which they are one, as the shadow is one with the body, silence with sound: they are identical and changeable with it.[8]

Note: Croce does not claim that history itself is imbued with logos, and that historical periods should thus be understood as the progression of spirit through human affairs. Instead, thought itself is by necessity periodic—that is organic, dialectical, and dramatic—and therefore thinking history is as well. Although historians have come a long way both from teleological accounts of history and mere chronicles of events, Croce's premise that periods are an indispensable heuristic tool for historiography is still widely accepted.[9] Thought cannot be separated from its shadows and its silences, and history cannot be either.

III.

Primo Levi would have rejected Croce's dialectics. He did not believe that silence makes us talk, that shadows make light. His belief in rationality remained unshaken even through the unspeakable experience of the *Lager* that the more dialectically minded have described as the culmination of the dark

---

8   Benedetto Croce, *History: Its Theory and Practice*, trans. Douglas Ainslie (New York: Russell & Russell, 1960), 112.

9   Cf. e.g. Jacques Le Goff, *Faut-il vraiment découper l'histoire en tranches?* (Paris: Éditions du Seuil, 2014), 188.

side of rationality.[10] As Levi writes in the foreword to *Is This a Man*, a false conclusion does not cast a shadow on logic as such, but merely on the validity of the premise:

> Many people—many nations—can find themselves holding, more or less wittingly, that "every stranger is an enemy." For the most part this conviction lies deep down like some latent infection; it betrays itself only in random, disconnected acts, and does not lie at the base of a system of reason. But when this does come about, when the unspoken dogma becomes the major premiss [*sic*] in a syllogism, then, at the end of the chain, there is the Lager. Here is the product of a conception of the world carried rigorously to its logical conclusion; so long as the conception subsists, the conclusion remains to threaten us. The story of the death camps should be understood by everyone as a sinister alarm-signal.[11]

As much as Levi does not question reason as such—after all a "system of reason" should be able to recognize the validity of its premises—he questions what one would call the periodicity of logic, the rhythmical inevitability with which the syllogism proceeds from premise to conclusion, bypassing further moral considerations.

Nevertheless, Levi did not make any attempts to "think" or "understand" history—in fact, he rarely evokes the term. He understood his writing as a form of witnessing, and he manipulated its form to serve this task.[12] Deeply suspicious of rhetoric, he would have refused to approach history

---

10   Cf. Max Horkheimer and Theodor W. Adorno, *Dialectic of Enlightenment: Philosophical Fragments*, trans. Edmund Jephcott (Stanford, CA: Stanford University Press, 2002). German *Lager* is often used in this context to refer to a concentration camp.

11   Levi, *If This is a Man and The Truce*, 15.

12   Cf. Levi, *If This is a Man and The Truce*, 382.

rhetorically, neither in historiography nor in narrative or poetry. Levi's writing is not periodic, neither in its syntax nor in its perspective on history.

The Truce tells the story of the nine months in Levi's life between the liberation of Auschwitz-Buna in January 1945 and the return to his birthplace Torino in October of the same year—a journey that takes him through Poland, various parts of Russia, Romania, Hungary, Austria, and, of all places, Germany. Levi and some of his fellow prisoners are transported in a bizarre zigzag from one diplaced persons camp to another by the rather erratic Russian authorities, unsure of what to do with the camp survivors. Throughout the confusing and enervating journey Levi longs for Italy. Yet on the eve of his actual return he recognizes that he and his comrades were unwittingly given an invaluable gift by the Russians, the gift of time:

> What should we find at home? How much of ourselves had been eroded, extinguished? Were we returning richer or poorer, stronger or emptier? We did not know; but we knew that on the thresholds of our homes, for good or for ill, a trial awaited us, and we anticipated it with fear.... Soon, tomorrow, we should have to give battle, against enemies still unknown, outside ourselves and inside; with what weapons, what energies, what willpower? We felt the weight of centuries on our shoulders, we felt oppressed by a year of ferocious memories; we felt emptied and defenceless. The months just past, although hard, of wandering on the margins of civilization now seemed to us like a truce, a parenthesis of unlimited availability, a providential, but unrepeatable gift of fate.[13]

---

13   Levi, *If This is a Man and The Truce*, 378.

In this passage we find in close proximity the title-giving expressions for both the original novel and its German translation. What is called a "truce" is also described as a "parenthesis of unlimited availability," an impossible *Atempause* that in retrospect appears to be infinite. Albeit this is not one of Croce's ideal pauses that marks, for example, the watershed between war and peace (because the battle lies ahead), neither is it the turning point between deportation to the camps and the return home (because an odyssey does not complete a cycle, and a concentration camp prisoner does not return home). Rather, Levi is thrown from one state beyond history into another as the parenthesis of unlimited availability represents a benign echo of the experience of time in the camp. The parenthesis is not, as the German title suggests, an *Atempause*, a caesura between the past and the future, the silence that makes the sound. It represents the impossible availability of unlimited time.

The rhythm of the *Lager* is brutally regular and without respite. Time gives way to the merciless present tense of survival:

> Every day, according to the established rhythm, *Ausrücken* and *Einrücken*, go out and come in; work, sleep and eat; fall ill, get better or die.... And for how long? But the old ones laugh at this question. They laugh and they do not reply. For months and years, the problem of the remote future has grown pale to them and has lost all intensity in face of the far more urgent and concrete problems of the near future: how much one will eat today, if it will snow, if there will be coal to unload.[14]

The prisoner soon learns not to think about the future and to practice the "underground art of economizing on everything, on breath, on movements, even thoughts."[15] This breathless present-future is

> our sterile and stagnant time, whose end we were by now incapable of imagining...for us, hours, days, months spilled out sluggishly from the future into the past, always too slowly, a valueless and superfluous material, of which we sought to rid ourselves as soon as possible....For us, history had stopped.[16]

For a brief moment, when air raids and nearby fighting announce the advance of the Red Army, Levi "breathes a tense air, an air of resolution."[17] However, the depiction of the actual arrival of four Russian soldiers in the camp is devoid of any expression of relief or conclusion. At this point, the reader is still reeling from the account of the death of a prisoner named Sómogyi on the eve of liberation, whose body Levi and a fellow detainee are in the process of disposing of when the Russians arrive:

> In the evening and for the whole of the night and for two days without interruption the silence was broken by his delirium. Following a last interminable dream of acceptance and slavery he began to murmur: "*Jawohl*" with every breath, regularly and continuously like a machine, "*Jawohl*," at every collapsing of his wretched frame, thousands of times, enough to make one want to shake him, to suffocate him, at least to make him change the word.[18]

Sómogyi's anti-periods mark the ultimate inhumanity of man reduced to naked life, mechanical responses to orders no one

---

15 Levi, *If This is a Man and The Truce*, 138.

16 Levi, *If This is a Man and The Truce*, 122–23.

17 Levi, *If This is a Man and The Truce*, 147.

18 Levi, *If This is a Man and The Truce*, 176.

is giving anymore. Sómogyi's end is "expected" and "in sight," but his humanity has long expired.

The way Levi recounts the coincidence of Sómogyi's death and the liberation of the camp reminds us that he is not bearing witness to history anyway, not to its reversals and peripeteias, its periods and ideal pauses. He is bearing witness to "the work of bestial degradation, begun by the victorious Germans, [that] had been carried to its conclusions by the Germans in defeat,"[19] but more importantly he bears witness to the fact that this work has the effect of a self-fulfilling prophecy. Degraded to bestiality, the degraded become bestial. In this syllogism, the conclusion is not announced but brought forth by the premise. It is not necessary, Levi insists, to derive from it a negative anthropology:

> We do not believe in the most obvious and facile deduction: that man is fundamentally brutal, egoistic and stupid in his conduct once every civilized institution is taken away, and that the Häftling is consequently nothing but a man without inhibitions. We believe, rather, that the only conclusion to be drawn is that in the face of driving necessity and physical disabilities many social habits and instincts are reduced to silence.[20]

Thus the turning point in the history of the camp is neither the departure of the Germans (defeat), nor the arrival of the Russians (victory), but a simple gesture that speaks to the social instincts, that makes them break their silence. When the narrator and Charles, a fellow detainee, find a stove in the ruins of the bombed Lager, transport it back to their hut on a wheelbarrow, and manage to get it working, each of the other prisoners in the hut offer a slice of bread:

---

19   Levi, *If This is a Man and The Truce*, 177.

20   Levi, *If This is a Man and The Truce*, 93.

Only the day before a similar event would have been inconceivable. The law of the Lager said: "eat your own bread,
and if you can, that of your neighbour," and left no room
for gratitude. It really meant that the Lager was dead. It
was the first human gesture that occurred among us. I
believe that that moment can be dated as the beginning of
the change by which we who had not died slowly changed
from Häftlinge to men again.[21]

Levi dedicated an entire book to such human gestures that
occurred in the *Lager* entitled *Moments of Reprieve*.[22] It is these
gestures, not the liberation of the camp, that ultimately make
a future, *the* future, possible. They, as well, give time.

IV.

In *Is This a Man*, liberation does not bring instant relief. In
fact, the prospect of returning from bestiality to humanity
is fraught with facing the pain the prisoners have learned to
suppress along with their humanity. But during the narrator's
captivity one episode in particular offers a moment of respite:
significantly, as the vitality of breath recovers, the narrator
turns to poetry.

One day, Levi is given a break from forced labor and is
ordered to get soup from the camp kitchen with a fellow
French prisoner named Pikolo. It is an unexpected parenthesis, a possible *Atempause* from the merciless rhythm of the
camp. Levi and Pikolo seize the opportunity: "Pikolo was an
expert. He had chosen the path cleverly so that we would
make a long detour, walking at least for an hour, without

---

21   Levi, *If This is a Man and The Truce*, 166.
22   Primo Levi, *Moments of Reprieve*, trans. Ruth Feldman (London:
      Penguin Books, 2002).

arousing suspicion."[23] Even though this is a short parenthesis, as in *The Truce* Levi is given time, and what happens in this
pause foreshadows his later odyssey: during the detour Levi
recalls the canto of Ulysses from Dante's *Inferno*. Dante's *terza
rima*, composed of three hendecasyllables, has about the same
length as the four iambic trimeters Quintilian demands for
the period and like the period is characterized by an "elastic
pulse—the ceaselessly vital thrust-and-pull—of the movement which makes [it] one of the most flexible and satisfying measures ever devised for verse-narration."[24] But while
the winding periodical style is syntactically geared towards
conclusion, Dante's verses flow in a cascade motion towards
a *telos* far off.

With the vitality of Dante's verse, summoned to raise the
dead, Levi finds his breath and time begins to work again.
Memories come flooding in, memories of home, visions of
memories of return, almost too painful to bear, so that the
narrator begs his attentive listener to interrupt him: "oh,
Pikolo, Pikolo, say something, speak, do not let me think of
my mountains which used to show up against the dusk of
evening as I returned by train from Milan to Turin!"[25] Breath,
poetry, time and return are inextricably bound here. But arti-
ficial interruptions of the *Inferno's* flow are unnecessary, as
Levi time and again fails to recall the stanzas in their entirety:
"There is another lacuna here, this time irreparable...For-
give me, Pikolo, I have forgotten at least four triplets."[26] Of
course, the lacunas are no "ideal pauses," they represent not
the catching of breath, but the failure to reconstruct the vitality of the ceaseless thrust-and-pull. Under the conditions of

23   Levi, *If This is a Man and The Truce*, 117.

24   Dorothy L. Sayers, "Introduction," in *The Comedy of Dante Alighieri
       the Florentine. Cantica I: Hell (L'Inferno)* (Hardmondsworth: Penguin
       Books, 1960), 60.

25   Levi, *If This is a Man and The Truce*, 120.

26   Levi, *If This is a Man and The Truce*, 120.

a hell more hellish than Dante's, time, breath, and memory return only temporarily, and only in fragments.

Soon the narrator and Pikolo have completed their detour and the *Atempause* has come to an end. Levi closes the chapter with the concluding verse of canto XXVI: "'And over our heads the hollow seas closed up.'"[27] In Dante, these concluding verses are solitary lines, separated from the regular *terzina* structure. They do not bow to the periodic rhythm, and often they contain surprising, unanticipated information or perform a transition, opening a door to the next canto. Thus, while the verse contains an image of shipwreck and doom, it is no mere ending, let alone a conclusion. Rather, it points ambiguously to the future: on the one hand it contains an element of hope since we know that Ulysses survives and returns; on the other hand it may just open a door to another circle of hell.

V.

Levi's accounts of the *Lager* do not correspond to the historian's rhythm of pauses and periods. In writing, Levi had to free himself a second time from the iron grip of the camp that extended way past its material historical existence. To this purpose, he sought a different type of period, one that would allow for rhythm and order beyond man and his fallible logic. In a memoir from 1975 entitled *The Periodic Table*, he finds it in chemistry, a field of inquiry that even before the war appeared to contain an antidote against historical master narratives: "[Chemistry] led to the heart of Matter, and Matter was our ally precisely because the Spirit, dear to Fascism, was our enemy."[28] The young Levi saw in Mendeleev's periodic table and its symmetries a poetry "loftier and more solemn

---

27   Levi, *If This is a Man and The Truce*, 121.

28   Primo Levi, *The Periodic Table*, trans. Raymond Rosenthal (New York: Schocken Books, 1984), 52.

than all the poetry we had swallowed down in *liceo*; and come to think of it, it even rhymed!"[29] After the war, the nexus of literature and chemistry reverses, and Levi becomes a writer as soon as he manages to derive from his daytime profession a stylistic ideal that allows him to articulate his testimony:

> My very writing became a different adventure, no longer the dolorous itinerary of a convalescent, no longer a begging for compassion and friendly faces, but a lucid building, which now was no longer solitary: the work of a chemist who weighs and divides, measures and judges on the basis of assured proofs, and strives to answer questions... I now felt in the writing a complex, intense, and new pleasure, similar to that I felt as a student when penetrating the solemn order of differential calculus. It was exalting to search and find, or create, the right word, that is, commensurate, concise, and strong; to dredge up events from my memory and describe them with the greatest rigor and the least clutter.[30]

The stylistic ideal derived from the Periodic Table is anti-periodic. Events dredged up from memory shall not be dissolved in the flow of hypotactic superstructures. Instead, they shall be called by their names, with precision and rigor. In the same vein, autobiography shall not attempt to integrate the events of a life into one over-arching narrative. Instead, Levi insists in the last chapter of *The Periodic Table*, autobiography is an exercise in a particular type of historiography he calls "micro-history," once more stressing the incommensurability of material life experiences and ideal historical arcs:

> The reader, at this point, will have realized for some time now that this is not a chemical treatise.... Nor is it an

---

29   Levi, *The Periodic Table*, 41.

30   Levi, *The Periodic Table*, 153.

autobiography, save in the partial and symbolic limits in which every piece of writing is autobiographical, indeed every human work; but it is in some fashion a history. It is—or would have liked to be—a micro-history, the history of a trade and its defeats, victories and miseries, such as everyone wants to tell when he feels close to concluding the arc of his career, and art ceases to be long.[31]

VI.

In January 1945, when Primo Levi encountered four Russian soldiers in the deserted Auschwitz camp, the Romanian poet Oskar Pastior was transported by the same Red Army to a Russian labor camp in the Ukraine. Romania had been part of the Fascist axis until 1944 when it sided, under Russian military pressure and after a coup d'état led by the monarchy, with the allied forces. After Russia occupied Romania, between seventy and eighty thousand members of the German speaking minority in Romania were sent to labor camps in Russia as part of "compensation" for Romania's Fascist policies. Pastior grew up as part of this minority in Sibiu (*Hermannstadt*) in *Siebenbürgen*. He was seventeen when he was sent to the Ukraine. When he returned, he was twenty-two.

In 1960, Pastior published his first book of poetry (in German), and he continued to publish after defecting to the West in 1968. His experimental sound- and nonsense poetry bears affinities to Dada, the *Wiener Gruppe*, and Oulipo. For the novel *Atemschaukel* (English: *The Hunger Angel*), an account of his years in the gulag, he collaborated with German-Romanian writer Herta Müller. Initially, Müller and Pastior had planned to write the novel together, but Pastior's sudden death in 2006 left the project in limbo. Having conducted

---

31   Levi, *The Periodic Table*, 224.

extensive and detailed interviews with Pastior, Müller eventually decided to write the novel on her own. The final text, published in 2009, thus constitutes a multilayered exercise in prosopopoeia, not the least because Müller's mother had also been a prisoner of the camps. It is a novel written in two voices: through Müller's prose the reader hears some of Pastior's poetic diction, and the richness in detail betrays the fact that the novel is based on factual experience. To what extent Müller's prosopopoeia was successful, how much her voice expressed her own or Oskar Pastior's vision, immediately became subject to debate.[32]

Levi's and Pastior's camp experiences are incommensurable. No analogy would do them justice. Pastior spent five years in a brutal and in many cases deadly work camp fueled by nationalist resentment, the spirit of revenge, and the megalomaniac character of the Russian communist project. Levi spent a year caught in the extinction machine of the Auschwitz death camp fueled by the ideology of racism and an inconceivable will to meticulously orchestrate the mass murder of people labeled as sub-humans. If we know anything from their testimonies we know that time and death had a different meaning in these places. But both writers were caught in the wheels of history in a way that does not neatly correspond to its chronicles, a fact that is highlighted by the contingent facts that Levi's liberation coincided with Pastior's imprisonment and that Levi's odyssey on the way home to Turin led him through Ukraine during Pastior's first year of captivity. Both stress the feeling of being removed from time and history in the camps, and neither of them felt time and history just picked up when they were, at once fortunate and burdened, able to escape. Nor did the war end for either one in 1945.

---

32   Cf. Sophia Gabrielli, "Der lange Schatten der Vergangenheit," accessed February 17, 2016, http://www.uibk.ac.at/literaturkritik/ zeitschrift/978389.html.

Pastior found himself caught in the shadow of the Second World War even after it had ended. The fighting may have come to an end, but for Pastior the ordeal had just begun. In the novel, Müller/Pastior find a memorable phrase for the blurring of historical periods. In various instances the narrator uses the phrase "it was the second peace," or "it was the third peace," instead of "it was the second or the third year of captivity." The novel is written in a style that abounds in such metonymies, just as it abounds in metaphors; particularly salient are compound metaphors such as *Hungerengel* ("hunger-angel"), *Atemschaukel* ("breath-swing"), or *Herzschaufel* ("heart-shovel") easily achieved in the German compound-heavy idiom but often awkward to translate. This style pursues a strategy very different from Levi's quest for the *mot juste*. While Levi attempts to discover the right order of words and things,[33] Müller/Pastior pit language *against* experience. As in the metonymy of the "second peace," only poetry can make the contradictions of reality visible; at the same time, language is used as a spell to ban such reality. One effect of this writing is that the novel reads like a *Künstlerroman*: the reader witnesses the discovery of poetry as a defense mechanism against the experience of the camp. Like metaphor, camp and poetry become compounded.

Some critics saw this camp-poetry as inappropriate for testimonial discourse, echoing Adorno's dictum of the barbarism of lyrical poetry after Auschwitz: "The era of gulag literature that left us feeling asphyxiated [lit.: "that takes our breath away"] has come to its natural end and will not be reanimated with [Müller's] second-hand sounds of celestial harps and angels' choirs."[34] This assertion by Iris Radisch, leading critic at the German newspaper *Die Zeit*, is remarkable

33 Cf. Levi, *The Periodic Table*, 41–42.
34 Iris Radisch, "Kitsch oder Weltliteratur? Gulag-Romane lassen sich nicht aus zweiter Hand schreiben. Herta Müllers Buch ist parfümiert und kulissenhaft," *Die Zeit*, August 20, 2009; my translation.

in more than one way: first, because she sees it as the duty of camp testimonials to convey to us the prisoner's state of suffocating claustrophobia; second, because she ties the ability of literature to achieve this to the authenticity of a first-hand account; and third, because she sees *The Hunger Angel* as a caesura that marks the end of the era of authentic testimonial. Literary history, then, has its ideal pauses too. For Radisch, *The Hunger Angel* sets that dramatic period that announces the end of something old and the beginning of something new, in this case the transition of *Lager* literature from communicative memory to cultural memory.[35]

Pastior/Müller's syntax, however, does convey some of the suffocating experience of being arrested in permanent limbo. Their sentences are decidedly paratactic and often elliptic, while frequent iterations create the impression of hyperventilation rather than celestial music. In its syntax, this novel is much closer to Levi's writing than in its wording. In fact, because he wanted to adopt "the calm, sober language of the witness,"[36] Levi forced his voice to calm down past hyperventilation in order to present Auschwitz as a case, not as experience. While the "breath-swing," the unconscious chiasmus of respiration, is never quite achieved in Müller/Pastior's sentences, Primo Levi's *If This Is a Man* is predicated on a certain catching of breath necessary for the witness to give a coherent account in front of the jury.

---

35   Cf. Aleida Assmann, *Erinnerungsräume: Formen und Wandlungen des kulturellen Gedächtnisses* (Munich: C.H. Beck, 1999), 13–14. The term "communicative memory" signifies forms of collective historical memory that rely on oral transmission, while the term "cultural memory" signifies forms of collective memory that rely on more mediated forms such as literature, film, monuments, etc.

36   Levi, *If This is a Man and The Truce*, 382.

VII.

The fact that something as natural and unconscious as respiration becomes thematic indicates that it has lost its natural and unconscious nature. In *The Hunger Angel*, the protagonist's "breath-swing" is either arrested or in a state of hyperventilation ("My breath [lit.: the breath-swing] teeters over, I have to pant."[37]). During the daily roll calls, Pastior learns to control his breathing in order to not stand out from the other prisoners:

> I practised forgetting myself during roll call, and not to separate breathing in from breathing out. I practiced rolling my eyes up without lifting my head, to look for a corner of cloud where I might hang my bones. If I was able to forget myself, and found the celestial hook, it kept me upright.[38]

This grotesque hangman marionette is suspended from time, history, and its corporeal humanity altogether. Like Levi, Müller/Pastior describe the experience of becoming one with the *Lager*, of being entirely subjected to its orders and rhythms, and losing with this becoming-space any sense of time. For Pastior too, history had stopped in the camp: "we were blinded by hunger and sick for home, withdrawn from time and outside ourselves and done with the world. Just as the world was done with us."[39]

When Pastior returns from the gulag, time continues to be out of joint. One reason is that every word, every object, potentially echoes memories of the camp. No period is possible in this life, because the camp has created an impossible future: "Everything that's yet to come is already here."[40] One

---

37   Müller, *The Hunger Angel*, 26.
38   Müller, *The Hunger Angel*, 20; translation modified.
39   Müller, *The Hunger Angel*, 39.
40   Müller, *The Hunger Angel*, 242.

of these echoes is in the ticking of the clock in his parent's living room: "On the wall, the ticking was my breath-swing."[41] The meta-metaphor of the ticking of the clock as the breath-swing highlights the asynchronicity between the periodical, regular time of the clock, and the irregular, suspended experience of time of the camp survivor. It insists that the former will always succumb to the latter.

Pastior's memories are often accompanied by shortage of breath. But sometimes he manages to calm himself down with the use of metaphor: "When the objects gang up on me at night, choking me, I fling open the window and hold my head out in the fresh air. A moon is in the sky like a glass of cold milk, it rinses my eyes. My breath again finds its rhythm. I swallow the cold air until I'm no longer in the camp."[42] We do not know whether the mental image of the moon as a glass of milk stems from Pastior's or Müller's repertoire. Surely, it is a metaphor that lends itself to Radisch's criticism as the archaic image of being washed with milk comes dangerously close to kitsch. It is yet another curious coincidence that Levi in the concluding paragraph of *The Periodic Table* evokes the image of a glass of milk *while describing the very act of concluding*. The passage may serve as another example of Levi's material ideal of writing and Müller/Pastior's use of metaphor. In his last chapter, Levi describes the imagined journey of a carbon atom, "the element of life":[43]

> [The carbon atom] is again among us, in a glass of milk. It is inserted in a very long chain, yet such that almost all of its links are acceptable to the human body. It is swallowed; and since every living structure harbors savage distrust toward every contribution of any material of living origin, the chain is meticulously broken apart and the fragments,

41   Müller, *The Hunger Angel*, 253.
42   Müller, *The Hunger Angel*, 26–27.
43   Levi, *The Periodic Table*, 225.

one by one, are accepted or rejected. One, the one that concerns us, crosses the intestinal threshold and enters the bloodstream: it migrates, knocks at the door of a nerve cell, enters, and supplants the carbon which was part of it. This cell belongs to a brain, and it is my brain, the brain of the *me* who is writing; and the cell in question, and within it the atom in question, is in charge of my writing, in a gigantic miniscule game which nobody has yet described. It is that which at this instant, issuing out of a labyrinthine tangle of yeses and nos, makes my hand run along a certain path on the paper, mark it with these volutes that are signs: a double snap, up and down, between two levels of energy, guides this hand of mine to impress on the paper this dot, here, this one.[44]

This last sentence, in syntax and semantics, sets a period. Does this mean that with *The Periodic Table* Levi has managed to narrate his life, as a micro-history of a trade or an atom, in a way that allows for an ideal pause, a next chapter? The real meaning of this conclusion begins to reveal itself only once one realizes that Levi wrote this story before he was transported to Auschwitz and later decided to include it as the last chapter in *The Periodic Table*. And that the *me* who is setting the period here, this one, is no longer the *me* that is setting the period there, that one.

44   Levi, *The Periodic Table*, 232–33.

THEATER IN WARTIME

Greg Alan Brownderville

For the play we got ourselves in love. Otherwise
        I didn't know her.
There were no other players. For three weeks
        of rehearsals, we lived together,
going by our characters' names, smelling like each other.
        The city turned into a war. Explosions
                gashed sky
        day and night, left both of us
                sick to the marrow.

The day of the first performance, the bombs
                louder, closer,
        we made love again and again.
When the hour came, like a demented mailman, the city
                made no sound. We stepped out
        into the smoking ruins and held each other.
Then trusted our feet, soles clicking
        toward the playhouse. I hoped
                it still existed.

        No one else there, doors bolted shut.
I took a dead potted plant from the street and flung it

through a ground-floor window, kicked out
the jagged fangs of glass, and climbed in.
      I doubted
she would follow, but she did.

    We busied ourselves with exercises, the normal
        routines.
  Got dressed, patted on our makeup.
Then readied the equipment as best we could, adjusting
    the lights to an all-purpose setting.

And strode onstage. *So soon?*

    We looked into each other. The void
gnawed away
              at my peripheral vision. *Now,*
    I thought. *The crew, the crowd—*
they'll all appear, and the apocalypse
    unhappen.
        Now.

    The first line
was mine.
      Simple. *Say the line.*

I couldn't. I could not
  speak words. She waited
for a moment,
        a few moments,
    then stepped back.
Her face darkened and wilted
    like a page cast into a fire.

COUNTING CARDS
A POETICS FOR DEPLOYMENT

Susannah Hollister

> deploy, *v*.: To unfold, display. Of a body of troops: To open
> out so as to form a more extended front or line. (*OED*)

When packing for a war zone, a deck of cards is an obvious choice. Most soldiers fit one into a rucksack or combat
uniform, issued items that seem designed for slipping extra
items into their many side pockets. A preventative measure of
a kind, a deck of cards promises to protect against boredom
or unwanted conversation, and will serve without a wireless
signal or powered battery.

My now husband deployed to Afghanistan in 2010, and he
took with him a lightly used, ordinary, Bicycle-brand deck. I
don't remember where it came from or even whether I knew
he packed it. But within a week of his departure we were playing a game—if game is the word for the system we devised.
A very simple, wholly necessary game. It required two decks,
the one he kept and one that I did.

The rules were as follows:

Both players
    Live through a week.
Player one
    Pick a card.
    Tell player two what the card is.
Player two
    Find the same card in your deck.
Both players
    Tape the card to a wall.
    Reverse roles and repeat.

That's it, and it's how we marked time. The cards in a deck would see us through exactly one year. Even in the face of powerlessness and uncertainty, as we were then, neither of us is much inclined to look for coincidences, much less take our cues from them. But the reality of his departure must have readjusted something in our shared sensibility, and we seized on the kind of numerical match that, typically, we'd overlook: fifty-two cards, fifty-two weeks. We started counting.

Our counting system worked for us, I now believe, because it emptied the time of its content. Unlike the Army-designed "personal identification playing cards" that featured photographs of most-wanted Iraqis, the ordinary cards we used had no strategic motive. They featured only the usual geometric shapes and stock faces. For us, each card, each week, went un-annotated. Our accumulating record showed nothing of my husband's rudimentary living conditions at the eastern border with Pakistan, where missiles not infrequently flew onto his base, nor of his daily route to the provincial police headquarters through an area US forces patrolled for IEDs, nor of his work training and supplying security forces charged with protecting a political structure to which they felt little allegiance. Our record showed nothing, either, of my just-rented house in Austin, Texas, where all my acquaintances were new, nor of the drought slowly killing the redbud tree in my front yard, nor of the classes I taught in twentieth-century poetry and poetics—classes that eventually helped me figure out why I was taping cards to my wall, and why I was still teaching.

We didn't want to forget any those things, and we haven't. We take it is as a responsibility of military life (though not a unique one) to register and continue to reflect on the full reality of war—for those in a war zone and those at a distance, on all sides. That's our ongoing task. But it's not what got us through the year. For *that*, we needed abstraction. While each taped card put a number on our respective walls (mine, solid and freshly painted white; his, plywood), those numbers were arbitrary and repetitive, not sequential. We watched the rows of cards grow and the remaining stack of cards diminish. But we kept ourselves from counting from one to fifty-two and knowing too precisely how much of the year had passed and how much remained. The cards gave us an image—not a description or a number, just an image—that announced time was passing for us both.

It's a complicated advantage of twenty-first-century war-fare that families can often stay in frequent, sometimes near-constant communication, and we had various means of keeping in touch. We were determined to experience the year together, building our still-new relationship in the cir-cumstances as they were. Every day, we reached each other by Skype's chat feature, where we could watch each other's words appear, line by line, in real time. Knowing the details of our days, often as they happened, let us think we were shar-ing time, not merely passing it.

We met teaching English and Philosophy at the United States Military Academy at West Point, and for both of us reading and writing is a way of thinking, a way of process-ing experience and also of having it. My husband gave me a Kindle as a present when he left, and we thought that reading books at the same time or at each other's suggestion would be high among our ways of coping with deployment. If we couldn't share the same immediate environment or daily routines, we could share the same imaginative worlds. But though we did exchange books, and though all year we were each reading at least two or three at time, neither of us finished the ones we sent each other. We didn't write many letters, or emails of substance. Online chatting was convenient; it was also ephemeral. On some server, the data of our chat sessions might be preserved, but if that occurred to us, our lack of the skills to retrieve it buried the thought.

We must have sensed that recording our experience as it passed would thwart us. Or maybe we just weren't capable of doing it. Especially in a medium expected to last, acts of describing require, or create, time's full spectrum: past, present, and future. In personal communication, perhaps more than other forms, the writer at the time of writing thinks ahead to the time of reading. The reader at the time of reading thinks back to the time of writing. Neither gets to sense the other's present moment. Instead, both sense the time between their separate acts, the time that distinguishes present from future or present from past. Focusing on those passages requires a confidence that the one stage extends continuously into the other. Under the constant threat of physical harm, to oneself or to loved ones, that confidence isn't there, ready to be drawn on. It needs tending.

Again, we avoided documenting the year not because we'd want to be able to forget particular feelings of fear or distance, much less specific reasons for danger or worry or responsibility, when they were behind us. Rather, we avoided documenting because we wanted and needed to treat present time as present. Thinking into the past meant admitting that one wasn't sure of the other's present, only of one's own. Thinking into the future meant imagining a safety we couldn't trust. Put another way, looking forward and back creates narrative tension, and narrative wasn't our genre. We didn't know it, but that year we were writing a poem.

Reading together introduced a similar problem, and I think that's why we didn't do it. To read a book that matters to someone else is to connect to experiences that person has already had, not to current ones. To read the same book you know another person is reading lets you share, however imprecisely, an alternate time. The time of reading replaces and becomes the present—but only as long as you both keep reading. The moment you put the book down, the unshared present returns. If we could have read the same pages without stopping, from the day of my husband's deployment to the day of his redeployment (the military's misleading term for coming back), I suppose that might have worked.

As much as we needed and wanted to live only in present time, we also needed and wanted to perceive our mutual survival. Our card game was our way of doing both. Every Saturday, when one of us would pick a card and the other would find its match (we took turns), we gave ourselves evidence that he'd survived a week in a war zone and our relationship had survived a week of deployment.

Our way of counting could have been even less representational. We could have used blank index cards or tally marks. Instead, we used something familiar and at hand, something with its own associations: games of chance, games of strategy, occasional big wins, likelier big losses, addiction. So in a way, our choice of marker reminded us of risk and the luck we'd need to come out the other side. But that reminder was importantly oblique.

Primarily, our chosen marker introduced numbers to set against the linear count of weeks passed and weeks still to go, and symbols to set against the content of our lives. We could play at thinking the chosen card significant: every week has one or six of something, or a man (Jack, King) or woman (Queen), and those things or those people have some relation to work (spades), feeling (hearts), beauty (diamonds), or harm (clubs). But any claim that a particular card fit a particular week was a deliberate stretch, a joke, a way of affirming the cards' meaninglessness. Our basic approach to reality was one thing we could maintain, and we tried. Really, the numbers, faces, and suits created another story—or more accurately a non-story, a sequence of empty symbols that overlapped the linear count of weeks and the qualities of our days. From within our present time and without disrupting it, they gave the year a set of stops and starts, and, with that, a way to keep feeling.

▣ ▣ ▣

Literature wasn't our means of experiencing the year together, but it was and is my work. My suit of spades. That year, I was teaching a new course in poetics and thinking about the teaching I'd done the year before, when my students were future Army officers in their first year at West Point (plebe year), having chosen to enter the Army while the country continued two of its longest wars.

West Point's core curriculum has long included literature courses, and the introduction to literature I taught from a staff syllabus devoted five of fifteen weeks to poetry. Cadets, accustomed to memorization, were responsible for learning a set of over seventy-five terms, ranging from allegory and anaphora to volta and zeugma. If non-readers of poetry are likely to consider it inaccessible, they are equally likely to consider it unserious, and the course was designed to sway cadets from either view. Versification offered the kind of rigorous, systematic approach cadets knew from their initial military training and other coursework required for the bachelors of science all graduates earn.

The theme organizing the course was knowledge, a word with its own definition at West Point. "Cadet knowledge" refers there to pieces of language cadets must memorize and recite on demand. These include such things as military songs, quotes from generals, the capacity of Lusk Reservoir, an antiquated definition of leather, an answer to the Gertrude Stein-like question, "How is the cow?" ("She walks, she talks, she's full of chalk, the lacteal fluid extracted from the female of the bovine species is highly prolific to the nth degree.")[1] The syllabus evoked arbitrary memorization so as to move beyond it, expanding the theme of knowledge from its substance to its development and uses.

When my classes got to the unit on poetry, I handed out a long chart grouping the poetic terms into categories. I don't know whether reading to fill in the chart helped my cadets enter into the poems we read, or stopped them at the point where they spotted an entry for the "examples" column. Their scavenger hunt through our anthology led them to minute details of language and form, and maybe some cadets stayed with those details long enough to feel them. As I taped cards to my wall a year later, one of the categories on the chart came to seem especially important: the one called "syntax and line" and including "caesura," "end-stopping," "enjambment," and "stanza break." I hoped some of them happened to dwell on that section. I hoped some of them tried reading poems for lines as well as sentences and noticing where the two diverged. If they did, they opened up a kind of knowledge they're sure to need: how to inhabit time two ways at once, how to stay both alert and human.

The turn of the poetic line gives verse its name and offers a definition of the genre. Theorists as different as Giorgio Agamben, Rachel Blau DuPlessis, and James Longenbach, when they set out to distinguish poetry from other kinds of literature, look to line endings. "Versus," the Latin root of "verse," refers to a line or row made by turning, as a plough does at the end of the field. The legal use of "versus" retains the sense of direction, a turning toward or against, and looking to line endings means looking to the relationship—often the opposition—between line and sentence. Line alone isn't a defining category, Longenbach claims; its ways of confirming

---

1   Casey A. Neff and David A. Jones, eds., *Bugle Notes 2007–2011: The 99th Volume* (West Point: Directorate of Cadet Activities, 2007), 264.

and denying a poem's syntax are what make it so founda-
tional. Agamben focuses on enjambment, DuPlessis on cae-
surae and white spaces, Longenbach on lines of all kinds: end-
stopped as well as enjambed, metered as well as free-verse.[2]
Their accounts share an argument that poetry's unique capacity is the sustaining of two strands, distinct if sometimes
overlapping: line and syntax, sound and sense, substance and
time. DuPlessis put poetry's doubleness in terms that could
describe the deployment-year card game my husband and
I devised. She sets her attention "where thinking in poetry
is both poised and ongoing, in a streaming of lines that one
could read as a constellation, but which also embodies the
experience of temporality and ceaseless questioning." Taking
George Oppen's later poems as an example, she finds "the
effect . . . is to be both solid in time and streaming, broken up,
interrupted with other connections in time to other objects
and events."[3]

To read a poem, then, and to read it for the two strands
of its language, is to enter a seemingly contradictory state:
fixed and changing, out of time and in it. When we instruct
students in reading poems aloud not to pause at the ends of
enjambed lines, we are teaching them to feel an ending without marking it. The voice follows only the syntax, while the
mind follows the lines as well, sensing an interval within and
against the progression of time or the structure of thought.

This habit that poetry builds, of at once sensing an interval
and continuing uninterrupted, is one my husband and I both
needed during his deployment. By now my cadets, most of
whom were commissioned as Army Lieutenants in 2013, are
likely to need it themselves. Military deployment is, of course,
only one of many contexts that require intense, unbroken

---

2   Giorgio Agamben, *The End of the Poem: Studies in Poetics*, trans. Dan-
     iel Heller-Roazen (Stanford: Stanford University Press, 1999), 109–
     15; Rachel Blau DuPlessis, *Blue Studios: Poetry and its Cultural Work*
     (Tuscaloosa: University of Alabama Press, 2006), 198–205; James
     Longenbach, *The Art of the Poetic Line* (St. Paul: Graywolf, 2008).

3   DuPlessis, *Blue Studios*, 203, 199.

focus on one's present time and circumstances and, at the same time, an intact ability to feel. Any situation that threatens well-being calls for that, especially if it has duration. And we need it even when we're out of harm's way. It may be the same capacity we draw on every time we put all our attention in one direction, when we work our hardest (spades), when we love well (hearts).

⬛ ⬛ ⬛

In 2010–2011, I wanted all of my husband's attention on his safety, where my attention was, too. He described, in chat messages now vanished, the heightened state he was sustaining all year: senses on constant alert, like wires carrying currents, ready to come alive at the slightest touch. He said it became second nature, continuing even as slow hours dragged, and I took some comfort in knowing he wouldn't let himself feel comfortable. But I spent the year scared for him, and uncertain about what life was ahead for us together. Perceiving existence while it is in danger, I found, keeps survival from being one's only possible act. Threats to oneself or to a loved one risk reducing experience to those threats alone, at the expense of all other thoughts and feelings—at the expense of the capacity to have other thoughts and feelings.

I've said my husband and I needed to confirm our mutual survival, and we needed to do that so that we could also do more, so that we could keep the other parts of ourselves present and active: the parts that love, the parts that question, the parts that make us fully human. Without that ongoing confirmation, I don't think I could have stood in front of my new students, or listened to what they said. I don't think I could have made friends or even chatted with neighbors. I don't think I could have kept being in my relationship with my husband, either. Confirming survival while still tending urgently to it let us continue our own humanity, and continue perceiving that of others—intimates and strangers both. Being in our relationship, not just keeping it going, that year meant knowing my husband beyond my anxieties for his safety. And as much as I wanted him to stay whole, I wanted him to see others whole: me, but also those he served with and those he opposed.

I'm suggesting a connection here between reading poems and living under existential threats. The two activities could hardly look more different, and the first may require an ease and attention that the second prevents. But the quality of attention they involve is precisely what leads me to consider them together. It is a sustained and busy focus—uninterrupted but mobile and sensitive, noticing everything. I'm fortunate to have more experience (and more training) with poetry than with existential threats, so I can speak with greater confidence about the one activity. Reading is rereading. But even in a single pass through a poem, the practiced reader notices the texture of its words together with the thoughts those words carry. Memorizing seventy-five different aspects of poetic style is worthwhile only when it allows that doubleness, when it stops being "knowledge" and creates a skill. I'm convinced by recent claims that, hard as it tries, the human mind cannot multitask, and I don't consider this skill to require that. The attention I'm describing ranges widely from within the single focus it never leaves—in DuPlessis's words, "poised and ongoing."

Neither teaching English to West Point cadets nor marrying an Army officer qualifies me to comment on military training or decision-making in war. But my brief and indirect experience with existential threats does help me understand my investment in this literary genre. Reading a poem well lets us read a poem well. When I teach poems, I want my students to have that experience. I also want them to think about why that experience matters, and to recognize the kind of attention they're practicing—attention that, elsewhere, can help them stay not just alive but also whole. And I want them to know how to regard wholeness in others, as well, especially when my students are training to be military leaders in a country waging war.

◨ ◨ ◨

A poem many of my West Point cadets disliked was John Berryman's "Dream Song 14." It begins, "Life, friends, is boring. We must not say so." By the point in the semester when I introduced this poem, I was feeling irreverent and suspected my cadets were too. I thought they'd laugh at Berryman's Henry and appreciate his resistance to expectation and authority. They didn't. Faces were blank, hands were on tables, unraised. At first I guessed they disliked the poem because they couldn't identify with Henry, and I was disappointed. I'd hoped they'd found more ways to read than looking for themselves in poems. Then I suspected they disliked it because they did identify with Henry but stopped there, sensing only the ugliness of complaint and not yet the ways the poem moves Henry beyond himself. They often seemed bored, in the way that comes from being too busy and having too little control over one's own actions and time. And they were all too familiar with prohibitions on expression, like the one that completes the poem's first line. They could have taken Henry's grievances as a way to confirm and voice their own, through the safe distance of anthologized literature. Some more critical cadets, I knew, shared a few of Henry's very complaints: about "great literature," about the romanticizing of leaders, about the rhetoric of capital-V Values.[4] But they didn't side with Henry, or against him for that matter. After a semester and a half of cadet life, they knew to avoid bitterness and self-pity.

4   John Berryman, "Dream Song 14," 1964, *The Dream Songs* (New York: Farrar, Straus and Giroux, 2007), 16.

I played for them a video of Berryman reading the poem aloud, partly to discourage identification, and his reading seems nearly as full of pauses as of words. He gives time to every mark of punctuation, adding some where they don't appear in the text (between "moreover" and "my mother," for one). And he stops at every line break, even the enjambed ones. The recording should have directed attention, as the poem itself does, to the difference between sound and sense. But I didn't emphasize that difference in class that day, and sense prevailed, keeping my cadets quietly disdainful—stuck at complaint or, perhaps, on Berryman's long beard, thick glasses, and continual shaking and nodding of his head.

If I taught this poem again—I haven't yet—I'd use it to teach a sense for endings within an ongoing line of thought. Its form helps us do that, and its ideas comment on the need for such doubleness. Here, the ongoing line of thought is embittered and isolated and doesn't resolve or find a way out. But we do find a set of endings within it, an alternate pattern that shows us a different mode of experience. The first line contains two complete sentences, of just six in the eighteen-line poem. Both carry the confidence of completed thought—and here thought is complaint. But they do not satisfy. Another line begins, and soon sentences lengthen and lines end with commas or no punctuation at all. After the opening lines, enjambments take over and show the annoying insistence of Henry's chastising by his mother (and others):

> and moreover my mother told me as a boy
> (repeatingly) 'Ever to confess you're bored
> means you have no
>
> Inner Resources.' I conclude now I have no
> inner resources, because I am heavy bored.

Henry starts listing the sources of his boredom, and as his list gains momentum, enjambments return, revealing and building tension between thought and expression. These are the poem's closing lines:

> And the tranquil hills, & gin, look like a drag
> and somehow a dog
> has taken itself & its tail considerably away
> into mountains or sea or sky, leaving
> behind: me, wag.[5]

At the level of syntax, Henry's frankness, his willingness to flout authority, brings not catharsis but growing agitation. The enjambments, in the tension they create, confirm the frustrations in Henry's words. But the enjambments also open up an alternative: expression released from self-pity.

The poem keeps to the form Berryman uses throughout the *Dream Songs*, three six-line stanzas that alternate between two longer lines and one shorter one. The variation emphasizes line length, and even when the pattern has become familiar, the short lines can feel cut off, as if poet or speaker couldn't come up with more to say. This poem's three-word ending — "behind: me, wag" — notably so. Berryman reminds us of line endings, then, every three lines, whether those lines are end-stopped or enjambed. When Henry's thoughts carry over from one line to another, we have two experiences — an experience of the fragmentary line and an experience of the continuing rant — and can sense the same in our speaker. Henry goes on with his complaints, but there is another dimension to his language, one defined not by complete thoughts, but in seemingly arbitrary pieces. After the line about hills and gin, the lines, taken as lines, don't sound much like complaints. They lose their bite. They're more like observations, or like nonsense. Their incompleteness of meaning ("and somehow a dog," "into mountains or sea or sky, leaving," "behind: me, wag") moves them away from the syntax of complaint. From

---

5   Berryman, "Dream Song 14."

all the memorizing my cadets did, they knew how to stop reading for meaning and sense structure instead. They would have been ready to take in the poem that way, line by line, if I had encouraged them to.

Every time Berryman runs Henry's language over his line endings, he shows us inner resources. Not the ones Henry's mother talked about, but real ones that keep feeling extending beyond the familiar structures of thought. This poem that has questioned and ridiculed notions of value ends with an image for skewed priority: "wag." If to wag the dog is to overemphasize the less important part of something, the last line makes Henry himself that less important part—even as it affirms his wit. The ending tells us that the self *is* a part, not wholly isolated, as Henry feels himself to be. It also tells us we need to rethink the social order that put him in that position. The poem starts us on that rethinking, repeating the word "me" six times (only "bore," in its several forms, and "and" get more appearances) and shifting its position in the line. The ending states that the self has been "le[ft]/ behind," but the shape of the last line nests "me" between two words and two punctuation marks, suggesting a different, more included condition.

∎ ∎ ∎

Berryman's consistent form—his regular irregularity: long, long, short—gives an example of fixed, imposed endings. Like the weekly routine my husband and I devised, it guarantees that experience will stop even as it keeps going. Though the meter isn't strict, the line will end after roughly five beats, or two. So if our card game was a poem, of a sort, it too fulfilled a regular form, seven-beat fourteeners, maybe. Free verse would have been more challenging, requiring us to generate the endings and beginnings we needed. But as Longenbach points out, any line, whatever its length or rhythm or relation to its neighbors, can expand the effects of the words it holds.

One line, though, is the last. "A point of crisis," Agamben calls it. The last line ends but does not break into another, and so stops us from experiencing resistant intervals. If poetry is defined by the difference between line and syntax, a poem's last line does not qualify as poetry. It rejoins the domain of prose, where sentences end only once—or, as our eyes move down the page, the domain of silence. Agamben asks whether there, in the shift out of poetry, enjambment's alternatives close up. He concludes they don't have to. With the right choice of words, "the double intensity animating language does not die away in a final comprehension; instead it collapses into silence, so to speak, in an endless falling. The poem thus reveals the goal of its proud strategy: to let language finally communicate itself, without remaining unsaid in what is said."[6] In the silence or "endless falling" that follows a last line, poetry's defining doubleness becomes a kind of ghost—present in a purer, resolved form when freed from its body, language. Such an ending evokes possibility, even revelation, and also evokes death. To experience it as possibility requires a confidence that what is falling is language, and not a life. Or that spiritual existence is enough.

Every poem rejoins prose. Clock time keeps going, and when we can, we stop overlaying it with an arbitrary or meaningless pattern of our own choice or devising. Because my husband works for the occupying force and not the occupied country, he got to leave the war zone, more or less at the anticipated time. The endings we marked for ourselves as we kept going that year led to a fuller ending in his safe return—which I marked for him by scattering my deck of cards on the floor just inside our rented front door. So for us, the two strands that carried us through his deployment did join. Survival and the perception of survival became one and the same, and more certain. But endings do bring ghosts. Ours are the ghost of abstraction, the ghost of fear, the ghost of alternate endings.

6   Agamben, *The End of the Poem*, xiii, 115.

ACE OF HEARTS

Susannah Hollister

Someone else
 might know how
many birds are
 behind the window's
song. One.
 Or more than a dozen. If
each throat throws
 the same pitch,
how to tell.
 Someone else might
know how to ride
 this edge, this edge
between
 bad luck and best friend,
between advantage
 kept warm and
triumph still inflicted.
 Between a single spot
repeating into corners,
 making itself
oblique. Then a bird-
 body lands, rounds

down and points up. Half
        a heart. Isn't the throat
the real home of emotion,
        if not the stomach.

CIVILIZATION AND ITS MALCONTENTS
ON TEACHING WESTERN HUMANITIES IN "THE NEW TURKEY"

William Coker

I.

A statue of Kemal Atatürk greets visitors at the entry to the university where I teach. On its base is inscribed a motto whose implications for university life are as broad as its meaning is puzzling for those who have just arrived: "Biz medeniyetten ilim ve fenden kuvvet alıyoruz": "from civilization we gain knowledge, and from science strength."

What does the first half of this motto mean? When I've asked my students I've found that no one else seems to have noticed the inscription. It is part of that official language one hears everywhere spoken and nowhere seriously listened to. For me the import is all in the word *medeniyet*, whose dictionary meaning is "civilization." I came here six years ago to teach "Cultures, Civilizations, and Ideas."

What is the importance of "civilization" for our academic program? Students have asked me to share my "thoughts on civilization" as if it were a topic on which views varied. The oddly outsized presence of this word in the local discourse made me try to find out what I could about *medeniyet*.

A glance at the word's etymology will not get you far. *Medeniyet* has the same origin as "civilization," echoing the Arabic *medina* ("city"), just as our word echoes the Latin *civitas*. Cultures of Islamic heritage conventionally oppose *medeni* ("settled, urban") to *bedevi* ("rural, nomadic"), from the same Arabic root word as "Bedouin." I gradually realized that in modern Turkish usage, *medeniyet* really means something more like "modernity." Family law as instituted in the first years of the secular Republic is called *medeni kanun*, as opposed to the Islamic law of the Ottoman caliphate. It was *medeni kanun*, passed in 1926, which outlawed polygamy and gave women the right to divorce.[1] That is to say, the word *medeniyet* has become inextricably tied to the cultural revolution of the 1920s and 1930s, and its legacy for the country since then.

Is this what I am teaching my students: secular modernity as modeled by the West, and put into practice in Turkey in the aftermath of the country's own war of national liberation? If so, I would be part of a tactical alliance of western-trained academics carrying out a project of nation-building that goes back to the republic's origins in the aftermath of the First World War.

Having defeated the western imperialist powers that occupied Ottoman Turkey after its defeat in the war, Mustafa Kemal set about transforming the new republic into a nation-state along the European model, relying on his Republican People's Party (CHP) as the mainstay of a one-party state. The achievements of his revolution from above are undeniable, even if its manner of application sowed the seed of future conflict. Women attained the right to vote and entrance to liberal professions earlier in Turkey than in many western countries. For the first time, the mass of the population gained access to schools and literacy, opening up an intellectual and professional milieu previously the province of a narrow Istanbul elite and mission schools reserved for non-Muslims. State-directed industrial development brought Turkey into

---

1   Turhan Feyzioğlu, "Atatürk ve Kadın Hakları," *Atatürk Araştırma Merkezi Dergisi* 2.6 (July 1986): 585–601.

proximity to the new Soviet Union, with which it enjoyed good relations, even if, from a Soviet standpoint, Atatürk still counted as a "bourgeois nationalist."

It bears repeating that on all three of these fronts—education, the role of women and industrial self-sufficiency—the legacy of republican Turkey is now massively under attack. This is not to overlook justified criticism of the original structure. A neocolonialist attitude toward the east of the country, long feudal in structure and thus deemed less "civilized" than the developed west, is still evident in many Turks who cling to secular republican ideals. So is the mistrust toward Kurds and Arabs, whose culture and language have not seen recognition from a state in which "Turkish" formally refers to citizenship. It does not help that members of these groups have taken part in rebellions that the state put down with a heavy hand, both in the republic's formative years and more recently, in the form of the armed militants of the Kurdistan Workers' Party (PKK). Having taken the West as its favored interlocutor, from whom the nascent republic sought recognition as an equal, many Turks have also internalized one feature of the colonial states whose armies Mustafa Kemal's men evicted from Anatolia: the claim to a *mission civilisatrice* toward its less "civilized," more "backward" countrymen.

This other side of the incipient republican project had already come in for criticism in certain corners of the Left before its wholesale dismantlement by the forces of counter-revolution. There can be no doubt that this is the proper word for what has transpired in Turkey since 2002, though it did not begin then. The Justice and Development Party (AKP) in power since 2002 is the culmination of a long-term conservative populist revival that began with the Adnan Menderes government at the beginning of the Cold War and gained steam in the 1980s and 1990s with that era's attacks on state ownership and the labor movement. With the organizational basis for left-wing politics severely curtailed, Recep Tayyip

Erdoğan and his party were well poised to benefit from a global conjuncture linking financialized capitalism to conservative cultural retrenchment.

There is no better symbol for this dire combination than the attempt in 2013 to turn Istanbul's Gezi Park into an Ottoman-themed shopping mall. The "infantry barracks" (*topçu kışlası*) the government's contractors planned to reconstruct to house the new mall had played host in 1909 to a military rebellion seeking to restore absolute monarchy and disrupt the constitutional order established the previous year by the Young Turks (*Jön Türkler*), whose campaign to reform the Ottoman state anticipated the founding of the republic.[2] Both an enclosure of public space in the service of capital and a monument to cultural reaction, the *topçu kışlası* project ignited a protest movement unlike any the country had yet seen in the era of neoliberalism. The project's dual symbolic significance explains why I saw so many of my students demonstrating in downtown Ankara in the summer of 2013, not only committed socialists but also those whose political profile seemed limited to admiration for Atatürk and national sovereignty and who were utterly disengaged in my class. They too have something to lose from "the new Turkey," and something to gain from joining the resistance.

II.

One chant I heard on the street in the summer of 2013 was *Tür-ki-ye la-ik-tir, la-ik ka-la-cak!* ("Turkey is and will remain secular"). Yet the question of secularism in Turkey has always been more complex than meets the eye. The French model

---

2   "Taksim Military Barracks," Wikipedia, Last modified April 16, 2015, http://en.wikipedia.org/wiki/Taksim_Military_Barracks. See also Ömür Harmanşah, "Urban Utopias and How They Fell Apart," *Jadaliyya*, June 28, 2013, http://www.jadaliyya.com/pages/index/12456/urban-utopias-and-how-they-fell-apart.

of *laïcité* differs considerably from the American notion of a "separation of church and state." In the French model, implemented since 1923 in Turkey, the state acts aggressively to protect secular public spaces, limiting the reach of religion. Yet in proscribing certain religious observances, the state of necessity finds itself in the position of giving others de facto sanction. *Laïcité* (in Turkish *laiklik*) is both more anti-clerical and more entangled in religious differences than its Anglo-Saxon cousin.

The irony of modern Turkish history, as others have pointed out, was that the movement to create a secular nation-state in Turkey also rendered the territory nearly mono-religious. On the eve of World War I, Christians comprised as much as 19% of the population of what would become the Republic of Turkey.[3] Both the massacres and forced migrations of the Armenians during the war, and population-exchange agreements signed with the governments of Greece and Bulgaria afterwards drastically lowered this figure. Today Christians, still the largest non-Muslim religious community, make up less than 0.1% of the population.[4] Whether deliberately or not, Atatürk's abolition of the caliphate coincided with a gradual emptying out of the country's religious minorities. At present, only the syncretic Alevis (Turkish Alawites), whose numbers are not certain, but who may amount to as much as 20% of the population, remain as a large religious minority motivated to resist the return to official orthodoxy.

Alevis have historically been disproportionately active in radical leftist politics in Turkey. Individual students who have told me of their Alevi identity have soon afterward revealed their extensive participation in the Gezi Park demonstrations. All six of the young men killed by police and their civilian

3   Ahmet İçduygu, Şule Toktas, and B. Ali Soner, "The Politics of Population in a Nation-Building Process: Emigration of Non-Muslims from Turkey," *Ethnic and Racial Studies* 31.2 (2007): 358–389, at 363.

4   İçduygu et al., "The Politics of Population," 363.

supporters during the Gezi protests were Alevi.[5] Some Alevis play a significant role in the mainstream center-left as well. One of them is Kemal Kılıçdaroğlu, current chairman of the Republican People's Party (CHP), whose own religious identity has become fodder for AKP rhetoric questioning his loyalty and tying him to the Syrian Alawite Bashar El-Assad.[6]

Once when I visited an Alevi shrine near Ankara I saw something surprising. One of the icons portraying early leaders of the faith, with the faces of caliphs Ali, Hasan and Hüseyin gracing three corners of a rectangular silver plate, featured a fourth and familiar face in the lower left corner: Atatürk. When I asked one of the young men from the community about this representation, he told me that the image included the Republic's founder out of respect for a political vision in which Sunnis and Alevis could live together in peace.

There being no independent institutional "church" in Islam, it is not unusual in predominantly Muslim countries for the state to oversee the training and accreditation of the clergy, and the upkeep of religious sites. Historically this has been true of many secular regimes, as it is of those with a religious affiliation. Atatürk established the Directorate of Religious Affairs as a government bureau tasked with keeping control over religious practice and teaching so as to make sure it did not threaten the state; today's Directorate acts to disparage women's groups and promote conservative Sunni doctrine.

---

5   This figure includes Berkin Elvan, who died in March 2014 at the age of fifteen, after spending 269 days in a coma induced by a police shooting him in the head with a gas capsule. Considering two other youths who died in protests indirectly linked to Gezi, Ayfer Karakaya-Stump calculates that seven of the eight civilians killed in connection with the Gezi movement "taken in a broad sense" were Alevi. Ayfer Karakaya-Stump, "Gezi'yi Alevîleştirmek," *BiR+BiR*, March 18, 2014, http://birdirbir.org/geziyi-alevilestirmek/.

6   Constance Letsch, "Syrian Conflict Brings Sectarian Tensions to Turkey's Tolerant Hatay Province," *The Guardian*, September 3, 2013, http://www.theguardian.com/world/2013/sep/03/syria-crisis-threatens-turkish-tolerance.

A turning point came in the aftermath of the military coup of 12 September 1980, though not many could have recognized this at the time. Junta leader Kenan Evren's decision to use Sunni Islam as a "cement" to bind together a society hitherto riven with violent political factionalism has had long-lasting consequences.[7] The successor governments opened many more specifically religious schools than had been in operation before, beginning the transition which some AKP politicians have now promised to complete by turning all public high schools into religious institutions providing certification to imams.[8]

III.

My first engagement with the 1980 coup came in another context. In the spring of 2009, my first year at the university, the founder and his son, then Rector, held a reception for US Ambassador James F. Jeffrey, to which they invited all American faculty. The hosts put on a video presentation on the university's history. This film took the form of a series of still pictures with accompanying spoken narrative. The speaker noted that the Turkish constitution in force on the eve of the military coup of 12 September 1980 specifically outlawed private universities. The slide showed a hand crossing out this provision in red ink. With the next slide came the statement that as the military leaders rewrote the constitution, "construction had already begun on the Rector's building" on central campus.

In 1982 the new constitution was approved by 92% of the voters in a referendum in which the ballot was not secret (voters were given a transparent envelope into which to slip their ballot before handing it back to the election official).[9] Private universities were not the only beneficiaries of the coup. Management benefited at the expense of labor, with union density in Turkey declining from roughly 30% of the population, on the eve of the coup, to 10% in 1999, and roughly 4% today.[10] One of the first actions of the coup government was to cut public sector salaries. The junta's shock doctrine corresponded to a reign of terror on the police front, in which thousands of leftists and some oppositional rightists were imprisoned, tortured, or disappeared.

In the wake of the coup arose a new "Kemalist" discourse whose goal was to neutralize the Left behind a façade of national unity. Kenan Evren worried aloud that if the "Turkish youth" continued to follow "ideologies other than the one Atatürk brought us," they would end up "becoming anarchists."[11] In mind was not the Atatürk who advocated state-owned factories and strict public secularism. The same coup government that erected statues of the founder all over Turkey also introduced mandatory religion classes in public schools, teaching the principles of Sunni Islam.

Temporarily banning from political activity the major politicians who had held the arena in the 1970s, the junta cleared the way for the rise of World Bank economist Turgut Özal,

---

9   When put to a mock "referendum" in 2008 by the Young Civilians' NGO, without the transparent ballots, the constitution in force in Turkey since 1982 was rejected by about the same margin that had originally approved it: 90% of the "voter" said "no": see "90 percent vote 'no' on Constitution in Young Civilians' public referendum," *Today's Zaman*, November 1, 2008, http://www.todayszaman.com/national_90-percent-vote-no-on-constitution-in-young-civilians-public-referendum_157542.html.

10 "Soma: the Aftermath of Tragedy (a Report)," *LeftEast*, August 27, 2014, accessed January 28, 2015, http://www.criticatac.ro/lefteast/somareport1/. See also Aziz Çelik, "Trade Unions and Deunionization During Ten Years of AKP Rule (in Turkey)," *Perspectives Turkey* 3 (2013): 44–48.

11 "EVREN'İN RADYO-TELEVİZYON KONUŞMASI ... (12 Eylül 1980)," *Bianet*, September 11, 2001, accessed January 26, 2015, http://bianet.org/bianet/siyaset/4542-evren-vatandaslara-sesleniyor.

who became first Prime Minister and then President over the course of the decade. Özal oversaw the reconstruction of the economy along neoliberal lines and deepened the NATO member state's ties to the United States through assistance in the first Gulf War. It was in this environment that private universities, and the western-style "great books" programs some of them have adopted, first appeared in Turkey. For better or worse, this history provides one of the contexts in which we teach.

IV.

For a professor to lament his students' ignorance is no more dignified than for a psychiatrist to complain that his patients are crazy. I don't know how common the latter is, but the former is both pervasive and hard to resist.

At the beginning of the semester, when I have just first read out the students' names and asked them each to tell me and their peers one thing that we must absolutely know about them, I sometimes add a question: what do you want from this class?

Of course the smart-aleck answers—"I want to pass this class," "I want to get credit for this class so I can graduate," "what I want from this class is a good grade," etc.—often come first and thickest, but there is one more that I have heard enough times to make it worthy of comment: "critical thinking." This answer usually accompanies a certain visible confidence in the student declaring it: a desire to show that we are playing the same game. And then I in turn begin to get cocky: "What is critical thinking, then?" I ask. Or, a bit cheekier: "of what is critical thinking critical?" This question usually annoys the students. "What does he want from me?" they seem to think, "I've already given him the answer he wants, now why is he asking me to take it apart?" "Critical thinking" has become one of the "right answers" that requires no further reflection.

Not only is "critical thinking" an undefined entity, it also plays into the semi-colonial dynamic that governs the students' encounter with western educational authority. One student told me that I should try to go easy on him and those of his peers who had attended public high school in Turkey. Referring to other classmates, graduates of English-language private schools, he said, "Some of our friends have been to American high schools—so they've had critical thinking." With allowances due to non-native English, it is hard to think of "critical thinking" as something one can "have."

Another telling discussion unfolded online, this time with colleagues, over what stance to take toward students' involvement in the Gezi Park demonstrations. One colleague wrote that she did not wish to get involved in their disputes but thought she could help them better navigate the arguments of both sides by teaching them "critical thinking." Am I alone in thinking this is another mask for "the white man's burden"?

All the same, it is difficult to dispense with the term. Some of us rely on the difference between criticism and critique, between claims that "such and such is bad" and an analysis that reveals the internal logic of the other position: hopefully contradictory. Ostensibly neutral, critique still lives off the expectation of criticism. Once the snags in the discourse we are analyzing have come to light, we discard it. Thus a good question to answer in any attempt to define "critical thinking" is: what do we hope to criticize?

As I understand it, critical thinking has two proper targets: (1) oneself, and (2) the prevailing dogmas of the social environment. Were "critical thinking" to mean simply the license to throw mud at sacred cows, it would not draw such resistance. The problem is not that people blindly obey authority. The problem is that any culture's true *doxa* are the ones its individuals have internalized in the process of their own self-formation. Classroom teaching is among other things an experiment in counter-interpellation.

The surest way to get conformist dogma is just to ask people to state freely their own opinions, without any specific prompt to focus the mind. Of course, professors' views are also socially formed, not free of dogma or ideology. Some professors simply substitute their own dogmas for those of the broader society and force them upon their students. Ideally the text intercedes.

V.

No doubt like many young people in different parts of the world, my students live at the intersection of market logic and resurgent cultural conservatism. Knowledge must be either marketable or morally edifying: both pressures weigh on them. They have the most difficulty with those aspects of literary texts that distance them from neutral description of the world: fictionality, metaphoricity and irony. The question of whether any given text is a "true story," and if not, why we are reading it, always takes up time at the beginning of the semester. When students make the transition to analyzing fiction as fiction, their first attempts often look clumsy.

One prevalent tactic is to look for some kind of conspiracy theory about the text—characters who turn out to be figments of the protagonist's imagination, hidden symbolism to be unearthed, subtle avowals of atheism slipping past church censorship—whatever demands "deep" thought to "uncover" the "true meaning" from the surface layer of deception. I've always been more inclined to think of "close reading" as surface reading: just look at the words on the page and tell me what you see. All of this insistence on "depth" can be bewildering.

I give my students exercises in synthetic perception: they collect sentences from the text featuring a common figure of speech or motif and comment briefly on each one, then look for connections between them. The final step is to fill in the gaps by writing an eight hundred-word essay quoting and analyzing each chosen sentence in a separate paragraph. The students find these exercises harder than the "five paragraph essay," in which a student typically writes: (1) "in this paper I will say A," (2) "A," (3) "again A," (4) "this example also demonstrates A," and (5) "to sum up, A" (with A usually in place before the student begins reading the text, much less writing the paper). My exercise improves some students' grasp of composition, but without dislodging the conspiracy theories. Their persistence has taught me that "close reading" is not so simple a matter as I had assumed.

The study of literature in Turkey, so far as I have been able to discern, remains haunted by the assumption that reading is an activity for gathering moral lessons. Turkish colleagues have told me of their high school literature classes organizing every reading of a text as a hunt for its "main idea" (*ana fikir*), a one-sentence summary ideally beginning with the words "you should..." One might say that they tend to read texts anagogically.

VI.

The scourge of the *ana fikir* is the first thing I need to expel when class begins. To shock them out of it, I begin the semester with a short story that offers no space for self-congratulatory moralizing. There is no right place to stand with regard to Jorge Luis Borges's "Brodie's Report."

This six-page story consists of a fragmentary manuscript discovered by an editor folded up between the pages of his copy of the Arabian nights. For a short story written in 1970 about events occurring in the Victorian period, it begins with a remarkably eighteenth-century conceit. The manuscript, which the anonymous editor then "makes known to the world," relates in the first person the exploits and observations of the explorer and erstwhile missionary David Brodie from his time among a people he calls "the Yahoos."[12]

The allusion to Swift carries over into the tone of the story, which records outrageous details as if they were the most ordinary things in the world. Brodie explains the measures taken to anoint the Yahoo king: "Immediately upon his elevation he is gelded, blinded with a fiery stick, and his hands and feet are cut off, so that the world will not distract him from wisdom."[13] Some of my more astute students wonder what kind of wisdom this can be; others find similarities to Plato or Sufism.

Brodie goes on to discuss how the Yahoos "drink cats' and bats' milk and fish with their hands," make no distinction between man-made objects and natural ones, or between parts of speech—though their language, based on pitch accent and subtle conceptual clusters, has a complexity all its own. Poets are *homines sacri*; once someone has stirred the tribe with a poetic utterance, "he is no longer a man, but a god, and anyone may kill him."[14] Brodie comments, "they believe, like the Jews and the Greeks, in the divine origins of poetry."[15]

Pointing to this and other commonalities, Brodie summarizes, "in a word, they represent culture, just as we do, in spite of our many sins."[16] Who are "we"? The inexplicable weirdness that Brodie has exposed at the heart of Yahoo culture reflects, without him knowing it, on him and his own culture as well, even before he concludes, "we have the obligation to

12   Jorge Luis Borges, *Collected Fictions*, trans. Andrew Hurley (New York: Penguin, 1999), 402.

13   Borges, *Collected Fictions*, 403–404.

14   Borges, *Collected Fictions*, 407.

15   Borges, *Collected Fictions*, 408.

16   Borges, *Collected Fictions*, 408.

save them."[17] Living in the Middle East in the early twenty-first century, we know what that means! But once again, who are "we"? Is "our" culture—the culture of our students and their university—in any way touched by Brodie's unwitting critique of culture?

Students take different sides in the confrontation of cultures staged by this story. Some call the Yahoos "savage" or "animal," others denounce Brodie's imperialism. Some grasp the absurdity both of what Brodie depicts and of Brodie himself. Their laughter shows that they get it. Brodie contorts himself spectacularly in order to take the Yahoo customs at face value. What the piece really satirizes is the anthropological pretense to objectivity, which justifies imperial meddling. In the end, the joke is on Brodie, but without turning the Yahoos into "noble savages" whom we should admire in ahistorical sentimentality about the world before the "white man."

VII.

Whether lacking a sense for the distinction or simply out of confusion over plurals (which in other contexts is clearly a feature of the English/Turkish divide), my students almost invariably refer to my class as "humanity class." For all that, humanism itself does not seem to loom large in their intellectual preparation.

One of the most interesting debates I have with my students every spring concerns the question of what, if anything, distinguishes the human species from the rest of the animal kingdom. The array of answers to this question from humanist philosophers—reason for Descartes, mimesis for Rousseau, "trade" for Adam Smith, "free conscious activity" for the early Marx—becomes a laundry-list of the key concepts of these thinkers: at worst a good tool for exam preparation. The

---

17   Borges, *Collected Fictions*, 408.

discussion heats up when a student, often a science major, denies that there is any such essential distinction.

One thing the positivist students are really passionate about is post-humanism. With the zeal of Voltairian atheists rooting out superstition, they decry all claims for human uniqueness as pernicious religious dogma. The glory of Galileo was the proof that we are not in the center of the universe, that of today's biological research that we are not unique. What they have against being unique, I think I can guess. In their minds human uniqueness means the obligation to enact a divine plan. It is a façade for theocratic despotism.

The only fully articulated worldviews that these students seem to have absorbed are religious and biological determinism. Their attacks on the one invariably take the form of the other. Philosophical anthropology is unknown to them, as it likely is for most westerners who have not studied the Humanities and for many who have. One is who one is always by virtue of God's or Nature's designs, never out of one's own initiative or that of those with whom one lives. It does not seem to deter anyone that the two positions are mutually compatible, as Feride Acar and Ayşe Ayata have found upon inspecting the curriculum of Turkey's Imam-certifying religious schools. There, they write, the divinely ordained separate natures of men and women are clarified through reference to biology.[18]

VIII.

When I arrived on campus six years ago, one of my first pleasant surprises was the feistiness of the female students, who in some cases outright dominated their male counterparts in

---

18   Feride Acar and Ayşe Ayata, "Discipline, Success and Stability: The Reproduction of Gender and Class in Turkish Secondary Education," in *Fragments of Culture: The Everyday of Modern Turkey*, ed. Deniz Kandiyoti and Ayşe Saktanber (New Brunswick, NJ: Rutgers University Press, 2002), 90–114.

discussion. That this was a surprise reveals something about the prejudices with which I entered the classroom. My mind-set at the time reminds me now of those tourists who come away from Turkey delighted with how "modern" and "developed" it is, because they don't see women in burkas carrying water while camels meander across the road. It is hard to make sense of initial observations when one is measuring them against an exaggerated image of the Middle East.

In more recent years I have been trying to gauge to what extent the macho ethic actually prescribes indifference to book learning, so that performance in school is not what marks a posture of social dominance. Such inferences are hard to quantify. It is also hard to shake off the sense that the cultural landscape is slowly shifting in accord with the preeminence of a Prime Minister (now President) who has said, "I do not believe that men and women are equal."[19]

I now have classes in which the young men sit on one side of the room and the women on the other. Not all or even most of my sections have this profile, but it is striking how much has changed on this front in the last six years. Cultural change is hard to specify; not all of my colleagues share my assessment or my observations. What is striking, and hard to deny, is the decline in students' knowledge of aspects of western culture that go beyond Hollywood cinema fare.

In fall semesters past, I introduced the three weeks we would spend reading Sophocles *Oedipus the King* with tongue-in-cheek questions like, "Who's feeling Oedipal today?" and "Raise your hand if you have an Oedipus complex." This used to be a sure-fire way to get a laugh from most of the room. Then we could talk about how these terms misname what is going on in Sophocles's play. In the last few years, I have largely lost the students who know what the "Oedipus

---

19   "Recep Tayyip Erdoğan: 'Women Not Equal to Men,'" *Agence France-Presse/The Guardian*, November 24, 2014, http://www.theguardian.com/world/2014/nov/24/turkeys-president-recep-tayyip-erdogan-women-not-equal-men.

complex" is. If they have heard of Freud, it is in most cases because whoever taught them the first-semester course had had them read *Civilization and its Discontents.*

One former department colleague, who speaks Turkish fluently and is deeply versed in the country's cultural and political life, told me once that he feared that the students enjoying the most success in his classes were simply those most immersed in American pop culture. It was a remarkable admission for someone otherwise committed, in a recognizably poststructuralist fashion, to the primacy of language and even the view that "there is no cultural difference." For all that the promoters of tourism wax cliché-ical about Turkey "forming a bridge between East and West," a little time spent learning the rhetoric of Turkish newspapers reveals that the West is something monolithic and Turkey is not a part of it. Increasingly, this monolith is defined in geopolitical, not cultural, terms.

I have tried to address this question with my students, with results not always to my satisfaction. As an extra-credit question on the final exam of the first semester course, I asked, "These texts have come to be known as 'classics of Western culture,' although at the time they were written, the 'West' did not exist. Do you find this designation correct or incorrect, and why do you think they have been given this title?" Students who found the time to answer this question at length were divided as to whether or not they agreed to ascribe *Gilgamesh* or *The Iliad* to something called "the West." Those who evinced skepticism on this regard cast their objection in every case in geopolitical terms. Those who accepted the designation of such works as "western" tended to praise their expression of "advanced," "modern," or "scientific" values, without giving examples. There may not have been time for detailed discussion, or it may just not be possible to discuss works of literature in such vague and programmatic terms.

I linger on this moment of failure because it exposes a problem that one cannot easily dispose of in such interdisciplinary "humanities" courses. It stands to reason that "the West" we discuss in "great books" courses is not so much an object of study independent of those books as something we construct and reconstruct in the classroom by studying them. We choose these six books, say, and not others, as founding texts of western culture because they enable us to found the West that we want founded: universal in the scope of its claims, but also reflective, open to self-criticism and reform.

Central to the "great books" education I received, and which indeed formed the cornerstone of my own college education, is the notion of "the West" or even "Europe" as a cultural unity, however riven by doctrinal and philosophical conflict, and transcending politics, though only in the sense that it provides the matrix for political disputes. To someone raised in this environment of liberal humanism, the notion that "the West" refers to NATO, or "Europe" to a glorified free-trade zone seems almost blasphemous.

It is worth pondering to what extent this exalted idea of Europe is really an American idea, like the consternation of American tourists who flock to Europe for its gothic cathedrals only to find them empty on Sunday morning. No doubt the notion of Europe as a cultural unity is underwritten by the institutions and power structures that have given the West its recent hegemony: among them not only the EU, but also the United States. It is nonetheless valid to ask what is lost when one sees "culture" as a mobile Potemkin village camouflaging the infantry of such power blocks.

One who treats "culture" as a weapon in the war of civilizations is Yusuf Kaplan, a writer respected in circles close to the ruling party AKP. In his recent column in the progovernment newspaper, *Yeni Şafak* ("new dawn"), Kaplan advocates "demolishing" my university along with two others, which he claims "pursue the agenda of other cultures." His alternative is to found new universities "along the model of the Ivy League," capable of spreading the culture of the new

Turkey as ably as the Ivies have spread American culture.[20]
He seems incapable of thinking outside of western categories,
even while trashing the West.

It is clear from Kaplan's proposal that he sees intellectual
life as a global power struggle, in which educational institutions serve the agenda of one "culture" or another in the fight
for hegemony. This kind of civilizational thinking brings him
into proximity to Samuel Huntington and his admirers. It is
not clear that a scrupulous western conservative should find
much to disagree with in Kaplan's assessments. Suffice it to
recall Cardinal Joseph Ratzinger's opposition to Turkey's EU
candidacy and his counter-suggestion that the country would
be more at home in some kind of parallel organization proper
to the Islamic world.[21]

In the same letter, Kaplan exhorts outgoing Prime Minister and incoming President Erdoğan to root out the culture
of consumerism, which he evidently sees as a threat to that
of faith and family. Kaplan does not ask himself whether a
state can really end consumerism by cultural fiat, without
a revolutionary disruption of capitalism itself, nor does he
confront the fact that it is precisely the new credit economy
that serves as the AKP government's economic basis. Since
2008, when the US Federal Reserve lowered interest rates
to near zero in response to the financial crisis in the United
States, Turkey has been able to lower its own rates to expand
credit domestically without closing an interest rate gap that
has lured foreign capital away from the core economies
and toward developing countries where rates of return are
higher. Thus relatively high interest rates continue to attract
speculative foreign investment while an expansion of credit

20 Yusuf Kaplan, "Erdoğan'a 20 öneri," *Yeni Şafak*, August 15, 2014,
    http://www.yenisafak.com/yazarlar/YusufKaplan/erdogana-%20
    20-oneri-55353.

21 "Ratzinger on Turkey in EU, European Secularism," *Catholic World
    News*, August 11, 2004, http://www.catholicculture.org/news/fea-
    tures/index.cfm?recnum=31436.

stimulates consumption. Turkey's large and growing current account deficit bears eloquent witness to the economy's reliance on speculation, rather than production.[22] The economic growth to which Turkey's conservatives owe their political dominance rests entirely on factors inimical to their stated ideology: consumer extravagance and financial speculation.[23]

Kaplan's civilizational thinking bears the same weakness as his wistful critique of consumerism: an inability to confront the system of production that underlies both the consumer mentality and the present mode of "civilization" in both East and West. How could he do so, without losing his grip on that unique Turkish-Islamic virtue called on to explain what AKP apologists at home and abroad describe as the country's rise to global power?

Kaplan's ideology may be riven with contradictions, but let's not forget that ideology is precisely that: disavowal of the economic foundations on which cultural life rests, so that a sober analysis of our social relations can give way to fantasies of who we would like to be. It is not inconsequential which fantasies one chooses. The choice to substitute the magnificent Süleyman—or for that matter the Alevi-slaughtering Yavuz Sultan Selim—for Atatürk the liberator and modernizer means abandoning one national ego ideal for another. National unity is always a fiction, but that fiction can be differently inflected. In the old Turkey, "Turk" was held to be an ethnically neutral term, denoting citizenship, while "Kurd" remained unacceptably sectarian and ethnic. In the new Turkey, the death of a Muslim Brotherhood militant in Egypt is

---

22   Erinç Yeldan, "Turkey's Debt-Ridden Growth," *Social Europe*, April 30, 2013, http://www.socialeurope.eu/2013/04/turkeys-debt-ridden-growth/.

23   Erinç Yeldan, "Patterns of Adjustment under the Age of Finance: The Case of Turkey as a Peripheral Agent of Neoliberal Globalization," *Political Economy Research Institute:* Working Paper Series 126 (February 2007), http://scholarworks.umass.edu/cgi/viewcontent.cgi?article=1100&context=peri_workingpapers.

grieveable,[24] while that of a dissident teacher in a small town on the Black Sea is not.[25]

Living in the crosshairs of ideologies makes it desirable to recognize what ideology in the singular is, just as people living on a fault line may want to learn about tectonic plates. An easier way to approach this matter than steeping oneself in Marxist theory is to read literature. Fiction has its own way of engaging us, but it is the way we are most often engaged. Rather than try to assimilate fictions to what we consider the real world, by asking "is this a true story?" and "what is the main idea?" we can treat literature as an invitation to move in the opposite direction.

IX.

So where does it all begin? The *Epic of Gilgamesh* is the first text on our syllabus. Some repeat that it is the "oldest story ever told," or the earliest text of world literature. I do not know whether either claim is true. Some see the story in more personal terms, as the tale of a man who reluctantly acknowledges the certainty of death. The moral of the story is that we die. Didn't we already know that?

The epic whose Babylonian title was "he who saw the deep" may be named for its hero, but it begins and ends with a panorama of his city, Uruk. "See its wall like a strand of *wool*, view its parapet that none could copy."[26] A string of impera-

---

24   "Mısırlı Esma için gözyaşı döktü, Berkini anmaya gerek görmedi," *Diken*, March 12, 2014, http://www.diken.com.tr/misirli-esma-icin-gozyasi-doktu-berkini-anmaya-gerek-gormedi/.

25   "Turkish PM Erdoğan Blames Opposition for Hopa Clashes," *Hürriyet Daily News*, June 1, 2001, http://www.hurriyetdailynews.com/default.aspx?pageid=438&n=erdogan-blames-the-opposition-parties-for-hopa-clashes-2011-06-01.

26   Andrew Robert George, trans. *The Epic of Gilgamesh*. (London: Penguin 2003), 1.

tive verbs invites the reader—or listener—to inhabit the city enriched and put on trial by Gilgamesh's exploits. These lines reappear word for word at the close of the epic, when the celebrated king returns from his failed quest for immortality; the city awaits him and his guest, Ubar-Tutu, as a consolation. "[A square mile is] city, [a square mile] date-grove, a square mile is/clay-pit, half a square mile the temple of Ishtar."[27] What if we see, not Gilgamesh, but the city of Uruk as the protagonist of the epic?

The urban society whose achievements the epic trumpets is also a world of blistering oppression. With the collection of food in grain silos, which *The Epic of Gilgamesh* monumentalizes in its opening lines, comes a class division that is everywhere present in the epic and nowhere explicit. Some hoard the grain that others have harvested; some get to move into the city to engage in more profitable work while others remain on the land. The dichotomy pitting city-boy Gilgamesh, descended from the gods, against pastoral Enkidu, animal but peaceful, may be obscurely about this split, as much as it reflects the kind of binary opposition that structures many a myth. Once Enkidu and Gilgamesh clash, the brash king leaves off pursuing the women of the city and sets off with his new friend to attack monsters, for his glory and for Uruk's. In other words, an internal revolt forces Gilgamesh to seek enemies elsewhere, transferring his aggression onto foreign policy.

As the city harvests wood from the cedar forest whose guardian demon Gilgamesh and Enkidu have killed, the wilderness is both desanctified and destroyed. This success permits the heroes to domesticate the gods. With the god Enlil's sacred space annexed to the empire of human needs, the brothers in arms offer him in compensation a new door for his temple at Nippur. The gods move into the city as captives, serving human desire. The last card they have to play

---

27   George, *The Epic of Gilgamesh*, 2.

is death. They play it effectively, though the effect is not one of psychological realism. Enlil intones, "Because they have killed the Bull of Heaven... let Enkidu die, but let not Gilgamesh die!"[28] The story must go on, with Gilgamesh as its human protagonist.

The epic of origins telescopes its pathos into the life of one man. The work of reading the epic is to decipher this move, extracting the story of the culture from that of its hero. At the end of the epic Gilgamesh returns from the ends of the earth where he has failed Utanapishti's initiatory immortality test and lost the plant of eternal youth, whose name, evocatively, is "old man grown young," which appears to be the etymology of the name "Gilgamesh" as well.[29] Failing to live up to his name, then, Gilgamesh falls out of myth and into something quite different: literature. His refuge at the end is the city, which he shows to his new companion Ubar-Tutu, erstwhile boatman to the eternal Utanapishti, in the same words sung by the anonymous narrator on the epic's first tablet. Gilgamesh's private quest has failed. What is left is its public residue, the city: both a victory against death and a site of domination, revolt and struggle. "Civilization" is a double-edged sword.

I recount this reading here as a reminder of what reading literature in the university classroom can teach. A story is not merely an invitation to empathy. It is not only a meditation on our mortality, but also a reflection on what we are but do not commonly feel ourselves to be: agents in the creation of the social structures and narratives that transcend us, and which are our collective answer to death. A story need not always be deciphered in this way to be pleasurable or useful, but such deciphering is what the classroom has to offer. This

28 George, *The Epic of Gilgamesh*, 55.

29 George, *The Epic of Gilgamesh*, 99; cf. Stephen Mitchell, *The Epic of Gilgamesh: A New English Version* (New York: Free Press, 2004), 10. Cf. Rivkah Harris, *Gender and Aging in Mesopotamia: the Gilgamesh Epic and Other Ancient Literature* (Norman, OK: University of Oklahoma Press, 2000), 194.

is the case especially when the professor speaks a language different from your own; or asks you to fill in the blanks of the fragmentary text, and find differences of meaning behind passages of word-for-word repetition...when a text you've been told is a founding classic of "western culture," but was actually written to the east of you, lies before you with blank spaces on the page and variant versions for you to compare, inscribed or performed in intervals hundreds of years apart, translated imperfectly from one foreign language to another. The words on the page are no one's property.

Civilization is both a victory against death and a subtle imposition of its terror upon others. Whatever terror we educators inflict on our students, let us make it serve noble purposes. We cannot be neutral. The world has not given us that luxury.

DEPARTURE ENTRANCE

Denis Ferhatović

Departure

Some are staying
Some are going
Exodus

Those staying are
Also going
To hell

The angel of God is a killer
He goes after the first-born

Seven plagues,
One after another

They are:
AIDS, hurricane, flood
Cancer, California conflagra-
tions
Coronaries
Incurable depression

God destroys their temples
Scatters their bank-benches
Sets their shopping malls
On fire

No more oil for cars,
No more electricity
The country crammed
With corpses

When the Lord comes down,
The idols sink into pandemonium

Sail / Veil

Sailveilveilsail
SEGL: a stamp (<sigillum)
the sun
the rune for the sun
S

It protects the Chosen Ones
It envelops them
It develops them, pulls them into the future
It wraps them the way it will wrap
Naked Christ's body when it's taken down
From the Cross

It is the pillar around which the world is organized
It is the staff with which Moses hit the ground
It is the vine that waxes fruitful and multiplies
It is the male principle touching the female principle
At one point they inter-
Penetrate

The four directions meet at one point
Past, present, future meet at one point
It is God Almighty's
Seal

It is my—your humble poet's—
Signature.

African Woman

Zipporah
I am a bird, I am everything
I sing for Moses out of my bright throat
Under my wings I hold the world
I have everything I need right here
In my purse
Whatever you want for an exodus
Breath mints, a map, dental floss
You'll want your teeth to gleam
When delivering a song of praise
On yet another foreign shore
Amidst dead Egyptian bodies
Armored, half-naked, naked
There they are lifting bracelets
And torques off that dark-
Eyed youth
His mother will never see him again
His beloved never embrace him
I have to look my best
As the commander's wife
I with my ornaments provide support
The center to which nations flock
Easily allegorized
But I tell you: Resist
Think how heavy these jewels

The Beasts Of Battle

Maybe it sounds gruesome   but aren't you a fan of
          sustainability?
This is just that, or, if you prefer,   Nature's own recycling.
Meet the wolf,   the eagle,   the raven.
They have R.S.V.P.'d   for the post-battle dinner party.

On the menu this evening   eclectic, fun Egyptian:
Croquettes of equestrians   in a ragout of their horses' liver;
Wild-caught spear-men served   on their spears cooked *al
          dente*;
Boiling Red Sea soup   with bits-and-pieces (various military
          ranks);
Pharaoh's flank, seasonal desert herbs,   choice of mashed
          ministers;
Chilled honey-lemongrass chiefs of staff   with a chocolate
          drizzle of fear.

Moses Describes the Raising of the Red Sea

Now you see with your own eyes, my beloved people
What I've done, myself, with this hand and rod
The sea-ridges are upright, the waves forming walls
Fields to step on, dotted only with tiny puddles
A dappled, patterned, protective landscape
This is a foundation, a chthonic roof on which
No man or woman has ever walked, nor will
And yet it betokens the path all righteous shall take
The high-way to heaven, we need only believe

Drowning Egyptian 1

his majesty god on earth his head forever upright
he a ziggurat of triumph why did he ever leave me
what monstrous wonder standing sea crashing down
until yesterday in our land they were guests
until their god no-name no-face intervened
he crushed my childhood running in the fields
my youth he demolished whispers and laughter
flower of manhood shrivels down in me
blotted forever by their one-god's power

Drowning Egyptian 2

s . . . or . . . row?
blub blubblu

Drowning Egyptian 3

sun moon cat crocodile
I see myself in a crimson loincloth
sun moon cat crocodile
arms caked with healthful mud
legs caked with shining mud
I see myself offering a sacrifice

crocodile moon sun cat
I call upon the Nile ever-fertile
on this journey to beyond
I loved one of their women
she now (crocodile moon
sun cat) wears jewelry of war

is it a blasphemy or a weakness
sun crocodile moon cat
sun crocodile moon cat
to wish her here with me
about to drown, arm in arm
in a clinch that ends time
upon a voyage to another world

PROFANATIONS
THE PUBLIC, THE POLITICAL AND THE HUMANITIES IN INDIA

Prashant Keshavmurthy

Shall She not find in comforts of the sun,
In pungent fruit and bright green wings, or else
In any balm or beauty of the earth,
Things to be cherished like the thought of heaven?
—Wallace Stevens, from "Sunday Morning"[1]

chhor literature ko apnī history ko bhūl jā
sheikh o masjid se ta'alluq tark kar, iskūl jā
char din kī zindagī hai koft se kyā fāyda
khā double-rotī clerky kar khushī se phūl jā[2]

Quit "literature" and, as for "history," don't be a fool.
Break with sheikh and mosque, go to "school."
Life's brief as a blink—why be bothered?
Breakfast on "loaves," push a pen, be cool!

---

1   Wallace Stevens, "Sunday Morning," *The Collected Poems* (New York: Vintage Books, 1982), 67.

2   K.C. Kanda, *Masterpieces of Patriotic Urdu Poetry: Text, Translation and Transliteration* (New Delhi: Sterling Publishers, 2005), 89. All translations from the Urdu in this essay are mine.

The political and the public in the modern world

In December 2013 a judge of the Indian Supreme Court recriminalized homosexuality under Section 377 of the Indian Penal Code by overturning the Delhi High Court's earlier decriminalization of it. The Supreme Court judgment declined to even engage the constitutional reasoning adduced by the Delhi High Court when it "read down" 377 "in order to decriminalize private, adult, consensual sexual acts."[3] This reasoning argued that 377 infringed Article 14 of the Constitution, "which deals with the fundamental right to equality" and "Article 15, which deals with the fundamental right to nondiscrimination" and "Article 21, which covers the fundamental right to life and liberty, including privacy and dignity." Simply disregarding the specifics of this reasoning, the judgment showed what a former judge of the Delhi High Court has termed an "exaggerated deference to a majoritarian Parliament." In other words, it violated a fundamental right by citing the numerical minority of the homosexual community. Rather than a republican commitment to fostering a polity whose majorities and minorities were shaped by debates around legally protected values it was the numerical majority of the mob that determined the law. In this the Supreme Court bent its knee before the leaderships of every religious community in India—legions of offended holy men—who, over the four previous years since the Delhi High Court's judgment had been smugly defending what they claimed were the (heteronormative) traditions of a primordial and changeless group. What is the pre-history of such offense as it comes to form communities or harden their presumed edges? In answering this question this essay aims

---

3   Leila Seth, "India: You're Criminal If Gay," *New York Review of Books*, March 20, 2014, http://www.nybooks.com/articles/archives/2014/mar/20/india-youre-criminal-if-gay/.

to specify the importance of the humanities to post-colonial South Asia.

In what follows I begin with a normative observation regarding all modern political thought, namely that it must necessarily validate the crowd as a political actor and grant ontological primacy to the everyday. This double condition, the essay argues, constitutes every modern public. It then argues that the numerous demands in India, dating to the 1920s, to censor this or that text hurtful to this or that "religious sentiment" originate in colonial and post-colonial perversions of the public. It examines the earliest case of offended religious sentiment, that surrounding a 1924 pamphlet allegedly offensive to the prophet Muhammad, interpreting the event as a displaced or fetishistic effect of the failure of mass political movements. It then reads a corpus of late nineteenth century Urdu Muslim Reformist literature as a case of the emergence of a dominant form of religious community in reaction to political disenfranchisement. The last sections of the essay argue that post-1991 or post–economic liberalization India reveals comparable emergences of religious community. It ends with a critique of a trajectory of Euro-American defenses of the humanities as indifferent to post-colonial localities and argues for the role of the humanities in fostering an Indian public as a profane world of commonly interpretable ambiguity.

Beginning at regionally varying dates in the eighteenth and nineteenth centuries across the world any mode of thinking describing itself as *political* in whatever sense has had to simultaneously satisfy two minimal conditions: regard the crowd as a legitimate political actor, and grant ontological primacy to the everyday. These two correlated conditions also minimally define *the public*. The former condition originates in the awareness that the people, not the king, are the real locus of legitimate power. The king's once sacred body then vacates an altar whose emptiness, in a sense, begins to constitute

democracy.[4] It begins to constitute democracy in the sense
that the people's awareness of the impossibility of legitimate
power inhering in an individual's body justifies their sense
of its dispersal across themselves. Henceforth, the signs of
political legitimacy would increasingly be sought and scrutinized, not in an individual's mysteriously inherited radiance,
but in the masses of ordinary bodies seen in an ordinary light.

This brings us to the latter condition. The people is made
up of bodies standing in the sort of quotidian light that Vermeer, the seventeenth-century Dutch painter, helped make
imaginable. Rather than otherworldly effulgence Vermeer's is
a tranquil window-light, suffusing a woman's stole and cheek
as she holds a dully gleaming metal jug in a basin. Cloth,
flesh, wood and metal each come into their own in this profane, diaphanous, and impartial medium. To be political in
the modern world has meant to gaze at it in this light, to grant
that this everyday object-world was more real than any other.
After Asadullāh Khān Ghālib (d. 1869), canonized as the last
practitioner of the traditional Urdu (and Indo-Persian) ghazal,
objects in the ghazal never shone so brightly. Displacing the
wine, goblets and gardens that were allegorically always more
than themselves in the traditional ghazal, the railways, tele-
graph and bread loaves ("double-roti") of Akbar Allāhābādi's
(d. 1921) ghazals dramatized the impossibility of such transcendence in a colonial political economy.[5] Henceforth, the
legitimacy of political aims was increasingly to be determined,

---

4   I am indebted for this phenomenological theory of the modern
     political to Claude Lefort, *Democracy and Political Theory* (Cam-
     bridge: Polity Press, 1988): "Power was embodied in the prince,
     and it therefore gave society a body. And because of this, a latent
     but effective knowledge of what *one* meant to the *other* existed
     throughout the social. This model reveals the revolutionary and
     unprecedented feature of democracy. The locus of power becomes
     an empty place" (17).

5   I am indebted for this interpretation to the essays on Akbar Alla-
     habadi by the great Urdu literary critic Muhammad Hasan Askari
     in his posthumously published collection of essays, *Vaqt kī rāginī*
     (Tune of the Time) (Lahore: Quasain, 1979).

not in the name of the next world, but according to whether and how it entailed a transformation of such this-worldly and everyday object-relations.

Before it was judged to be totalitarian, democratic, fascist, republican, socialist or communist, political thinking had to satisfy this double condition to be considered political at all. And to be political thus was to grant the reality of the public. This placed the practice of politics under a distinctly modern burden: the people were constrained to derive their norms of action by *interpreting the public*; that is, by interpreting the dispersal and ambiguity of the signs of legitimate power. Not that pre-modern politics entailed no such ambiguity and interpretation. But such ambiguity in the pre-modern world had still been confined to royal and aristocratic bodies. It had a locus. And so, too, did its interpretation which was legitimately undertaken only by specialists of one sort or another: priests, jurists, an aristocratic peer-group... Now, it was the people at large who scrutinized the signs of the political at large. From this collective scrutiny of an ambient object-world arose the necessarily tentative interpretative consensus over the necessarily provisional norms by which a state was to be organized. To be political in the modern world has thus meant granting the necessity of popular interpretation of the everyday as the means for the disclosure of norms of state.

This throws into explanatory relief the numerous and vehement demands in India, beginning in the 1920s, to censor this or that text "hurtful" to this or that "religious sentiment." Each such demand assumes the unambiguousness of the signs in question. (Even apparently unambiguous hate-speech is hardly unambiguous when we ask whether, why and to whom it might be important to pay attention to it at all.) This impatience with interpretation is a discomfort with the idea and reality of the public. It is a fear of the semiotic ambiguity inherent in even the most rudimentary forms of representative democracy. It is a demand that legitimate political authority be relocated in unambiguously identifiable bodies.

Not in the king's body, to be sure, but not in those of the people at large either. Rather, it is in the body of a demographically determined group mistakenly taking itself for a primordial, monolithic and changeless entity.

The early twentieth century beginnings of outraged religious sentiment

Dina Nath Batra, the complainant who filed a case in 2011 under Section 295A of the Indian Penal Code against Wendy Doniger's *The Hindus: An Alternative History* (2009) for insulting all Hindus, also spoke in the name of what he takes to be such a group. He follows in a long line of Hindu, Muslim, Christian and other such litigants each of whom claimed injury to the "religious sentiments" of their respective group. What is remarkable about Batra's forbears is not that they all similarly mistook colonial census identities for primordial ones. This is, after all, a commonplace by now among those aware of the effects of the colonial census on identity formation among colonized populations: social groups repeatedly identified under specific census categories increasingly internalized such governmental identifications, coming in time to naturalize them. The colonial censuses, the first of which was conducted in 1872, were data-collection projects including categories of "religion," "caste" and "race" that were intended to facilitate governmental control of subject populations. But among the most conspicuous and long lasting of its unintended effects was the crystallization of "agentive political identities" in place of what had been "fuzzy" group identities. As Sudipta Kaviraj puts it, "Surprisingly, the colonial administration changed identities by implanting cognitive practices which objectified communities, changing them from an earlier fuzzy or underspecified form to a modern enumerated one. Processes of enumeration of the social world, like mapping and census, irreversibly altered social ontology by giving groups a new kind of agentive political identity. This was not political agency in itself, but a precondition for the development of a political universe in which political agency could be imparted to large impersonal groups—like castes or religious communities."[6] This was the cognitive seed of a familiar South Asian act of categorization and its concomitant of caste and religious rioting: holding a random Muslim or Hindu responsible for what other Muslims or Hindus unknown to her did elsewhere.

However, this is no longer a remarkable theme by now in the historiographical and social scientific scholarship on South Asia. Rather, what is remarkable is how central to the formation of such community identities the emotional response to signs has been. Beginning as statistical identifications, community identities—especially those of religious communities—in modern India seem to have then been consolidated around rage at the hurt caused by signs taken to be unambiguously meaningful. A certain kind of electorally effective and socially dominant religious subjectivity in twentieth- and twenty-first-century India seems to have been defined—and to have defined itself—as an intensity of emotion formed like a never-closing cicatrix around a core of hurt.

Counterbalancing the formation of such "emotional communities" in the late nineteenth and early twentieth centuries was the imperative felt among native elites to "reform" their respective communities.[7] Reform, always an elite preoccupation, resisted the anxious decisiveness with which signs were decoded as "hurtful" or "offensive." After all, Reform

6   Sudipta Kaviraj, January 1, 2009, forum entry, "The Post-colonial State: The Special Case of India," *Critical Encounters Forum*, accessed June 13, 2015, http://criticalencounters.net/2009/01/19/the-post-colonial-state-sudipta-kaviraj/.

7   Barbara H. Rosenwein, "Problems and Methods in the History of Emotions," *Passions in Context: International Journal for the History and Theory of Emotions* (2010), accessed June 13, 2015, http://www.passionsincontext.de/index.php?id=557.

assumed the *need* for reform and therefore depended on granting the validity of certain criticisms of group customs and practices. Instructive here is the archive of the legislative assembly debates of 1927 on the popular demand of Muslim populations in the Punjab and North West Frontier Provinces to amend the law concerning offense to religious communities. The historian Neeti Nair has shown that the debates undertaken in the wake of popular unrest over the publication in Lahore of *Rangilā rasūl*, an Urdu pamphlet first alleged by Gandhi in his *Young India* to have been unmentionably offensive to Muslim veneration for the prophet Muhammad, evince an openness to the ambiguities of the text and affair: "The *consensus* that was section 295A left much to be desired. However, the *process of negotiation*—the speeches, the interruptions, the contingency, even the urgency—reveal the possibilities for conversation and dialogue that were still available in 1927."[8] Nair upholds such openness as a model for the deliberative practices the Indian polity must adopt today.

However, this openness, as Nair herself notes, only characterized the miniscule minority of Indians who had the power to decide, in however limited a way, on the laws of the colonial state. It was only such Indians who responded to British Orientalist denigrations of Islam or Hinduism, not by threats of violent disorder, but by writing tracts, travelogues, novels and poems. Furthermore, a consideration of the wider body of Reformist writings discloses even an elite anxiety over the indeterminacy of the signs of the religious identity of a place, person or thing. I pause here to interpret a case of such Reformist anxiety over the ambiguity of signs for it will let us understand the earliest entwinement in India between the political (as I have described it in the opening paragraphs of this essay), the public and religion-as-hurt-sentiment.

8   Neeti Nair, "Beyond the 'Communal' 1920s: The Problem of Intention, Legislative Pragmatism and the Making of Section 295A of the Indian Penal Code," *Indian Economic and Social History Review* 50.3 (2013): 317–40.

In 1892 Maulānā Shibli Nu'māni, an internationally celebrated Indian Muslim historian, (Urdu-Persian) literary critic
and theologian of his day, traveled by sea from Bombay to
the Ottoman Empire, journeying through Cyprus, Istanbul,
Syria and Egypt. Of this journey he kept a journal that he later
published under the title of *Safarnāma-i rūm va misr va shām*
(*A Travel Account of Turkey, Egypt and Syria*).[9] He claims that he
had not intended to write a travel account but that European
prejudices with regard to the Turks had led him to do so.
Even well-meaning Europeans, he observes, remain bound by
the islamophobic prejudices they are raised with. His aims
in writing it are therefore corrective and pedagogical: to correct prejudiced European travel accounts of Turkey that form
the basis for European histories, and to instruct Indian Muslims by documenting exemplary "progress" among Turkish
Muslims.

The Turkey or Ottoman state of Shibli's time, we must
remember, was the only one of the three great early modern Islamic states—the other two being Safavid Iran and
Mughal India—to still be extant. Moreover, its emperor,
Abdulḥamīd II (1876–1909), had only recently achieved radical
advances in the movement to modernize or "reorganize"—
"reorganization" or *tanzīmāt* bespeaking the bureaucratic
character of this modernity—of his state on European mod-
els. Shibli intends therefore to focus on the "developments
and reforms" of the Muslim world, especially Turkey.

The turn of the century preoccupation with lost Mughal
sovereignty among North India's Reformist Muslims—a sovereignty they understood as Muslim in the wake of the formal
end of the Mughal state in 1857—led them to regard the still
regnant Ottoman empire with special attention: in it they saw
a Muslim empire that was modeling itself through technological and institutional reforms on Europe, the very ambition
of Sayyid Aḥmad Khān, the founder of what became Aligarh

9   Shibli Nu'māni, *Safarnāmā-i rūm va misr va shām* (Ā'zamgarh: matba-
     i ma'ārif, 1940).

Muslim University, and his colleagues like Shibli Nu'māni. Shibli thus discusses formerly Ottoman Cyprus, when he passes through it, in terms of the history of its political sovereignty under Muslim and then British rule. Furthermore, everywhere in his travels he singles out educational syllabi, technology, and such empirical aspects of a society as clothing and food, treating them as indices of a polity's development.

Shibli desires and is at pains to discover signs of a continuous Muslim world. That he conflates all Arabs in the Ottoman territories with Muslims and vice versa signals this desire. The historical motivations for this desire lay both in the Pan-Islamism adopted as a policy against European meddling in Ottoman affairs by Sultan Abdulḥamīd II as well as in the sense of shame at their civilizational "decline" (*inḥitāt*) pervasive among intellectuals and literati in the Arab world of the time. From Bombay to Aden, writes Shibli, he had been "longing to see a Muslim" and, in Cyprus, when he hears a boy in a seminary recite from the Qur'an he is filled with an emotion of wonderment: "At the priest's signal the boy recited a few verses from the Qur'an. It affected me strangely. It occurred to me: what was the affecting power in these holy words that, becoming electric power from East to West, shot across from the distant deserts of Arabia to the far-flung islands of the Mediterranean and still survives?" The "affecting power in these holy words" became "electric power" in its rapid global spread: the metaphor succinctly formulates the Muslim Reformist goal of a modernity for a single if heterogeneous global Islam that would validate and include Western technological inventions.

A presupposed universal Muslim nationality (*qaumiyat*) is what allows Shibli to imagine Ottoman Muslim and Indian Muslim identities as separate and comparable at once. This separateness of identities serves him in his observations of Ottoman educational developments as he compares the state of "the old education" (*qadīm ta'līm*) in Turkey and India on a single yardstick to conclude that it was hardly much better in Turkey in respect of the governmental neglect into which it had fallen: "Although I like the modern educational system [*nayī ta'līm*], and like it well and truly, I am nonetheless a great supporter of the traditional educational system and I think that it is needed—indeed deeply needed—for the survival of the ethnicity of Muslims [*musalmānoṇ kī qaumiyat qā'im rehne ke liye*]."[10] Muslim ethnicity includes Ottoman Muslims as much as it does Indian ones, enabling Shibli's project of comparison.

However, what complicates his inquiry by threatening his ability to recognize and be recognized by his Muslim subjects of inquiry are the ethnic diversity and non-Muslim peoples of the Ottoman Empire. In Aden, his first foreign port of call, he observes Somali boys flock to the edges of European ships like his own in little boats and pull faces at the Europeans to win coins flung at them from decks, retrieving these coins from the ocean. Deeply hurt, Shibli laments the wretched pass Arabs have come to. But when he discovers on shore that Somalis are not considered Arab, he feels relieved.

In another episode, he is eager to talk to the Arab Muslim Hajj pilgrims on his ship, approaching and addressing them in Arabic on the very topics they happen to be discussing. But he is bewildered when they barely register his presence. One of them then asks him, "What is your religion [*maẕhab*]?" "Islam," he replies. "What sort of Muslim wears a hat like that?" the man responds. Shibli then realizes that they had taken him for a Zoroastrian (*majūsi*) because of the "red Iranian hat" he had worn. Having persuaded them that he was a Muslim, he observes that they then warm to his company.

In the first anecdote, Shibli appears exclusively concerned with the dignity and then discreteness of his object of inquiry: Arab Muslims. It does not trouble him as much to see Somalis lose their dignity because they were not considered Arab. He is relieved because this experience accentuates by differentiation the discreteness of Arab Muslims. The second incident

10   Nu'māni, *Safarnāmā-i rūm va misr va shām*, 88.

concerns the religious identity of the inquirer himself: the outer signs on Shibli's person do not correspond to his inner identity of belief. He appears a Zoroastrian while being a Muslim. This remains a constant problem for Shibli throughout the travelogue: the non-correspondence of outer signs of religious identity with inner religious self-identification. This infelicity—felicity being precisely the performance of socially apparent signifying conventions in harmonious accordance with inner qualities—constantly threatens through misrecognition or non-recognition both the identities of the inquirer who seeks to recognize Muslims and that of the Muslims he seeks recognition from.

This very problem also motivates and structures the historical novels, the earliest instances of the genre in Urdu, by ʿAbdul Ḥalīm Sharar (1860–1926). Each of his novels presents a medieval Muslim hero who, in his initial naïveté, is seduced by an intentionally infelicitous (this intentional aspect differentiating the narrator's motivated infelicity in Sharar from Shibli's accidental confusion) performance of signifying conventions. He is the object of the dupe of a Christian, Jewish or Hindu woman. His dealings with her and her people—always erotic and military at once—lead him and us through a progressive rending of this deceitful veil of signs to recognize the truth of the insincerity that it had concealed. This rending of veils arrives as the relieving clarification of who and what is Muslim, Christian, Jewish and Hindu. Almost every such novel ends with the conversion of the non-Muslim woman, now in love with the Muslim hero, to what Sharar presents as the more magnanimous faith of Islam.

Anger at European Orientalist denigrations of Islam inspired Sharar and Shibli in their literary-intellectual projects to keep rehearsing a logic of anxious semiotic clarification, to traverse over and over a narrative vector that established the edges and boundaries of a religious community. In this they bore a strange affinity with the nineteenth century colonial administrator, Colonel William Henry Sleeman

(1788–1856). In his lifetime, as today, Sleeman was associated with the eradication of "thuggee," the practice attributed to what was imagined to be a pan-Indian secretive group of men, women and children of garroting highway travelers and making off with their property. These "thugs" were distinguished from other criminals by their ability to mimic any other Indian identity through disguise. Sleeman's achievement was to marshal the floating signifier of the thug into the identity categories of colonial law; "to synthesize various and discrepant occurrences as a semiosis under centralized control; against *thuggee*—conceived of as a vast, well-articulated, and centralized conspiracy—could be opposed the concentrated power/knowledge of the state."[11] However, unlike Sleeman's exegetical victory over the thug that was invested by the colonial state with legal authority, Reformist exegesis had almost no legal effects. This is why Reform may be characterized as a kind of disambiguating gaze turned from what should normatively have been a legally fostered public to the anxious discovery of signs of a census-defined religious community.

It is worth noting here that Muslim Reformism typically disparaged Sufism because Sufism celebrated the ambiguity of the everyday, exulting in a millennial tradition of allegorical Islamic interpretations of ambiguous signs whereby, as in the case of the great Indo-Persian Sufi litterateur ʿAbdul Qādir Bedil (1644–1720), the Hindu god Krishna was a phenomenal manifestation of the Islamic cosmogonic principle of Love.[12] By contrast, Reformist discourse aimed at disambiguating the everyday into religiously identified discreteness. The resulting volume and prolixity of Muslim Reformist discourse, like that of its Hindu and other counterparts, was inversely proportionate to the political power of its authors. It was

---

11   Parama Roy, *Indian Traffic: Identities in Question in Colonial and Post-Colonial India* (Berkeley: University of California Press, 1998), 65.

12   ʿAbd al-Qādir Bedil, *Chahār ʿunṣur* (The Four Elements), in *Āvāz-hā-yi bedil*, (Tehran: Muʾassasa-yi intishārāt-i nigāh, 1386/2007), 482. *Chahār ʿunṣur* is Bedil's autobiography.

precisely because India's Reformists were legally curtailed by the colonial state in their abilities to mobilize the people at large for transformations in the public at large that they responded by producing an anxious semiotic that obsessively clarified the limits of religious community. (This is why the numerous recent attempts to transpose onto modern India Jürgen Habermas's concept of "the public sphere," originally invented with reference to the civic openness of the salons and coffeehouses of the Westphalian states of eighteenth century Europe, are mistaken.) This is why the genesis of literary realism in the early Urdu novel and the inauguration of the modern discipline of literary criticism in Urdu were, in this sense, tied to Muslim identity. These were elite, particularistic and discursive assertions of religious identity in response to the real impossibility under colonial rule of satisfying what I began this essay by characterizing as the two necessary conditions for any modern thinking to be considered political: investing the people in general (rather than only Muslims or Hindus) with legitimate political power to transform a quotidian world that was held in common.

It is therefore not a coincidence that the controversy over *Rangilā rasūl* erupted in "the summer of 1924, shortly after the failure of the Non Cooperation–Khilafat movement to secure *swaraj* [i.e. self-rule] in one year."[13] Nair does not spell out the implications of the timing of the event. Popular vulnerability to injury to religious sentiment grew as a displaced response to the failure of mass movements for popular sovereignty in colonial India. The failure of political practice— that is, the failure to adequately locate legitimate power in the people and adequately transform their everyday—found its fetishistic resolution in defending religious sentiment. A fetish, as Freud and Marx conceptualize it, is an image with which fetishists cover up a lack unbearable to themselves. It is, in this sense, not a solution as much as a provisional

---

13   Nair, "Beyond the 'Communal' 1920s," 318.

resolution by a displacement of emotional attention. Here, then, we begin to glimpse the outlines of a dominant formation of mass religious identity in modern India: the fetishistic hyper-investment in traditional items of faith in displaced response to political disenfranchisement.

The similarity of post-1991 India to post-1922 India

Is it any accident, then, that between 1947 and 1991—decades of a government-regulated economy in India—it was the central or a provincial government that banned this or that text rather than a social group demanding it of the government? Or that they peaked in the decades after 1991 when the liberalization of the Indian economy withdrew governmental protections from agrarian, educational and other sectors of the economy, leaving increasingly vast sections of the population to cope with price rises determined by international corporate finance? The tension is thus not, as Jehangir S. Pocha argues, between the "secular western liberalism" that inspired Gandhi, Nehru and Ambedkar and the "old feudal notions of society" that "too many Indians still cling to."[14] The history of the politics of giving and taking offense to religion—and of religion itself as an offended subjectivity—has nothing "feudal" about it. It is a thoroughly modern pathology whose etiology lies in a fetishistic response to the failures of politics in its accountability to the public. Exploiting the popular impatience with the imperative to interpret among India's increasingly disenfranchised people, the Hindu Right, like its Muslim and other counterparts, discovers offense in books, movies and paintings as easily as one reads advertising copy.

---

14   Jehangir S. Pocha, "Shut Up India!: Free Speech is Failing in the Wolrd's Largest Democracy" *The World Post*, posted February 21, 2014, updated December 1, 2014, http://www.huffingtonpost.com/jehangir-s-pocha/india-censorship_b_4832838.html.

"Reflecting the sensitivities of many Hindus," Reliance Fresh, one of India's prominent convenience stores and headed by Mukesh Ambani whose proximity to Narendra Modi of the Hindu Right is well known, has stopped the sale of all meat products.[15] In 1936 the German philosopher Walter Benjamin observed at the end of a famous essay: "Mankind, which in Homer's time was an object of contemplation for the Olympian gods, now is one for itself. Its self-alienation has reached such a degree that it can experience its own destruction as an aesthetic pleasure of the first order. This is the situation of politics which Fascism is rendering aesthetic."[16] What we see being created and normalized in India today is religion as a taste for offense, as an aesthetics of offense that needs to interpret signs as little as the tongue needs to curl in disgust at the taste of meat. Once it becomes as normal among masses of Hindus as a turning of the stomach, religion-as-hurt-sentiment will ensure solidarities of fetishistic rage among the millions forsaken by the free market.

The post-colonial specificity of the humanities in India

All the prominent Euro-American defenses of the humanities have been indifferent to the specificity of the humanities in post-colonial societies. José Ortega y Gasset's *Mission of the University* (1930), which arguably inaugurated a modern Euro-American tradition of defenses of the humanities, is problematic for more than just this reason.[17] Its call for a higher educational system that empowered the student belies

---

15   http://www.globalmeatnews.com/Industry-Markets/India-s-Reliance-stops-selling-meat-products.

16   Walter Benjamin, "The Work of Art in the Age of Mechanical Reproduction," *Illuminations* (New York: Schoken Books, 2007), 242.

17   José Ortega y Gasset, *Mission of the University* (Transaction Publishers, 1991).

its apparently democratic character by its justification for a "general" education preceding a "vocational" one. This justification assumes as correct the economic principle by which scarcity determines the order of priorities. By this principle, students ought to be empowered to make the most of their inevitably brief student careers by determining the content of general cultural knowledge and then that of technical or vocational knowledge. In this sequence "culture" would ideally ensure that the student body didn't contribute to the formation of the sort of "masses" Ortega condemned in his larger work, *Revolt of the Masses* (1930). The "mass man" or "mass woman," in his conception, was characterized by a refusal to reason and thus by an absence of public morality. A humanistic education was a safeguard against a descent into such mob-rule. In this patronizing interpretation the people does not exist, only the mob does.

Josef Pieper's *Leisure: the Basis of Culture* (originally given as lectures in Bonn in 1947) draws on Aristotle and St. Thomas Aquinas among other ancient and medieval thinkers to argue that leisure is not idleness but the freedom to reflect in more than analytical and instrumental ways on reality.[18] Such intuitive and non-instrumental reflection is, he argues, the highest affirmation of being human. However, this critique, attentive though it is to the historical transformation in the philosophical conception of thinking into nothing but analytical labor with Kant, is uninterested in the public and historical trajectories of the public. By extension, then, it doesn't help us explain the situation of the post-colonial humanities.

Among the most prominent defenses of the humanities that claim to include the post-colonial world within their scope of reference is Martha Nussbaum's *Not for Profit: Why Democracy Needs the Humanities* (2010). One of her key arguments for the humanities is that they enable individual moral maturation and therefore model democratic citizens. But her

18   Josef Pieper, *Leisure: The Basis of Culture* (South Bend, Indiana: St. Augustine's Press, 1998).

argument is indifferent to the local or South Asian history of the public implicit in the democracy she invokes. Not all democracies are the same, nor are all moral thinkers. If this sounds like a commonplace it is one she forces me into formulating when she writes: "One of our world's most creative democratic political leaders, Mahatma Gandhi, one of the primary architects of an independent and democratic India, understood very well that the political struggle for freedom and equality must first of all be a struggle within each person, as compassion and respect contend against fear, greed and narcissistic aggression."[19] But Gandhi was also responsible for consolidating a Hindu solidarity by objecting in 1932 to the provision to grant Scheduled (formerly "untouchable") castes separate electorates. He argued that such a provision would only separate these groups from the Hindu community. So, in that year he signed a pact with his detractor and leader of these low caste groups, Bhimrao Ramji Ambedkar, by which separate electorates were withdrawn but the low-caste groups were granted increased representation for ten years. By this action, Gandhi helped naturalize as a primordial Hindu community what had been a category of the governmental census. It was to this very solidarity that he had helped consolidate that he fell victim when, in 1948, he was assassinated by a member of a Right Wing Hindu group. It is because she ignores such moral complicities and politico-historical complexities that Nussbaum appears able to speak from a position of moral transcendence, drawing without distinction on Gandhi, Rousseau, Tagore and Socrates.

Any defense of the humanities relevant to and practicable in India must take account of the post-colonial historical dynamic by which its public has only come into being through a contest with a kind of religious community. This is also why general or disciplinarily specific calls, such as

19   Martha Nussbaum, *Not for Profit: Why Democracy Needs the Humanities* (Princeton: Princeton University Press, 2010), 29.

those contained in Peter Brooks' *The Humanities and Public Life* (2014), for "ethical reading" that are indifferent to historical locality (or implicitly and predictably assume Euro-American localities as universal) are of little use.[20] It's this post-colonial dynamic that I have tried to capture by my politico-historical-literary interpretation, in the foregoing sections, of the formation over the last hundred odd years of a certain kind of modern religious community in India. And it's this dynamic that leads me to assert, against Simon During, that the humanities can't accurately be characterized through a relativistic sociology as just another life-practice like sport.[21]

Unlike sport or any of the other practices During cites, the humanities are bound up in their very nature with natural language. This is why the visible and audible practice of the humanities in as many publically accessible (rather than privatized) forums in India as possible is one way to retain the idea of the public—with the interpretable ambiguity intrinsic to it—that is crucial to the political. This is because the methodologies of the humanities rest on three assumptions: that the valuable meanings of a text in a natural language are not its obvious ones; that it is through interpretation that a text's valuable and non-obvious meanings become available to the reader; and that the protocols for such interpretation can, in principle, be learned and taught by anyone regardless of class, caste, gender, theological conviction and other identities. The first two assumptions distinguish the humanities from the natural sciences that aim to describe their objects, in the non-natural language of mathematical algebra, in terms of exactitudes. The last distinguishes them from theological traditions of scriptural interpretation. This is why neither natural

20   Peter Brooks, ed., *The Humanities and Public Life* (New York: Fordham University Press, 2014).

21   Simon During, "Stop Defending the Humanities," *Public Books*, March 1, 2014, http://www.publicbooks.org/nonfiction/stop-defending-the-humanities.

science qualifications nor theological competence have ever been held in any theory of democracy to exclusively authorize participation in the public of any democracy.

If the utilitarian market logic of neoliberalism has led to the forsaking of the arts of interpretation that the humanities in India's public universities are tasked with teaching, it has also disclosed the need to renew them in response to the crisis of interpretation exploited by the likes of Dina Nath Batra. If we don't keep in public view the practice of humanistic interpretation we risk losing the public as a shared space of commonly interpretable ambiguity. On this space will depend any consensus on amending or removing retrograde laws like Sections 295A and 377 of the Constitution. On such a shared space will also depend the possibility of acting as a *people*— not only religious communities of affect—resolved to inhabit and interpret in non-exclusivist ways an irreducibly ambiguous world of signs, an ambiguity constitutive of any republic. Wallace Stevens' famous poem "Sunday Morning" concludes its meditation on a profane heaven by observing in the hieroglyph of pigeons' wings on the evening sky—"ambiguous undulations"—not portents of an ascent to another world, but a tranquil descent into shared ambiguity "as they sink,/ Downward to darkness, on extended wings."

VILLAGE COSMOPOLITANISMS
OR, I SEE KABUL FROM LADO SARAI

Anand Vivek Taneja

Introduction

You come from the rose-garden of Lahore laden with
  flowers
We come bearing the light of Banaras mornings...
And after that we'll ask, Who is the enemy?[1]

The famous Indian Urdu poet Ali Sardar Jafri wrote these
lines in a poem addressed to the Pakistani poet Ahmed Faraz.
In the poem, the long-shared experience of urban aesthetics—
the gardens of Lahore and the morning light of Banaras—so
much older than the boundaries of the nation states, under-
mine the taken-for-granted enmity of India and Pakistan. If
we can love the gardens of Lahore, and you can love the light
of Banaras, then how can we be enemies?

A version of this essay first appeared on the blog *Chapati Mystery*.
Anand Vivek Taneja, "Village Cosmopolitanisms: Or, I See Kabul from
Lado Sarai - I," *Chapati Mystery*, accessed May 6, 2015, http://www.
chapatimystery.com/archives/homistan/village_cosmopolitanisms_or_i_
see_kabul_from_lado_sarai_-_i.html.

1   For the original Urdu as well as a translation and commentary
     on these verses, see Irfan Ahmad, "In Memoriam: Ali Sardar
     Jafri, 1913–2000," *Seminar* 494 (October 2000), http://www.india-
     seminar.com/2000/494/494%20in%20memoriam.htm.

But if we're not enemies, then who is?

> Only that historian will have the gift of fanning the spark of hope in the past who is firmly convinced that even the dead will not be safe from the enemy if he wins. And this enemy has not ceased to be victorious.[2]

For Benjamin, writing in the shadow of catastrophe, the enemy was a much older one than the Nazi jackboots trampling over Europe in 1940, the year he wrote the *Theses on the Philosophy of History*. For him, the enemy was the conformism that threatens to overpower all tradition, and make it a tool of the ruling classes.[3] For me, Benjamin's idea of conformism is akin to what I call *presentism*: reading the past as merely a prelude to the historical inevitability of present states of affairs. Colonial historiography constructed Muslim rule in India as simultaneously cruel and effete, to make the colonial moment of its writing, the ongoing British conquest and subjugation of India, seem both inevitable and necessary. Hindus have always fought against Muslim oppression in nationalist historiography written in post-Partition India, thus portraying the birth of two separate and hostile nation-states as historical inevitability. History has been, by and large, a tool of the ruling classes and their investment in maintaining the *status quo*. Presentism is the enemy.

What would it mean, given all this History, to fan a spark of hope in the past? What would it mean "to wrest tradition away from a conformism that is about to overpower it"? What might we do with the light of Banaras when Banaras is the place from which Prime Minister Narendra Modi was elected to Parliament in 2014 despite (or because of?) being widely held responsible for the mass-killings of Muslims in the state of Gujarat in 2002?

---

2   Walter Benjamin, "Theses on the Philosophy of History," in *Illuminations* (New York: Schocken Books, 1969): 253–64, at 255.

3   Benjamin, "Theses," 255.

Modi's victory marks the triumph of a certain Hegelian view of the Indian past, in which a defeated and enslaved Hindu nation, long subjected to Muslim tyranny, finally rises to glory by overpowering its enemies. This view has become a kind of dominant common sense in Indian middle-class discourse, and can be directly linked to the ways in which our present has been grotesquely transformed: the partition of the sub-continent on religious lines, horrific anti-Muslim pogroms in Gujarat and elsewhere, everyday discrimination against and marginalization of Muslims. But as I discovered in the course of my wanderings and other research in Delhi over the last several years, this master-slave dialectic, inherited from colonial epistemology,[4] is certainly not the only vision of the past available in contemporary North India. In writing this essay, it is my hope that by recovering other ways of remembering the past, we might be able to imagine alternatives to the inevitability of the present, and different ways of inhabiting, and co-habiting, the future.

Many of my encounters with these alternative views of the past took place in the "urban villages" of Delhi. These are villages that were once part of the rural hinterland of Delhi, but have since been surrounded by the rapid postcolonial expansion of the city. While the agricultural lands of these villages were appropriated by the Delhi Development Authority to make way for modernist housing colonies, shopping centers, and the planned expansion of the bourgeoning city, the residential areas of the villages, the *abadi deh*, were left largely untouched by the state. Largely exempt from the zoning regulations and prevailing mores of the modernist middle class Delhi that surrounds them, these villages are zones of cosmopolitanism—both in the variety and kinds of people that live in them today, and in the old traditions of negotiation with difference which inform this contemporary hospitality, however commercially motivated it might be—often absent

---

4   Gyanendra Pandey, *The Construction of Communalism in Colonial North India* (Oxford: Oxford University Press, 2012).

in more "modern" parts of Delhi. The villages mentioned here include Lado Sarai, Hauz Rani, Mehrauli, Begampur, and Chiragh Dehli.

Lado Sarai: The Wall

The wall has been standing for centuries, a large imposing pile of mortared rubble, slowly crumbling into ruin. In the time that the wall has been standing, many things have been built inside its vast circuit—gardens, orchards, houses; tanks, tombs and shrines—and many of these had crumbled away to ruin. At some point a settlement of Jat farmers, a community of agriculturalists also renowned for their marital nature, took up the spaces between and around the tombs of fifteenth century Muslim noblemen, and the wall became the boundary marker for the agricultural land of the village.

Unless you were interested in such things as migration patterns and *longue durée* historical processes, this fortification wall that the Mughals identified as Qila Rai Pithora, the fort of Prithviraj, was a boring, bucolic, wall. I use the past tense because sometime in the 1990s, things began to change. The wall was suddenly in the news. For one, the wall now served as the boundary marker for a golf course, developed by the Delhi Development Authority on the former agricultural land of Lado Sarai village. Then, there was the statue.

A month after coming to power with a majority alliance in the parliamentary elections of September and October 1999, the Hindu right wing Bhartiya Janata Party (BJP) decided to build a cultural center, topped by a commemorative martial statue of Prithviraj Chauhan riding a horse, abutting the walls of the Qila Rai Pithora. Prithviraj Chauhan, the man whose name was associated with the crumbling wall, is the tragic hero of Hindu nationalist historiography, the chivalric Hindu hero who was cheated out of his kingdom by treacherous Muslim attack. The statue and cultural center were conceived at the same time as the BJP government began a project of rewriting school textbooks to hew closer to their vision of history, in which Muslims were fundamentally bad people, Muslim rule was eight hundred years of tyranny imposed on India, which was (and should return to being) an exclusively Hindu country. So, of course, Hindu machismo had to be written anew on the landscapes of the national capital.

Two and a half years later, when the cultural center was ready for its inauguration, the world had changed significantly. The planes had crashed into the twin towers on 9/11, the war in Afghanistan had begun, and now the Western world was, fully, completely, nakedly in alignment with the BJP's view of history and politics, in which Muslims equaled evil and tyranny. Eight months after Operation Enduring Freedom had begun in Afghanistan, on June 8, 2002, Lal Krishna Advani, the Deputy Prime Minister of India and leading member of the BJP, came to inaugurate the cultural center by the wall, and to unveil the statue of Prithviraj Chauhan. At the inauguration, he drew a ceremonial sword out of its scabbard, and talked about the ongoing War against Terror.

> The Union Home Minister, L.K. Advani, today said India would react in accordance with the "popular national sentiments" if Pakistan failed to end cross-border terrorism.
>
> "If Pakistan does not put an end to cross-border terrorism and India reacts in accordance with popular sentiments, it would be considered appropriate," Mr. Advani said here, after unveiling the statue of the Rajput warrior, Prithviraj Chauhan.
>
> The entire world had realised that Pakistan was encouraging terrorism in India and leaders, including the U.S. President, George Bush, and the British Foreign Secretary, Jack Straw, had expressed the opinion that permanent

peace could not be established in the region unless Islamabad stopped abetting terrorism.[5]

The walls of Qila Rai Pithora were burdened with the narrative of not just a National History, that of the last Hindu King being defeated by the Muslim invader for lack of national unity; but also a global history, where Prithviraj Chauhan was the first martyr of the War Against Terror, being fought continuously for eight hundred years against Islamic terrorists from Pakistan and Afghanistan.

Lado Sarai: The Village

In October 2005, I heard a very different narrative about Prithviraj Chauhan and the invader Mohammad Ghori in the village of Lado Sarai. The agricultural lands of Lado Sarai village had been gone for twenty years, acquired by the Delhi Development Authority as part of the Masterplan for developing the city, but the residential lands of the village, the *abadi deh*, were untouched by the city's zoning imperatives. The old *zamindars* or landowners of the village still lived on in Lado Sarai, and one of them told me the story.

This story begins with the good but childless king Anangpal Tomar of Delhi, the last of the line, so the story goes, of the mythical Pandavas. One day, in his old age, the good king Tomar decided to go on long pilgrimage, and leave the kingdom in the care of two relatives, Prithviraj and Jaichand. Prithviraj was given custody of Delhi and Ajmer, while Jaichand, the king of the "Jat belt" took care of Kannauj.

Prithviraj told Anangpal that his custody was useless unless he had authority which other kings would believe in. "Give it

5   Vinay Kumar, "'Retaliation If Infiltration Does Not Stop,'" *The Hindu*, June 8, 2002, http://www.thehindu.com/2002/06/08/stories/2002060804500100.htm.

to me in writing," he said. "No King can enter Delhi without the permission of Prithviraj." So Anangpal gave it to him in writing, and went off on his pilgrimage. Not much later, when he returned to his city, the gates were closed to him. No King can enter Delhi without the permission of Prithviraj. And so it was that Prithviraj came to rule Delhi.

Flashback. A trader from Afghanistan decided to start trading with India and thus expand his business and his profits. So he loaded his goods on camels and came to India, and to the court of the vigorous but childless king, Anangpal Tomar, along with his beautiful daughter. He offered Anagpal his daughter in marriage. "I know that you will have children with her."

The marriage was consummated, the child was conceived, but the older, childless queen was jealous. While the younger queen was pregnant she forbade Anagpal from meeting her, and when the child was born, she threw him out on a garbage pile, *ghor* in Sanskrit.

The child was picked up by a passing childless potter, who then brought him up as his own. When the child was seven years old, king Anangpal passed a judgement which dissatisfied his people. The potter's son suggested another way in which judgement could be done. The news spread like wildfire and reached the palace.

Fearing the king's wrath a servant from the palace went and told the potter who his son really was, and asked him to send the child off to Afghanistan, to his grandfather.

Years later Mohammad Ghori marched on Delhi to reclaim his inheritance, and Jaichand joined him. Prithviraj was defeated. Lad Singh, a soldier in Jaichand's army, settled in what was to become Lado Sarai village. His four sons lived in four domed structures, four *gumbads* which existed there prior to their settlement, and around these domes the village of Lado Sarai grew.

Karan Pal Singh, who was about seventy years old when she told me this story, also told me: There are three kinds of history. One is those written in schoolbooks. This is written by those in power, and cannot be trusted. Then there is the history by the person who sits with books and tries to make sense of the past for himself. The third is oral tradition, what people remember from what ancestors tell them. There is some truth in both of these.[6]

The Historian

In a recent essay, the historian Manan Ahmed writes,

> The South Asia we inhabit is a recent construct. It is a limited and restricted political space as compared to more than a thousand years of textual history and thousands more in material and cultural memory. The stories it currently tells are themselves limited, the imaginations it cultivates are themselves rigid. The geographies that seem so indelible, so permanent are mere shadows upon regional perspectives that are still legible movement and life patterns, in languages, in customs, and in cultural imaginations. Taking this *longue durée* look at the Indic peninsula compels us to imagine varied configurations for the future sixty years, hence.[7]

The story I heard in Lado Sarai, drawing on cultural memories different from those privileged by colonial historians and postcolonial nationalism, blew my mind. For one, here was

6   Slightly different versions of the two sections on Lado Sarai were originally published in Anand V. Taneja, "History and Heritage Woven in the New Urban Fabric: The Changing Landscapes of Delhi's 'First City'. Or, Who Can Tell the Histories of Lado Sarai?" in *Patterns of Middle Class Consumption in India and China,* edited by Christophe Jaffrelot and Peter van der Veer (New Delhi: SAGE Publications India Pvt Ltd, 2008), 157–70.

7   Manan Ahmed, "Future's Past," in *South Asia 2060: Envisioning Regional Futures* (London: Anthem, 2013), 46–52, at 46.

an account of the past where trade came before war. People from Afghanistan and India exchanged goods, in the chronology of this story, long before they exchanged blows on the battlefield. Through trade came kinship—the Afghan trader's daughter married to the king of Delhi. Through kinship came legitimacy. Muhammad Ghori, his name not a sign of foreign parts and irreducible difference, but of the most humble of domestic origins, takes over the throne of Delhi because it is his right, as a lineal descendant of the Pandavas. And the justice lies not just in his claim to Delhi, but in his persona—he had to go into hiding because he displayed a kingly aptitude for justice while still a potter's son.

Of course, there are many mythic elements in this story, but they also contain many truths inadmissible by the mythologies of nationalism. Well before the Battle of Tarain, there were connections, not just military and antagonistic, between Ghur and Delhi. "Mahmud of Ghazna (d. 1030), that foremost iconoclast, employed Hindavi commanders and battalions. Tilak, the commander of the Hindavi troops...rose up the ranks, eventually having his own quarter in the city of Ghazna. Some accounts of that city, as well as surviving architecture, reveals a multiethnic space where artisans, trades and crafts communities from Sindh and Rajasthan thrived."[8]

The lineal descent from the Pandavas; and hence, the positing of Ghurid rule as not break, but legitimate continuity, this too has precedent in pre-colonial historiography. When Syed Ahmad Khan wrote the "king-lists" that accompany the *Asar-us-Sanadid*, his canonical Urdu work on the historical monuments of Delhi, written in the mid-nineteenth century, he started the list of the kings of Delhi from the Pandavas (to be precise, from Raja Judhishtir), and continued through Puranic lists till it came to the Sultanate and Mughals.[9] The continuity with previous Indic forms of sovereignty, rather

8   Ahmed, "Future's Past," 49.
9   Syed Ahmed Khan, *Asar-us-Sanadid*, 2nd ed. (Delhi: Urdu Academy, 2000).

than rupture, was deliberately cultivated by the rulers of the Delhi Sultanate and the Mughals. We see this, to choose an example rooted in Delhi's landscape, in Firoz Shah Tughlaq's relocation of the Topra Ashokan pillar, associated in legend with the Pandavas, to become the majestic centerpiece of his new citadel, hoisted high upon a riverside pyramid.[10]

People from various castes and communities in contemporary Delhi, Muslims and non-Muslims, petition saint figures among the ruins of Firoz Shah Kotla, asking for justice. These "Muslim" ruins serve as the sites of memory of a political theology (or rather, *theologies*), which developed at different times on the frontier (both physical and conceptual) of "Islam" and its Others: theologies that didn't elide difference, but made hospitality, or rather, an openness to mutually comprehensible difference, central to the ethical ideas of premodern Indian states.[11] We see this political theology remembered in the deposition of petitions in a fourteenth-century ruin in contemporary Delhi, but also in the story told in Lado Sarai, where the boy-king Muhammad Ghori is recognized for who he is because of his *expression of judicial opinion*.

The Wedding Feast

The present has a powerful hold on our imagination. So we imagine the future as being an amplified version of the present, and we imagine the past as prelude to a foreordained

10   Finbarr B. Flood, "Pillars, Palimpsests, and Princely Practices: Translating the Past in Sultanate Delhi," *Res: Anthropology and Aesthetics* 43 (2003): 95–116.

11   Manan Ahmed Asif, "A Demon with Ruby Eyes," *Medieval History Journal* 16.2 (October 2013): 335–69, doi:10.1177/0971945813514901; Anand Vivek Taneja, "Saintly Visions: Other Histories and History's Others in the Medieval Ruins of Delhi," *Indian Economic & Social History Review* 49.4 (December 2012): 557–90, doi:10.1177/0019464612463843.

present, precisely aligned cogs and gears grinding towards the historical, tragic inevitability of the now.

> The words we use, informed by our immediate past, and already encoded with incomprehensible difference—*coercion, submission, conversion, conflict.* The categories we construct are already hegemonic—"Hindu," "Muslim," "invader," "indigenous." We take this ahistoricized words and categories and proceed to give them a universality that they don't deserve even for the here and now.[12]

If we can think of the past outside the prison-house of the present, then can we think of different possibilities for our present and our future? Was the present in Lado Sarai different because the past was remembered differently?

It seemed so in 2005. Lado Sarai was no haven of peace and brotherhood. The Jats, who are the dominant caste-group of the village, remembered banding together with people from other villages in the area and attacking Mehrauli in 1947, described in conversation as a Muslim *garh* or stronghold. But they also remembered giving shelter to Muslims from the neighboring village of Hauz Rani, because they were from the same *gotra* as the Jats of Lado Sarai. Even today, I was told, we eat at each other's weddings. There were many Muslims present in the Lado Sarai, migrants from UP, Bihar, and Kashmir, running small businesses and living as tenants of the Jats. One of the old men I interviewed in Lado Sarai proudly told me of how he had stormed into the local Police Station and gotten his young Kashmiri tenant out of illegal custody just by sheer force of personality (and some yelling). This was in the years immediately after the attack on Parliament, blamed on Kashmiri separatists, which had led to a near-war situation between India and Pakistan, and to "tenant verifications" by the Delhi Police which made it even harder for Muslims to

---

12 Ahmed, "Future's Past," 47.

rent properties in the planned colonies of middle-class South Delhi, such as Saket and Malviya Nagar, on the other side of the wall from Lado Sarai.

Another story, a few years later, in another of Delhi's urban villages. This time in Begampur, a humorous story tinged with nostalgia for the past, a father and son tag-teaming in telling me the story, their voices overlapping each other on my recording as they added and elaborated details.

> There must have been a time when there was a shared civilization (*mushtarka tehzeeb*) ... I still remember that story from the village, *Yeh le shank sa, kha bhi aur baja bhi.* (Here take this thing like a [conch] shell, eat it and blow it as well.) Where we come from, towards Meerut, there is a village entirely of Jats, with one Muslim home, that of a carpenter. One day he's sitting outside his house, looking very morose. The chaudhari (village headman) was passing by, and he asked, Master, why do you sit here looking so troubled? The carpenter said, My daughter is getting married. The chaudhari said, So what's the worry? She's a daughter of the village, we'll all get together to help out with the arrangements. The carpenter said, that's all fine, of course you'll help with the arrangements, but when the *barat* (the groom's procession) comes to the village, who will serve them food? You all don't eat meat, and I don't have any family here. The chaudari said, our boys will serve the guests, where's the problem? You just get someone to cook the food. So a Muslim cook (*khansama*) came and cooked the food, and when the wedding guests sat down to eat, all the Jat men of the village started serving them, with cloth wrapped around their faces, to keep out the smell of the meat. And of course, the ones who were eating didn't know who was serving them. One of the guests got served a piece of shank bone, without meat and said, *Are, boti de boti.* Hey, give me meat. The Jat replied, *ke boti boti kar riya hai, yeh le sankh sa kha bhi aur baja bhi.* Why're you going on

about boti, take this thing like a conch shell, eat it and blow
it as well. This is a famous story. See how mixed together
(*mile hue*) people were then. How much love there was. The
honour of the village shouldn't be lost...

The story of village togetherness, of a shared civilization
(*mushtarka tehzeeb*) that was recounted so fondly to me that
afternoon in Begampur was fundamentally a story of profound difference. In his famous speech of 1940, articulating
the Two-Nation theory and a separate homeland for Muslims, Muhammad Ali Jinnah pointed out that Hindus and
Muslims "neither intermarry nor interdine together."[13] True
enough, at least going by the story of the Jat village. The differences between the Jats and Muslims were so profound that
the former didn't even recognize the *ingredients* of the latter's
food—a misrecognition on which the whole punch line of the
story rests.

But that impasse in the story, that moment of misrecognition, which would become a sign of irreconcilable difference in nationalist historiography—*they neither intermarry nor
interdine*—becomes instead the fondly remembered moment
of bridging difference in the memory of the village—they
may neither intermarry or interdine, but that village throws a
damn fine party, face-masks and all.

A Brahmin Has Said That This Year Is Good

The common ground on which differences became mutually
comprehensible, at least in the story as it was remembered,
was the village itself. *Gaon ki beti. Gaon ki izzat.* The daughter

13   M.A. Jinnah, *Address by Quaid-i-Azam Mohammad Ali Jinnah at Lahore
Session of Muslim League, March, 1940* (Islamabad: Directorate of
Films and Publishing, Ministry of Information and Broadcasting,
Government of Pakistan, 1983), 5–23.

of the village. The honour of the village. To understand this common ground perhaps we need to take the metaphor literally—the ground that we stand upon, our shared geography, is our *common ground*.

To propose an alternative to the linear, teleological presentist modes of thinking history, Manan Ahmed sketches out an alternative model. Imagine, he says, three concentric circles. "The innermost circle, labeled 750–1250 CE, is where a specific dialogue of political theology is mostly concentrated, though it emanates outwards. The second circle, labeled 1220–1850 CE, is the site of development of a new political language, administrative and localized. The third circle, labeled 1480–1947 CE, is the space of a distinctly visible vernacular culture, though it permeates back towards the center."[14] To his model of three concentric circles, I want to add a fourth. We can think of this as the smallest circle—for it is a local, intimate circle, the circle of a shared sacred geography.

One of the unexpected findings of my research on shared sacred sites in Delhi, sites of veneration for both Hindus and Muslims, was how intricately these sites were connected to the ecology and topography of the city.[15] For instance, in his *Asar-us-Sanadid*, Syed Ahmad Khan wrote about Bhuli Bhatiyari ka Mahal, a small and mysterious structure built upon a fourteenth century Tughlaq check dam along the scarp of the *Pahari*, or hilly ridge, just to the west of the plain of Delhi. Bhuli Bhatiyari ka Mahal was the site of an annual *mela* or fair.

> This building has been built atop a high hill from which the natural scenery can be seen far and wide and especially in the rainy season the water flowing everywhere and the waving of the greenery in the wind all around gives wondrous pleasure . . . here there is a very big fair of *pavan pareechha* (testing the wind) in which all the city's

14   Ahmed, "Future's Past," 47–48.

15   Anand Vivek Taneja, *Time, Islam, and Enchantment in the Medieval Ruins of Delhi*, forthcoming.

Brahmins, [Hindu] astrologers (*jotishi*), fortune tellers and [Muslim] astrologers (*najumi*) gather to test the air and test it by planting a small flag (*jhandi*) and thousands of Hindus and Muslims spectators gather to watch.[16]

The mela was held annually on the full moon of the month of Ashad, which corresponds to the beginning of the monsoon in Delhi. By testing the winds the Brahmins and Muslim astrologers would predict how the rains would be that year, and hence how the crops would grow, and hence whether the year would be a prosperous one for the folks of the city and its hinterland, or a lean one. I like to imagine that this fair and its annual predictions was what Ghalib, the renowned poet of nineteenth-century Delhi, was playfully thinking of when he wrote this famous couplet:

Dekhiye pate hain ushaq buton se kya faiz
Ik birahman ne kaha hai key eh sal accha hai

Let's see what grace lovers find from idols
A Brahman has said that this year is good

⊡ ⊡ ⊡

One of the places that the Deccani nobleman Dargah Quli Khan wrote about in his account of his mid-eighteenth century visit to Delhi was what he called a *chashmeh* (a spring or well) near the *dargah* of the fourteenth century saint Hazrat Nasruddin Roshan Chiragh-e Dehli (d. 1356), a shrine located within the village of Chiragh Dilli.

> In truth you are the lamp of Delhi, rather you are the lamp and the eyes (*chashm o chiragh*, dearly beloved) of all

---

16   Syed Ahmed Khan, *Asar-us-Sanadid*, 1st ed. (Aligarh: Aligarh Muslim University, 2007), 267.

Hindustan. The pilgrimage to your tomb is on Sundays. In the month of Diwali the crowds are especially impressive. In this month the people of Delhi come on every Sunday to gain the bliss of pilgrimage (*ziyarat*). There is a spring/well (*chasmeh*) near the *dargah*, here they pitch tents and enclosures and bathe in the spring and often people find complete cures from their old diseases. Muslims and Hindus both make the pilgrimage in the same fashion (*yaksan*). From morning to evening the caravans of pilgrims keep coming regularly. In the shade of every wall and every tree they spread out carpets and give due praise to luxury and the happiness of hearts. It is a strange and wondrous excursion and amusement and an extraordinary spectacle. Everywhere there is color and music and in every nook and corner there is the sound of the *pakhawaj* and *morchang* (drum and jew's harp).[17]

Dargah Quli's account indicates that the fair associated with the saint Chiragh Dehli (The Lamp of Delhi) happened in the month of Diwali, a festival month in the Indic calendar, which does not necessarily coincide with the 'urs or death anniversary of the saint, which is calculated by the Islamic calendar. It was only when I was at the shrine of Chiragh Dehli, and saw the clay lamps lit in offering there, which are the same as the clay lamps traditionally lit during Diwali, that I made the connection. In the festival calendar of Delhi, every year, the festival of lamps (Diwali) was celebrated at the shrine of the lamp of Delhi (Chiragh Dehli), a festival at which all the chroniclers note that both Hindus and Muslims came together. Across different mythologies, histories and religious identities, the connotative equivalence of *chiragh* and *diya/deep* had created the possibility of a shared life-world.

---

17   Dargah Quli Khan, *Muraqqa-I Dehli: Farsi Matan Aur Urdu Tarjamah* (Delhi: Anjuman Taraqqi-e Urdu, 1993), 118.

⊡ ⊡ ⊡

In the June of 2010, I took a break from fieldwork and the heat of Delhi and went to Iran for a short holiday. When I came back, I brought small baubles I had picked up in the Shiraz bazaar for my friends at the shrine of Firoz Shah Kotla, Turkish apotropaic antidotes against the evil eye, made of blue glass. Everyone had been happy with these gifts but P (who is from the Balmiki community, and identifies as Hindu) was especially moved. He held the beads reverentially to his eyes and said, you brought these from Iraq? That's where all the *walis*, the saints, come from.

For P, a deeply local geography of sainthood could simultaneously be cosmopolitan, encompassing both the saints' origins and their ends without any contradiction. Compared with the subtlety of village cosmopolitanisms, it is modern nationalist thought, as exemplified by Vinayak Damodar Savarkar's limited and limiting ideas of sacred and nationalist geographies, which seem boorish and parochial. Savarkar (1883–1966), the originator of the Hindu right-wing ideology of *Hindutva* (Hinduness), argued that Muslims and Christians could never be patriotic enough because their sacred spaces lay outside of India—in Mecca, Jerusalem, and the Vatican.[18]

And as in the self-fulfilling prophecy of a Greek tragedy, the sacred spaces shared by Hindus and Muslims are disappearing, along with the rapid destruction and transformation of the city's ecology. The Fair of Wind Testing is long gone from the calendar of the city. By some accounts it stopped after Partition. Only a faint memory of it is left in the name of the Jhandewalan Temple, the Temple with the Flags, one of the most famous temples in Delhi. The temple now stands in the middle of a dense conglomeration of concrete, all traces of

18   Nivedita Menon and Aditya Nigam, *Power and Contestation: India Since 1989* (London: Zed Books, 2007), 37.

greenery and flowing water—and Muslims—now long gone
from the vicinity. The sacred spring which once brought Muslims and Hindus together near the shrine of Chiragh Dehli
is long gone, the stream-bed it originated in now carries the
untreated sewage of Delhi's southwards urban expansion to a
Yamuna which is all sewage.[19] The common lands of Delhi's
villages, the *shamilat-deh*, have rapidly been urbanized and
built over, taking many shared spaces of sacrality and social-
ity with them.

'Twas Useless to Mourn Destructions?

If we turn back to thinking of the four concentric circles of
South Asia's alternate histories, we will also have to think of
destruction radiating outwards from the center, like a mushroom cloud. The circle of shared geography, sacred and mun-
dane? Almost obliterated, by the massive transformations of
land use and land tenure, but still tenaciously surviving in
the shared sacrality of Sufi shrines. The long development of
political theology? Almost obliterated by nationalism and the
bio-political logics of postcolonial states, but still surviving as
a counter-memory of justice in the *darbars* of *pir babas*.[20] The
political languages of Indo-Persian culture have been widely
displaced by English, and in India at least, by highly Sanskri-
tized local vernaculars. But even then, when that master ora-
tor of the Hindu Right, Atal Behari Vajpayee, really wanted to
get a point across, he would often use an Urdu couplet.

For the largest circle of all, that of vernacular culture,
yoked to the technologies of cinema and radio, cable TV

---

19   Anand Vivek Taneja, "A City Without Time," *Indian Quar-
      terly*, accessed May 5, 2015, http://indianquarterly.com/a-city-
      without-time/.

20   A *pir baba* is the "generic north Indian term for (usually) Muslim
      saints." Taneja, "Saintly Visions," 561.

and YouTube, seems to have outrun the mushroom cloud of destruction, or at least seems to have grown faster than it. Bombay cinema, with its many lives, enables the creation of new cultural referents, and provides a common vocabulary; most crucially it keeps long-standing historical and cultural themes within living memory, particular views of love, of jealousy, of friendship, of the beloved that we can easily trace to the vernacular epics of the seventeenth century. Most of this is not a surprise, considering that that from the very beginnings of Indian cinema, the epics (from the *Mahabharata* to *Laila Majnun*) have been a popular source, and that the film industry has remained far more agnostic on the faiths of its workers than its surrounding society.[21]

Bollywood films and film songs are in the end, a commercial product, aiming for maximum popularity by going for the lowest common denominator. It's the common denominator itself which happens to be not a mathematical simplification, but a rich and complex amalgam of shared histories—including shared affects, shared joys and sorrows and pain. I have argued elsewhere[22] that the perceived "Muslimness" of Hindi cinema, and the popularity of "Muslim socials" as a genre is because "Muslimness" is metonymic for the shared premodern culture of North India—with north being a somewhat loose term, stretching at least as far south as the territories of the Nizam (the "Nizam territory" is still a distribution area for Hindi films which does not coincide with the boundaries of the linguistically organized state of Andhra Pradesh).

There is a scene in the film *Kabul Express*[23] that really gets the ability of Bollywood songs to encompass shared culture and shared histories across all kinds or borders. It's set in a jeep, traversing the war-torn landscape of Afghanistan. It's

---

21   Ahmed, "Future's Past," 51.

22   Anand Vivek Taneja, "Muslimness in Hindi Cinema," *Seminar* 598 (June 2009), http://www.india-seminar.com/2009/598/598_anand_vivek_taneja.htm.

23   Kabir Khan, *Kabul Express*, DVD (Mumbai: Yash Raj Films, 2006).

been a picaresque journey with an Afghan driver, an American war correspondent, two Indian journalists and a Pakistani "Taliban." As the journey nears its end, one of the Indian journalists tunes his short-wave radio, and through bursts of static we hear a famous song from the film *Hum Dono*[24]— "Main zindagi ka sath nibhata chala gaya"—a song from fifty years ago. The Indians and the Pakistani, part of a shared community of listeners because of the popularity of Bombay cinema across national boundaries, start humming, and then loudly singing along together.

It is a cinematic masterstroke. The sound track of the scene is diegetic—everything making sound is included in the frame. But the song coming through the shortwave radio blows the frame wide open.

Barbadiyon ka sog manana fizul tha / Barbadiyon ka jashn manata chala gaya, the song goes. It was useless to mourn destructions, so I kept on celebrating destructions. Not just one destruction but plural. *Barbadiyan*. The song was a huge hit when the film came out in 1961, perhaps because the incongruity of the jauntiness of the tune and Mohammed Rafi's singing, and the stoicism of the lyrics, captured something of the mood of South Asia, fourteen years after the horrors of Partition, fourteen years into the destructions integral to the making of the new nation state and its national citizens. The way to deal with destructions was not to mourn but to celebrate, to focus on independence not on Partition, to smoke like a chimney to forget all those thoughts and worries that arise unbidden. *Jo mil gaya usi ko muqaddar samajh liya / Jo kho gaya main usko bhulata chala gaya.* I accepted as fate whatever I found. Whatever I lost I kept on forgetting. People found new countries, new homes, new identities on the other side of the never ending *barbadi*. But the forgetting was never quite done—*I kept on forgetting.* The plot of the film *Hum Dono*, as it unfolds, about a man MIA in World War II and his look-alike who reluctantly takes his

24   Vijay Anand, *Hum Dono*, film (Mumbai: Shemaroo, 1961).

place back home, must have resonated hugely with those who saw it, for they knew about missing homelands and missing beloveds that you never quite forget, and the substitutes never quite being the same.

And so this bittersweet song makes Indians and Pakistanis bond as they drive across the *barbadi* of Afghanistan. The song leads to a shared smoke, and a moment of incongruous closeness despite the tensions of their journey. I've always said, the Pakistani says, *Madhuri Dikshit de do, Kashmir le lo*. Give us Madhuri Dixit and take Kashmir. It's a moment of hope in the bleak comedy of the film. Yes, of course, shared culture beats divisive politics. The beauty of Bollywood actress Madhuri Dixit trumps the acrimony over Kashmir. But, says the Indian journalist, Madhuri Dixit got married and went off to America. Ah, says the Pakistani sadly, All our good things go off to America. And then in a screech of brakes and bullets, the conversation ends and the madcap—and tragic—finale takes over.

All our good things go off to America. Tell me that's not true.

TERPSICHORE

Irina Dumitrescu

When Lady Philosophy finds Boethius mournfully composing verse in prison, she immediately sets upon the poetic Muses surrounding him. "Who has allowed these theatrical whores (*scenicas meretriculas*) to approach this sick man?" she asks. The Muses, according to Philosophy, do nothing to help the invalid, playing upon his passions rather than nourishing his reason. I heard, however, that a most passionate muse slipped back between the bars when Philosophy wasn't looking.

While writing my essay for this collection, I spent several months immersing myself in the memoirs of Romanian political prisoners. There is almost nothing that could make a person want to dance less. Reading these texts made me internalize the overwhelming sense of entrapment prisoners felt, even, sometimes, their paranoia. Though living in warm Texas, within walking distance of four supermarkets, I couldn't help but imagine the cold and hunger that gripped these prisoners, kept them frozen like stones. In the harsher prisons, inmates were forced to maintain a single position, facing the door, at all times, so as to be permanently under supervision. Even when sleeping, they were not allowed to turn their faces to the wall, an insidious rehearsal that deprived them of any real rest.

Imagine, then, my surprise, when one of the muses snuck in. Actually, many muses haunted these forbidding prisons, hiding sprite-like in pockets and under chamber pots. But I am thinking of the most audacious one: Terpsichore.

It is a day in the late 1940s.[1] A group of men in their late teens and early twenties have been imprisoned and accused of fomenting against the Revolution. It is important to note that they have little understanding of the political events around them, live in a village in the far northern end of Romania, and are much more concerned with hiding their passionate crushes on girls in their high school than in impeding the steady march towards a classless society. Gheorghe Andreica, age seventeen, has found himself in a cell with the older, more sophisticated Ion Ilban, age eighteen, and knowing that their time together might be short, he decides to learn manners from the worldly-wise Ion.

Gheorghe, nicknamed "Ghiță," has a problem. He knows how to do the country-dances, how to dance a "sârba" in a circle, or to twirl a girl around and around until "her heels sizzle." But until he learns what the waltz, tango, and foxtrot are, he'll never be able to face polite society.

Maybe it was the youth and energy of these teenagers that let the Muse know she was welcome, or maybe it was the fact that they seemed ripe for the occult mysteries of two-steps-back-and-one-to-the-side. But she slipped into the cell, and soon enough, the eighteen-year-old Ion was dancing alone with his arms wide open, and Ghiță was following right along. Ion taught Ghiță to move slowly and gracefully, "like the sea's waves when the afternoon breeze caresses them." When Ion explained that the dancing couple should keep a decent distance between their bodies, Ghiță confessed his ulterior motives: "I've seen that—with the tango most of all—the partners are very close. Man, most of them clasp their hands between their chests. Each one can feel the other's heart

1   Gheorghe Andreica, "Cu ghiozdanul la închisoare," in *Memoria închisorii Sighet*, ed. Romulus Rusan (Bucharest: Fundația Academia Civică, 1999), 7–104, at 39–43.

beating with the back of the hand. This is what tempts me the most."

And so the *scenica meretricula* Terpsichore made herself known. Poor Ion had a tough time explaining to Ghiță that one really has to let the girl make the first move, that this happens later at night, and that she knows perfectly well where her heart is. Ghiță complained that if the girl's mother takes her home early, he's lost an evening for nothing. Ion promised him he would win double of whatever he lost that night, leaving the precise nature of the winnings tantalizingly vague. His lesson learned, Ghiță declared himself a Doctor of Elegant Manners.

Did you remember that they're in prison?

Terpsichore has a special way with memory, and with time as well. When I first learned to tango, our instructor taught us to imagine that every song was the last time we would ever dance with that particular partner. The tango Ghiță was dreaming of has always been a space apart from time, and a fantasy of the end of time. *This is the last three minutes we'll ever have*, one must think, even while a remarkable quality of breath or a heavy shoe on one's foot gives this affirmation the lie.

Terpsichore teaches absorption, an attention to physical technique that erases the world outside studio, ballroom, or cell. When dancing, we enter the realm of the physical, an area beyond ideology or even bare thought. Memory works its way through muscles rather than mind, surprising the dancer with unwitting revelations. The rhythm that was out of reach during lessons happens spontaneously in the stairwell, the muscle that was uncontrollable in class submits when the dancer is waiting for the streetlight to change. As sexy as Terpsichore may be (and she did once allow Rita Hayworth to play her in a movie, after all), Ghiță's fantasy is about more than an erotic connection to a hypothetical village girl. He dreams of existence beyond space and prisons and politics. He dreams of an eternal and constant beat, felt, as if accidentally, through the back of his hand.

RUMBA UNDER FIRE
MUSIC AS MORALE AND MORALITY IN MUSIC
AT THE FRONTLINES OF THE CONGO

Judith Verweijen

We are like refugees. We move around like refugees, we live
like refugees, we eat like refugees. Yet, the refugees are better
off, they get humanitarian aid from the United Nations, but
we do not. Lieutenant Kalupala is fuming. The soldiers of the
armed forces of the Democratic Republic of the Congo, the
Forces Armées de la République Démocratique du Congo (FARDC),
never tire of pointing out their miserable living conditions
and the hardships to which they are exposed. There's always
hunger. If you're lucky you get food twice a day, but never
meat. Meat is too expensive. So there is rice and beans, or
ugali, the doughy stuff made from cassava or maize flour that
is a staple food in large parts of the eastern Congo. It's never
enough. So you buy extra food and if you lack the money you
smoke. *Bangi. Ganja.* Stuff, you know. It makes the hunger dis-
appear. But sergeant Affasha does not like to smoke. It's bad,
he says. It makes you *mjinga*. You get crazy and then you start
doing crazy things. The devil will walk behind you and you
lose control. He rather drinks. Alcohol. Not the strong liquor
in plastic bags like *Furaha* or *BT*. He mostly drinks *kanyanga*,
a brew made from cassava and maize waste. You drink just

I am grateful to Maria Eriksson Baaz for analyzing the transcription and
translation of the lyrics presented in this text.

some, in the morning, before you go to the roadblock. Then you feel much better, because the roadblock duty is long and boring. But *kanyanaga* helps. And it's very cheap.

The FARDC is a poorly resourced force. It lacks infrastructure, logistics and equipment. There are few barracks, especially in the interior of the vast country. Thus, soldiers either build their own huts from bamboo sticks and banana leaves or live in the houses of civilians. The makeshift *manyata* are far from comfortable. Given that soldiers are rarely given tarps, the improvised roofs cannot withstand the torrential rains that mark the rainy season. In cold, mountainous zones, the bivouacs do not offer sufficient warmth. Therefore, soldiers have to warm themselves around the fire. But there is often no charcoal and not sufficient time to let the firewood dry, causing them to have constant sore eyes from the smoke. Cold also fosters poor health and being sick is bad, for one simply has no money for it.

Congolese soldiers are paid around eighty dollars a month, a derisory amount in the light of the costs of living. Moreover, as for many other state agents in the Congo, there are no social benefits: no health insurance, no family allowances, not even pensions. And soldiers have to pay for everything themselves, including basic necessities like salt, sugar, soap, charcoal, buckets to fetch water, tools, and medicine. While many units have an *Omed* (*officier medicale*), these often have little more to offer than paracetamol, a painkiller. Most of the funds for health care are embezzled. Other funds, like for military operations, intelligence, rations or funerals, undergo the same fate. At every stage of the command chain, a part is "eaten," leaving the soldier at the frontlines with little more than the crumbs. So soldiers who are sick commonly have to pay for health care themselves, or simply leave huge debts at health-care centers. Only when you get seriously wounded on the battlefield does the military have any pity.

Major Dieudonné shows the huge scar on his belly. Soldiers love that, I have noticed, showing me their scars. Evidence of their bravery. And perhaps a road to intimacy? He lacks some vital organs. If it were not for *madame Jeanette*, a French doctor working for a humanitarian organization, he would have been dead. He was shot down in the fight against the CNDP rebels in Rutshuru in 2008. While he was lying in coma in the hospital of Kiwanja, the rebels took the town. All nurses, patients, and doctors fled. *Mais Dieu m'a envoyé madame Jeanette. Le Sauveur m'a sauvé.* It took him over a year to recover, then he was ready to go back to the frontlines. If you are not assigned a good position in the FARDC, you earn no *makuta*, and you have nothing to send home. And the kids need to go to school. So when he could get a position as an S2, an intelligence officer, of a brigade, he did not hesitate. But he needs to move around a lot, conducting investigations, gathering information, including in the most isolated zones. After long journeys by motorcycle on the bad roads of the Kivus, which change into rivers of mud in the rainy season, his thorax often hurts. Thorax, he emphasizes, the medical vocabulary giving more weight to his medical condition. Travelling is also dangerous. *Coupures de routes* or ambushes are a common phenomenon, not only by rebels but also by the multiple bands of bandits roaming the countryside. Being a soldier in the Congo is a *boulot du sacrifice*, Dieudonné emphasizes, you even have to be willing to make the ultimate sacrifice. But we get nothing. Civilians are ungrateful, they give you a *merci bapesa na mbwa*, the gratitude given to a dog. Civilians deride us. They spit at us when we pass by, they shout at us when we get into a minibus, *eeeeeeh soldat utalipa!*, fearing that we will not pay. In the time of Mobutu, civilians flocked to the military as we gave them food. Now it's the opposite. We are reduced to beggars, we have no value in their eyes.

The eastern Congo is littered with armed groups of all shapes and sizes. Nobody can keep count of them, for they wax and wane, almost like a natural phenomenon. The FARDC is supposed to fight this armed potpourri, but does so erratically and ineffectively. Some brigades collude with armed groups in their zone of deployment, concluding gentlemen's agreements of non-aggression and engaging in mutually beneficial economic activities. Other units conduct military operations, but lack means and motivation. In many cases, the rebels simply withdraw into impenetrable forests and mountains, only to return when the FARDC has left. The result is a rebel kaleidoscope, with ever-shifting pieces in constantly changing combinations. "Civilians," a superordinate identity category that ill captures the multitude of social roles played by non-combatants, further contribute to the volatility of the military landscape. In a militarized social order, armed groups are not an exogenous evil preying on society. They are an integral part of society itself, deeply woven into its fabric. Thus, civilians collaborate with and have multiple ties to armed groups, encompassing a range of forced and voluntary interactions. Similarly, the boundaries between the FARDC and civilians are porous, as they form part of the same social webs, allowing both military and civilians to capitalize upon the manifold threads spun between them. Despite the military's bad behavorial track record, in many zones awash with armed groups and bandits, the FARDC is seen as one of the lesser evils. The resulting "you can't live with, you can't live without" configuration introduces a profound ambiguity in civilian-military relations. This ambiguity further feeds into and is fed by the ambiguity that soldiers feel towards soldiering itself, hating and loving it simultaneously.

Rumba

Every morning at 4.00, lieutenant Kalupala wakes up to the tones of one of his favorite songs by Koffi Olomide, an old one, before going for morning prayer. It reminds him of his wife in distant Mbandaka. They used to listen to this song together. It reminds him of his children, whom he rarely sees, but he talks to over the phone. Especially his youngest son, he misses a father. Military staff in the Congo rarely get leave, especially those deployed at the frontlines in the east, for they cannot be missed for prolonged periods of time. At least that's what their superiors say. For those whose family is in the distant western part of the country, like Kalupala, visiting home is simply too expensive. Road infrastructure in the Congo has crumbled due to decades of mismanagement and war, turning the country into even more of an archipelago than it already was, with islands of accessibility amidst seas of isolation. There are no overland connections linking east and west, and a return ticket by airplane costs hundreds of dollars. Lieutenant Kalupala last saw his son after birth, eleven years ago. He has become a stranger to his own children, and to his wife. But he has no choice. The military is a *service commandé*. There is not much he can do but accept. God has predestined him to be a soldier, like his father. But he misses his family, a sense of home, a sense of "normality." Here in the east, there is always war, craziness, one attack after another. He has been fighting since 1996, when the First Congo War broke out. Since then, the country has never fully returned to a state that some would call "peace." Always war. He is tired of it. Home has become a mythical place, it's there yet it's not there. And this longing, this loss, is captured by Koffi Olomide's words. Koffi sings *absence ya moto olinga, ekomisaka lokola mwana ya etike*, the absence of the person that one loves, transforms those who loves into an orphan. And we are like orphans in the military, Kalupala says, we are abandoned by our superiors, by civilians, by our family. There is absence.

As for millions of Congolese, music is a basic necessity of life to Congolese soldiers. Congolese popular dance music that is, generally but inadequately called "rumba" or "soukous" as a catch-all term.[1] The Congolese often call it simply *ndule*, music. Enchanted by the rhythms and tones of Cuban

---

[1] This contribution uses "rumba" as a catch-all term, reflecting generic use.

music, itself a mixture of African and Latin-American styles, Congolese musicians started to color the rumba and the merengue with their own timbres from the 1930s onwards.[2] They added new instruments and introduced innovations in the *seben*, the percussion-dominated instrumental break with rapid rhythms that is characteristic of the rumba. In the 1950s, this evolvement culminated in the creation of orchestras with a distinct style, like l'African Jazz with its famous singer Le Grand Kallé, who produced the immortal song "Indépendance Cha-Cha." Celebrating the Congo's accession to independence in 1960, this song marks the starting point of the gradual melting of music and what might be termed "nation," the sedimentation of the rumba in collective consciousness. Its rhythms, lyrics and associated dances shaping and being shaped by representations of what it means to be "Congolese," music has become a cement that binds this bewilderingly vast and diverse nation together. Even in the Swahiliphone east, the mostly Lingalaphone music is a staple, and the choreography of the latest dance in fashion is mastered in detail. In fact, to many people in the east, rumba is the primary channel through which they become acquainted with Lingala language, which dominates its *paroles*.

One of the Congo's foremost artistic expressions, the rumba provides essential ways of making sense of, coping with, and commenting on the stunningly adverse conditions the country has faced over the last decades. The *paroles* of the rumba and the *cris* of the *batalaku*[3] reflect and are incorporated in common parlance, becoming and drawing upon popular expressions, containing wisdoms, guidelines,

---

2   For the history of Congolese rumba, see Gary Stewart, *Rumba on the River: A History of the Popular Music of the Two Congos* (London and New York: Verso, 2003).

3   Batalaku are "animators" who shout/sing short texts and melodies during the instrumental part of a song (*seben*) in order to liven up the music and dance.

reflections, social categorizations, aspirations and desires.[4] While generally not explicitly political, the lyrics and dances reflect important developments in society, whether related to political changes, economic decline, or the outbreak of wars.[5] Crucially, the rumba is one of the primary means of softening the harsh realities of everyday life by commenting on them with subtle irony or by normalizing them a shared fate. This also applies to the realities generated by the processes of militarization that have swept the country since the 1990s. Commenting on the *kadogo*, the very young soldiers from the east that engulfed the capital after the AFDL rebellion overthrew Mobutu in 1997, Koffi Olomide sings *moto asimbi mandoki batuna kambula na ye te* or "those who carry a gun, one cannot ask their age."[6] Civilians in the eastern Congo continue to draw upon this expression today to reflect upon and criticize the dominant position of the military, as I discovered during over a year of ethnographic field research for a doctoral thesis on civilian-military interactions.[7] Read in the light of the military's tendency to always claim a separate status and place themselves above the law, the meanings of Koffi's words have transformed into a more general expression indicating that "one cannot ask too many questions to the military." This transformation reflects the ways in which the signification

4   For an analysis of popular proverbs and parables in Congolese song texts, see Dieudonné Iyeli Katamu, *Proverbs, paraboles et argot dans la chanson congolaise moderne* (Paris: L'Harmattan, 2010).

5   These themes are developed in Bob White, *Rumba Rules: The Politics of Dance Music in Mobutu's Zaire* (Durham, NC: Duke University Press, 2008).

6   Representations of the military under Laurent-Désiré Kabila in lyrics are analyzed in Milau K. Lutumba, "*Atalaku*, the People's Eye and Memory from 'Ndombolo' to 'Plein na Plein': A Critique of President L.D. Kabila's Regime in Popular Music," *Présence Africaine* 163–164 (2001): 67–79.

7   See Judith Verweijen, "The Ambiguity of Militarizarion. The Complex Interaction between Congolese Armed Forces and Civilians in the Kivu Provinces, DR Congo," PhD. diss., Utrecht University, Faculty of Humanities, forthcoming.

of *paroles* constantly evolves, as they are appropriated, reappropriated and adapted to changing circumstances, like the rumba itself.

Just as civilians in the eastern Congo draw upon the *paroles* of the rumba to comment on the militarization of the social order, the military employs metaphors and expressions derived from popular *paroles* to comment on their interactions with civilians. Describing the perceived irreconcilable attitude and stubbornness of civilians in the east, an FARDC officer once evoked an expression he had heard in a song by Chancelier Desi Mbwese: *kunda ebembe aboya koyoka pardon ya ebembe*, the hearse refuses the apologies of the corpse. The words of the rumba also give meaning to other dimensions of soldiering, such as the desolation of life at the frontlines, poverty, and the anxieties of combat. Recognizable narratives of life, love, and death, these lyrics provide grids of intelligibility to digest adversity, express hopes and desires, and make sense of everyday life, with the omnipresent word *bolingo*, love, often serving as a container for a host of other concepts, and reflecting notions of abandonment, uncertainty and isolation.[8] But the electric rhythms of the rumba also provide, to civilians and military alike, a narcotic way out of sorrow, a way to enkindle erotic fire, to fire oneself up before difficult and dirty jobs, an outlet of energy that helps one to carry on *malgré tout*.[9] In these multiple ways, the rumba is a lubricant of both individual and social life, providing common frames of reference, shared musical, bodily and spoken languages, and enkindling similar passions and hopes. As such, it also breaks down the boundaries between civilians and soldiers, highlighting how, similar to other social phenomena,

---

8   Cf. White, *Rumba Rules*, 178–182.

9   Although Congolese music indeed offers distraction, I do not subscribe to the widely held view that, in the words of Didier Gondola, it turns on "an escapist ethos" that fosters "a fixation with the instant gratification of consumption with its immediacy and certainty," thereby paralyzing criticism. Cited in Katrina Manson, "Sounds of Kinshasa: Music, Dance and Culture Are a Lifeline in Congo," *Financial Times Magazine*, August 29, 2014.

the militarization of everyday life is reflected in and plays out through the dances and paroles of Congolese music.

Bolingo

The *ciné-video*, the movie theater of the poor, is cramped. For as little as 100 *francs congolais* (less than $0.10) you can forget the troubles of daily life. In isolated rural areas, where there is no electricity and few people can afford a television and video-player, the *ciné-video* is the foremost source of organized entertainment. Sergeant Affasha frequently goes. He does not have to pay, he says. They give him free access because he provides security to civilians. Affasha takes another sip of his *Furaha*. Only in the *ciné-video* he drinks that, he now says. It makes him all fired up when he listens to his favorite artists. He likes the music but even more the videos. The Congolese girls are the best dancers in the world! Look at that, he says. The synchronized movements of rows of invitingly dressed women vaguely resemble Kracauer's mass ornament, but there is too much energy, too much irregularity, too much individuality for this to be a mechanical mass ornament. The hip movements are phenomenal. Hips in a dizzying whirlwind. The *bazungu*, the white people, cannot dance like that. Affasha likes to dance as well. He likes the fast, energetic style called *ndombolo*, produced by megastars like Fally Ipupa, shooting rays of ecstasy into the dreariness of life in the village. It is fast like a machine gun he says, *pahpahpahpah*, without charging. When not hunting for the enemy, the days pass by monotonously in the village. We are *ku pori*, in the bush, a non-civilized space, a non-existing space for the outer world, but also a space of exception, especially for armed actors. Sergeant Affasha hates it. The dreariness. Always the same villagers. And there are no easy women in the village. They think you will marry them, that you will pay *mali* [dowry]. The only thing you can do is go to the mining site when you are on patrol. There one can find women who sell their body, *bamalaya, putes, ndumba*. But that costs a lot, you can only go there when the RCA (*Rations Calculées en Argent*), soldiers' salary, has been paid. He suddenly jumps up. He loves this song by Werrason, *le Roi de la Forêt*, from the album *Techno Malewa*. Le Le Le Le Le Le, Le Le Le Le le Le. The latest dance. Le Le Le Le Le Le, Le Le Le Le Le Le. There are almost no lyrics. Le Le Le Le Le Le. Le Le Le Le Le Le. He bumps against a person but he does not care. He is a soldier. He rules. Now.

Major Dieudonné is in a bad mood. His *copine* lied to him about other men she was seeing. Yes, he had a mistress, he confides. Many of the lower ranks take their wife with them on deployment, but those who can afford it do not want to expose their loved ones to the miserable conditions of nomadic military life. It's no life for women. So he often searches for a girlfriend in new deployment locations, to satisfy his needs. What else can he do? Just one, he says, in each place. He is afraid of diseases. But they are treacherous, women. They are only interested in soldiers for the money. If someone else has more to offer, they are gone. And he gets money irregularly. He was to make money out of the sale of wood from *muvula* trees, which is first quality hardwood, but it fell through when the customary chief refused them access to the envisaged part of the forest. He couldn't strike a favorable deal. It was *nzela mokuse*, a shortcut to money, but it failed. And he had already made some down payments. So he was short of money for a while and could not spend anything on his *copine*. He had to borrow money to buy her a *pagne* (cloth) for her birthday. But she still got dissatisfied. You see, we have a saying, *bolingo ya mbongo eyebanaka na tango ya mpiaka,* love that is for sale shows itself in times of scarcity. And the women in this region are very opportunistic, they only care about the money. He also worries about his wife at home. When he speaks to her on the phone her voice is cold. He has been trying to be good to her, always sending money for the children. But he distrusts her. How can he know what she is doing while he is at the frontlines? She is very beautiful. Dieudonné shows a picture on his phone. A typical woman from Kisangani. Beautiful but dangerous. And he fears she does not love him anymore. A common chorus among FARDC soldiers, *alingaka nga lisusu te*, my wife does not love me anymore. But Dieudonné is doubly hurt. He truly loved his mistress, she nourished him like vitamin. Aaaah, *Joyeuse*, ma fleur, *bolingo eleki trop,* love overflows. He feels as much pain in his heart as he does in his thorax after traveling. Like more vital organs are missing. He will not sleep tonight, unless he drinks some *Primus*, the most-sold beer in the Congo. He wants to forget tonight. How could she betray him? It's killing him, killing like the hunters among the Mai Mai,[10] those knowing how to shoot. He searches in his phone in his collection of songs. *L'amour n'existe pas. Il n'existe que des preuves d'amour*, says Koffi in "Fouta Djalon." The song fits his mood.

> Eh amour amour amour amour fulu nini obwaka nayo
>   mawa eh?
> Oh love, love, love, love in what trashcan have you
>   thrown compassion?
>
> Yo moko oteyaki nga kopumbwa
> It was you who advised me to fly
>
> Pona nini obotoli nga mapapu amour
> Why did you take away the wings, love
>
> Eh amour amour amour amour mpo nanini ozongisi nga
>   na zero
> Oh love, love, love, love, why did you return me to zero
>
> Nazalaki mohumbu na yo
> I used to be your slave

---

10   "Mai Mai" is a general name for smaller armed groups that appeal to discourses of autochthony and communal self-defense.

Pona nini okomi kopesa nga liwa avant l'heure ya
    la mort
Why did you try to kill me before the death hour

Eh amour okosuka na nga wapi e
O love, till where do we go

Bolingo pourquoi vraiment osili elengi
Love, why do you no longer give pleasure

Bonbon na nga pourquoi vraiment okomi ngayi
My candy, why have you become sour

Chiclet na nga vraiment osili sukali avant
My chewing gum, you have really lost your sweet flavor
    too soon

ha a a a an Diamo oo na

Diamona okomisa nga pondu ya matanga eh
Diamona you have turned me into the *pondu* [manioc
    leaves] of mourning

Moto nioso na linga akumba oyo ya ye partie
Every person who eats it, takes a piece away

Nga mboto osangisi nga na malangwa
Me a fish of value, you have confounded me with the
    fishes of the first price

Okakoli nga sans qu'otuna motuya na ngai
You have sold me without asking my price

Okomisi nga etula oyo ya simba zigida ah a a a an
You have turned me into an unsellable item at the market
    of Simba Zigida

Diamona ata kala okobanza nga e e
Diamona, one day you will think of me

Banzungu ya kala elambaka ba supu ya bien
The old casseroles make good soups

A près tout moyi ezuwaka se elongi
After all, the sun only reaches my face

Elengi ya makoso ezalaka na mokuwa a a a
The taste of pig feet is in the bones

Okati mandalala nanu na weyi te
You have cut the [palmtree] branches while I have
    not yet died

Somba sanduku olela nga dans pas longtemps
Buy a coffin, you will cry for me not within a long time

Eh bolingo okolela nga ee
Oh love you will cry for me

Ehh bolingo o o o o oh
O love o o o o oh

Visa ya bonheur bazwaka wapi eh?
The visa of happiness, where does one get it?

Ambassade ekangama na libanda ah
The embassy is closed

Tozali ebele molongo molayi.
On the outside we are numerous in a long queue

Tozozela ah
We are waiting

Ata na ndenge ya kundalupé, ata na ndenge ya kundalupé
Even in an illegal manner, even in an illegal manner

[*spoken*]
Pona nini moyi ezuaka moto se kobe na elongi, kasi na
    motema te?
Why does the sun reach the face of people and not the
    heart?

Moke eza ndambo te
A bit does not imply half

Motema Mabe

A vos ordres mon major, je pars tout de suite. The work of *Bureau 2*
(intelligence) never stops. It's *vingt-quatre sur vingt-quatre*. And
it's even worse for him, lieutenant Kalupala says, as he has to
do all the work. His *chef*, the S2 battalion, is from the rebellion. He knows nothing of the work of an intelligence officer.
He does not even speak French. How can he make a *procès-
verbal* (charge sheet)? He, lieutenant Kalupala, has enjoyed a
good education, he attended the *École de Formation d'Officiers*
in Kananga. Three years. Then he did the *École de Prévôté Militaire*, he was trained in the Military Police. So he knows the
law, he knows the *Règlement Militaire*. But his boss knows
nothing. A cow herder from Masisi, thrown into the army.
No military education, nothing! But appointed *major*. Those
are fake ranks, ranks from the bush. Given to people who
have no military mindset. Who only went into the military for
opportunistic reasons, to protect their kith and kin. Not the
country. They lack patriotism. We say *baleli grade bateki mboka*,
those who most need ranks, have sold out the country. But
he, lieutenant Kalupala, he has always remained loyal to the
government. He is a real patriot. Today, with the integration

of all those rebels, those who have always stayed in the loyal-
ist camp are called *ex-gouvernement*. But there is nothing ex
about it, he says. He has always served the government and
he will always serve the government. The lieutenant starts
arranging his things, he needs to go on a mission. Apparently, there have been *dérapages* (troubles) by some of the
newly integrated troops, deployed to an isolated area. And
the S2 of the brigade has pushed his superior to send him for
investigations. He lacks faith in Major Muombamungu, who
is from the same ethnic group as the soldiers that went on a
rampage. They will always protect their brothers, these ex-
rebels. That's how it works in this military today. Tribalism.
Everything is negotiable. *Politique des composantes.*

   They robbed several people of their phone, and some of
their money, on the way home. *Basoldats mubaya*. People no
longer dare to come to the *ciné-video* at night. How will he
make money now, the manager wonders. And the soldiers
who come here never pay. They just enter with guns, imposing themselves. *Nguvu iko yulu ya sheria*, force is above the law,
he says. If he asks them to pay, they tell him to "go and ask
Joseph Kabila."[11] And they drink a lot during the screenings,
they are loud and they disturb people. A bunch of *bamwizi,*
thieves. They live in total insecurity with this brigade. *Les
Malewa,* that's how they call them here. For they steal everyone's mobile phone, and many phones have this song, the
Malewa, as a ringtone. *Leta telephone ya malewa,* they will say.
They especially want the phones with double SIM-card holder.
Sometimes they grab your phone and they give it back if it's
not a double sim. We want the return of the *integrés,* the soldiers of the Integrated Brigade that was deployed here before,
the *ciné-video* manager continues. Regret enters his voice.
Those were good soldiers, we used to call them MONUC, after
the UN mission deployed here. They behaved professionally.
Well-educated military! There was even an officer who taught

---

11   Joseph Kabila is the current president of the DR Congo.

English at the local school. An exemplary brigade. But these new soldiers are different. *Watu ya Nord Kivu.* They are Rwandophones, you see. They speak the same language as the rebels of the FDLR. How can we tell the difference? They behave worse than a rebellion. All goats in the area have disappeared. Women no longer dare to go to the market. People do not cultivate anymore because their harvest will be stolen at night. *Tunateseka*, with this new brigade, *vraiment* we suffer.

□ □ □

Baraia habajue kazi ya jeshi. Civilians do not understand a thing about the military. They are stubborn. We tell them not to walk around at night because the enemy might be close, but they won't listen. Affasha is agitated. He got news about complaints made against his *pleton* by the *chef de groupement*, the highest customary chief in the area, who went to see the battalion commander. But it's the population itself who brings *fujo*, disorder. *Bamai mai ni batoto ya huko.* The Mai Mai are their children. Yesterday they found a wounded Mai Mai officer who was hiding in the village. You see! They are plotting behind your back. *Leo iko muraia, kesho iko adui.* Today it's a civilian, tomorrow it's the enemy. This tribe here has a very difficult mentality. They are not open to outsiders. It's not only the soldiers who face this problem. Other state agents are also seen as *batokambali*, those coming from far. The locals do not like it if outsiders tell them what to do. They keep their secrets, only speaking in their local language, which the soldiers cannot understand. They feel afraid here. If they get into a conflict with someone, this person might mobilize the Mai Mai who will ambush them. Especially the *chef de localité*, they distrust him. His uncle is an important officer in the Mai Mai. Before we came to this village, there were weekly food collections among the population to support the rebels. Now we collect the food. Otherwise it will go to the rebels. And we have to because we have nothing to eat. We haven't been paid for over three months. Three and a half months, no food, no nothing. The brigade commander says he has not received anything from the hierarchy, that there is a blockade in Kinshasa. *Anasema bongo,* he lies. Imagine, *maman,* three months without salary. And the civilians refuse to sell us on credit. Because of their difficult mentality. They distrust us. You go to a shop and they say *ulipe kwanza,* pay first. You see, the population here does not like those who speak Kinyarwanda. They believe we are not Congolese. So they complicate things.

At 19.00 Kalupala's phone is still out of the *réseau cellulaire.* We were supposed to have a *Primus* tonight, but maybe he got stuck on the way. The contingencies of travelling in the rural areas, one never knows when one will arrive. I decide to stay in and work on my field notes. The mood in the whole brigade is plummeting due to months of salary arrears, but certain officers make money out of that, I discovered today. Soldiers desperate to pay their rent and cater to their family's needs borrow money from higher officers at usurious interest rates, a system called *Banque Lambert.* This puts a large part of the soldiers in a position of exploitative dependence on their superiors, feeding anger towards them. *Tu es là?* Kalupala is knocking on my door. We stay in the same lodge. It's a shitty place but usually full of military staff, so perfect for my research. That platoon are *miyibi,* he says, thieves, not worthy the name of soldiers. They steal with the complicity of the commander, giving him a part of the *butin.* And worse, he found, one soldier also raped a woman, although it is not yet sure if it was a case of rape. Sometimes the sex is consensual but the parents start accusing the soldier as they hope to gain something out of it. Rape is business here, because of all this international money. But some soldiers really take women by force. Contrary to the *Règlement Militaire.* In the *Forces Armées Zaïroises* (FAZ) we would not rape, he contends, we were given very strict orders. The mission of the military is *kobatela population na biloko ya bango,* to protect the population and their goods, so you can't take the wife of another person. These young guys have had no education, he says. *Rien dans la tête*. They grew up during the war, all they know is fighting. And they are influenced by this music promoting obscenity. Artists like Fally Ipupa, *ils incitent à la débauche*. We were taught that if there are no women you have to persevere. But then they listen to such music. What music, I ask. I want to know more. He calls a friend whom he knows has an album of Fally. Together they translate.

Moto ya bilengi eza ko flamber
The heat of pleasures flames

il faut l'avoir vu pour ne pas l'oublier
You have to see it in order not to forget

il faut l'avoir gouté pour ne pas l'oublier
You have to taste it in order not to forget

tes jolis lexéts'e [*sic*] braquer nga arme à feu
Your beautiful lexéts'e [*sic*] like firearms

dans un combat sans mercie
In a merciless fight

Un fait divers na canapé ya salon
A "fait divers" on the sofa of the salon

e déclenché conjoncture ya sentiment
Has triggered the conjuncture of sentiment

mon agent secret te fait craquer
My secret agent makes you split

to tshutshi [*sic*] tonga na clandestinité
We have "tshutshied" [*sic*] the needle in the underground

Comme les chauve-sourris le soir
Like the bats at night

Nous aimons vivre dans le noir
We like to live in the dark

Tout ces secrets à se raconteur
All these secrets to tell

Tout ces baisers mbebu yuuu mbebu
All these kisses lips aaa lips

Butu ya mukuse bolingo ya liboma
Short night crazy love

Odope moteur ya fusée na feu d'artifice
You have enkindled the engine of the rocket with
    fireworks

Effet ya bombe epimenté elengi
The effect of a bomb has spiced up desire

petite dose esali grand effet
A small dose has sorted big effects

nazo comprendre te
I do not understand

mais ça me fais danser
But it makes me dance

miliki na nyampuli
Milk to *nyampuli* (sweet coconut milk)

nyampuli na miliki ehh
Nyampuli to milk

elengi
Delicious

paradisier nga oohh
Paradize me oooh

rotation d'amour sentijoie
Rotation of love joyfelt

libérer (glisser) na moselu ba vitesses
To free (glide) with velocities on slippery ground

loboko na nzungu eloko ya nyama ezosala
The hand in the cooking pot this giant work

le jeu de jus d'amour
The game of the juice of love

mongongo ezo tremblotter
Trembling voice

You see, nothing but incitation. This has a bad effect on soldiers, explains Kalupala. When they have not seen a woman
for a long time they start imagining things. They get bad ideas.
We used to turn to music for wisdom. Especially Lutumba
Massiya Simaro, *Le Poète*. He gives advice on all the important matters of life. Love, friendship, ungratefulness, jealousy, rivalry, disease. Really, they have developed it all. He
also likes songs that draw upon the bible. He is a Catholic
and the Bible is very important to him. So he likes the song
Esau from J.B. Mpiana. It refers to deception in life and that
acknowledgement is not of this world. Esau, the eldest son of
Isaac, was going to inherit all power, but they did not like him,
they tainted his reputation. So it was Jacob who obtained the
power. It's very similar to the situation in the FARDC, he says.

We believed that in the FARDC it was us, ex-FAZ, who were going to get the power. We are the older son. But in the end, they gave it to the ex-rebels, and they did everything to taint our reputation. We will not be recognized in this world. In this world, nobody is thankful to us. I have no money, no rank, nothing. There is nothing but *pasi* (suffering). But *Nzambe* (God) he knows that we sacrifice ourselves. Like Jesus. He knows that we are being tricked even by our own *bamikonzi* (superiors). Especially those in Kinshasa. While we are risking our lives here at the frontlines, they are driving around there in expensive cars. Having lots of money. You can hear it in the songs, you know, *mabanga*,[12] when they mention the names of important people. Colonel this and that, General X. Sometimes we do not even know these officers, but we hear that they have money through the songs. Some pay as much as $1000 dollars just for some artist to sing their name.

Suddenly his train of thought bends. He pauses, lighting a *Sportsman*. But we have to learn to be humble, he continues, even towards those from the rebel groups. If we only feel resentment we will be devoured by it one day. Even if he is a rebel and he has no education, he is still a colleague. And I need to greet him, even if I feel a pain somewhere in my heart. We have to be on the guard against *motema mabe*, evilness, just as Félix Wazekwa teaches us. We have to fight it also within ourselves. We have to master our anger. So I listen to *Mokuwa ya Bongo*, the bone of the brain, as they call Félix, *Sagesse Grave*.

Nzambé ozipa ebalé té kasi ezalaka peto,
God, you created rivers without any roof but they are
     pure and clean

---

12   *Mabanga* (stones) is derived from the expression *kobwaka libanga* (to throw a stone), which refers to the practice of citing or singing names of sponsors during performances or on recordings, commonly for payment.

motema ya moto ozipa boni etonda mbindo boyé
Why is the human heart, which is protected by the rest of
   the body, so dirty?

nabotama na mboka moko congo au coeur de l'afrique,
I was born in a country named Congo, in the heart of
   Africa

congo na biso etonda ba richesse,scandale géologique
Our Congo is full of richness, a true geological scandal

congo eza na ba diamant pé na or,zinc cuivre coltan cobalt
Congo has diamonds and gold, zinc, copper, coltan, cobalt

kasi na cours ya geographie babosanaki koyebisa nga que
   congo eza na richesse mosusu kombo motema mabe
But in geography class they forgot to teach me that there
   is another richness named evilness

motema mabé ezali kozanga kolimbisa,kozanga bolingo
Evilness is refusing to forgive, lacking the sense of love

koyoka motema pasi soki moninga azui
To feel bad when another person succeeds

motema mabé ezali koyina sans motif,kotonda jalousie,
   koboya kofuta moto asali mosala na yé
Evilness is hating people without any reason, being
   deeply jealous, refusing to pay somebody who did
   his job

motema mabé ebandaka tango okomi kobomba bolamu ya
   baninga
Evilness starts when you do not want to admit good
   things other people do

motema mabé ezali koboma bien public,kopanza sango ya lokuta
Evilness is destroying public goods, spreading false information about someone

kokanisela moninga mabé, na likambo asali na yé té
Having bad thoughts about somebody, based on things he did not do

Kokufa

For the umpteenth time, the mud is too thick to get the motorcycle through so we need to walk. Many soldiers are jealous of the black rubber boots that I brought but they are no redundant luxury. *Matope* or *potopoto* is omnipresent. Never thought mud would ever come play such a prominent role in my life. But I am happy to get off the motorcycle. Major Dieudonné's AK has been pressing against the flesh of my back. He needs to have it at ready, he said, when going through *La Forêt de 17*, a stretch of forest of seventeen kilometers that is plagued by regular ambushes. As with many crimes in this area, the main perpetrators are so called HUNI, *Hommes en Uniforme Non-Autrement Identifiés* or Non-Identified Uniformed Men. Ghost perpetrators, becoming screens that each person can project their own narratives onto. So the population says the ambushes are laid by the FARDC, dressed up as FDLR rebels and the FARDC says it are the Mai Mai and local bandits. Perhaps it is a bit of all. But in the Congo the truth does not always lie the middle. Major Dieudonné is nervous, the road is windy here and every bend potentially harbors an ambush. He prayed before we left towards the gold-mining area, where the *État-major* of his brigade is established. A long journey of around ten hours, depending on the state of the road, or rather the mud. The rain starts pouring. *Merde*, that implies further delays. We find a shack where people are drinking *mungazi*, palmwine. He needs some, his thorax hurts terribly. We share a bottle. A comfortable shelter.

The *commandant brigade* receives me reluctantly. He believes I am Major Dieudonné's girlfriend. There is not much I can do to reduce the confusion. We are hanging out almost every night. Major Dieudonné is a so-called key informant. I could also call him a friend. Could I? I have never been able to define friendship. There are affective and instrumental dimensions, but what's the composition of the mixture? I need access to insider data. But I also need to maintain distance. Tightrope. Will I be able to maintain the equilibrium? *Hali ya usalama iko sawa*, the security situation is good, the brigade commander thunders. He is clearly not of the educated kind. And he lies. He is trying to keep up a show for the *muzungu*, the white person, but I know that the Mai Mai have been regrouping in the hills nearby, where there are dozens of small artisanal gold mines. *Tunachunga baraia muzuri*, we guard civilians well. Again, he lies. I know for a fact that the chair on which he is sitting was looted from the office of the human rights defender with whom I have been working in this area since last year. A human rights defender who is also involved in the gold trade and rumored to sell to middlemen at the service of the Mai Mai. The contours of good and evil, victim and perpetrator, do not neatly overlap with the military/civilian divide. As I get spun in more deeply myself, the complex social webs linking the military and civilians mainly turn out to be colored in many shades of grey. I am seeing less and less black and less and less white.

Kalupala is jealous, I notice, upon seeing me with Major Dieudonné, who is parading me around like a prize bride. They rotated the second and third battalion, so he is deployed here as well. In the mining area. The main town here has a Wild West type of feel to it. Bustling with *femmes légères* (prostitutes), fortune seekers, misfits, demobilized and many layers of competing military and other state services. And a lot of *ambiance*. The nightlife in this place redistributes some of the money earned during the day. But for the moment there is crisis. The *Malewa*, as this brigade is called, has a stranglehold on the mining sector, and the production has plummeted. And gold is the main currency in this area. Kalupala approaches us with hesitation. He clearly does not want to show his boss that he knows me well from his previous deployment site. Jealousy is omnipresent in this military. But what to think of a force where superiors can take the women of their subordinates? A practice pioneered by Mobutu, but which has survived till this day. Kalupala needs to talk business. There is growing unrest among the *motards,* the motor-taxi drivers who constitute the main source of transport in this zone. One of the trigger-happy newly integrated soldiers accidentally shot down a *motard*, and now there is a *colère generalisée* (general anger). They are on a strike and are blocking the main road, levying fees to pay for the funeral. But they also want to see blood. It's a hotheaded lot, the *motards,* young guys with a macho type of subculture. They have attacked the *carporal* that fired the shot, almost stoning him to death. He is in the hospital now.

We have to celebrate anyway. It's *nouvelle année*, Major Dieudonné says. December 31st. He is already well on his way to getting drunk, one of his main weaknesses. The situation in town has remained tense. But dancing is inviting. Intel officers can never really party, the major explains. The war does not go on holiday. The war takes no rest. The FARDC always has to be on the alert. They get tired of it. To forget the war, only for one evening. To be like civilians. And dance. That's what he wants. Dance with me. The rumba is irresistible. One can simply not remain static. *Nzoto basala mpo eningana.* The body is made to move. But I only like the fast paced songs — dancing is a solo activity for me. Major Dieudonné insists. I need to dance the slow rumba with him. Koffi Olomide and Cindy Le Coeur, that singer with the chillingly beautiful high-pitched voice. We dance. Uncomfortably. His phone rings, he refuses to answer. I continue dancing alone. Nwa Baby by Mr Flavour, a Nigerian artist. Very hot at the moment in the Kivus. Werrason. *Techno Malewa*. The human rights defender teaches me how to dance *Mukongo ya Koba* (the back of the turtle). Many brigade members are on the floor. They are not like soldiers anymore. It seems as if the rumba dissolves the boundaries between the military and civilians, makes us transcend social identities. There are only people dancing and not-dancing. This is the second year on a row I am spending Christmas and New Year's Eve with the FARDC. Home has become a distant abstraction. Indeed, rumba blurs the bound-aries between social categories. Between researcher and what is called "research subject." His phone rings again. This time he answers. *Makelele* (trouble, noise).The shit is going down. An angry mob of *motards* has dragged the soldier out of his hospital bed to finish off the job. They clubbed him to death. There were only two *gardecorps* at the hospital entrance and they were easily overwhelmed. We hear shots in the distance. There is something terribly wrong. When does one stop danc-ing? This is rumba under fire.

A fine intelligence officer, Major Dieudonné says, a true ex-FAZ. Well educated. He died in the harness. Am I overly emotional because I have a hangover or does it touch me? At 03.30 Lieutenant Kalupala died. A brutal visiting platoon commander lost control of himself and started firing on the crowd, shooting down two *motards*. His name? A certain Affasha, one of those troublemakers. He was apparently on a mission to protest payment delays. Those shot down appear to have been civilian collaborators of the Mai Mai, as a gue-rilla attack followed soon after. No less than three bullets pierced Kalupala. There is no specialized surgery in this area. They tried to transport him to the nearest hospital but he died from blood loss on the way. That's life in the FARDC, *ma chérie*, we die by the dozens. It's a system of hell, the FARDC. As Koffi and Papa Wemba sing: *Système ya lifelu, veut dire moto ezopela mais tozozika te*, the system of hell/hell's system, there is an intense fire, but we do not get burnt. I mean the FARDC as a whole does not get burnt. The hell perpetuates itself. The analysis is depressing. Who will mourn for Kalupala? We need to pay honor to him, somehow. An improvised *kilio* (period of mourning). One of his friends proposes we listen to his favorite music. The oldies. He was someone from the old generation, after all. He did not like the new stars too much. *Le Poète*, we need *Le Poète*. I buy everyone a beer. *Testament ya Bowule*.

Oh Yawe, ndenge osala biso
Oh God, we are like you created us

Otinda biso awa na mokili
You sent us to this world

Moto na moto azali na lingomba naye asambelaka
Each person is part of a particular religion

Bamosusu ba sambelaka na Catholique
Some people are Catholic

Bamosusu na Mission Protestante
Some people Protestant

Bamosusu na Armee du Salut
Some are Salvation Army

Bamosusu na ba Musulman
Some are Muslim

Bamosusu na Kimbanguist
Some are Kimbanguist

Bamosusu na Mpeve ya Longo
Some are Mpeve Ya Longo

Bamosusu na Maikari
Some Maikari

Nzambe ndenge toyokaka
God we hear that

Mangomba nyonso wana na tangi
All these religions

Bayebi que soki moto akufi bayebi epayi akendeke
Know where we go when we die

Est-ce que, Yawe, okoki koyebisa bango mokolo mosusu
Yahweh, can you ask them to tell us one day

Epayi to kendeke te
Where we do not go

Nzambe po toyebi epayi towutaka te
God, because we don't know where we come from

Toyeba quand meme epayi to kendeke
Can we know at least where we go next

Okomona mwasi na mobali bavandi
You will see a couple together

Moko na bango akei
One of them dies

Oyo akotikala nzoto ya kokonda, kokonda
The one who will stay alive continues to lose weight

Mikolo ekoeka te alandi moninga, Nzambe mawa
A few days later the one remaining also dies,
   God it's sad

Toyebi epayi to kendeke te
We don't know where we go

Nzambe toztala bobele yo
God, we rely on you only

Bowule pesela biso mbote na bango banso
Bowule greet everyone who has died

oyo toyebi oyo ba kende
On our behalf

Bino ba angelu batu bozali pene pene ya nzambe
You angels, the people who are closer to God

Boyebisela biso ye te
Why don't you talk to him

Ah pitie
Ah mercy

Pinzoli ya likoko

Torn out of the web. Some threads remain. Some have dissolved but will be memorized. Imaginary threads to a distant
web. The field. Months have passed since I left. One morning
the phone rings. Do I already know that Major Dieudonné
has died? They think he has been poisoned. He was at a military base for regrouping and there was heavy competition for

appointments. However, he could have also died because of heart failure, given his fragile state. They simply don't know. They only know he is dead. *Pinzoli na nga lokola ya likoko* (my tears are like those of a fish) *na se ya mayi nani akomona* (under water who will see it?). The wisdom of Koffi consoles. He was not afraid to die, the major used to say. He knew he would not live long. Like most FARDC soldiers that I met. He will live on in the rumba.

Discography

Chancelier Desi Mbwese, "S.T.P. (S'il te plait)," from *Bénédiction: Tous ensemble*, Kiki Productions, 2007, compact disc.

J.B. Mpiana & Wenge BCBG, "Ezau (Nungu Nungu)," from *Anti-Terro*, Badive Music, 2004, compact disc.

Koffi Olomide & Quartier Latin, "Fouta Djalon," from *V12*, Sonodisc, 1995, compact disc.

———, "Parking ya Ba Baba," from *V12*, Sonodisc, 1995, compact disc.

———, "Phaseur," from *Loi*, Sonodisc, 1997, compact disc.

Koffi Olomide & Papa Wemba, "Wake Up," from *Wake Up*, Sonodisc, 1996, compact disc.

Werrason & Wenge Musica Maison Mère, "Techno Malewa Mécanique," from *Techno Malewa Sans Cesse vol. 1*, Diégo Music, 2009, compact disc.

Fally Ipupa, "Nourisson," from *Power "Kosa Leka," vol. 1*, Obouo Productions/Because Music, 2013, compact disc.

Félix Wazekwa, "Motema Mabe," from *Faux Mutu Moko Boye*, Kiki Productions, 2006, compact disc.

TP Ok Jazz, *Testament ya Bowule*, 1986, record.

ULYSSES

Sharon Portnoff

It had been 7 years and after all that labor—building a world
         from a bang—
I deserved a rest.

Your promises had begun to wear thin, and I wanted to return
         to my men—
Those souls vanished like an errant ship to the
Horizon.

"Stay," you say.
And begin again to weave your tale of immortality.
But already I was dead inside and wanted to go back to my wife.

Poor, silent Penelope.
Alone.

I pity and long for her.
I too want to be alone.
With no tale to tell.
As another will.

To yield to the crash of the waves—to let no one say
The world is what it is not and make it so.

Though it may go away with a puff of sails and a whimper.

ACKNOWLEDGMENTS

Thank you to Eileen Joy, who has supported this project from the start, beginning with her warm encouragement of the panel on "Humanity in Crisis: East (of) Europe" at the first Biennial Meeting of the BABEL Working Group in Austin, Texas, in 2010, and continuing through the invitation to prepare a volume on the topic for Punctum Books. I am also grateful to friends and colleagues who have helped along the way. Denis Ferhatović offered editorial advice, feedback, suggestions for contributors, and a wealth of ideas. Uwe Baumann's enthusiasm for the book at a key moment led to it growing beyond its original scope. Berit Andersson transcribed the interview with Cara De Silva and proofed citations throughout. Mary Kate Hurley and Carla Baricz read and commented on material in progress. Peter and Rita Albrecht made work on this volume possible by watching little Maxi. My husband Tim Albrecht helped shoulder the editorial burden, from correcting essays to choosing a title and cover photo. Our conversations about the importance of the arts and humanities have been one of the deep pleasures of working on this book. Most of all, I thank the contributors for their patience, beautiful writing, and heart. This book is dedicated to Mircea Trifu, poet, critic, editor, and much-missed grandfather.

CONTRIBUTORS

Inspired by Denis Ferhatović's essay, we asked the contributors to name one or more books they would never burn, even for fuel.

Tim Albrecht is a research associate at the *Zentrum für Literatur- und Kulturforschung* in Berlin, Germany. He holds a PhD in German literature from Columbia University and has articles forthcoming on Austrian authors Franz Grillparzer and Heimito von Doderer. He is currently working on a book on trust and international law in German literature in the early 1800s. He would never burn James Baldwin's *Another Country* and Norman Lebrecht's *Companion to 20th Century Music* for fuel.

Carla Baricz is a PhD candidate in the English Department at Yale University. She is the assistant editor and translator of Romanian Writers on Writing (Trinity University Press, 2011). Her stand-alone translations have been published in *World Literature Today, National Translation Month, The Fifth Impossibility: Essays On Exile and Language,* and her essays and reviews have appeared in *Words Without Borders, The Los Angeles Review of Books, Observator Cultural,* and *Magyar Lettre Internationale.* She is the author of the chapbook *Timp Rotitor* (Iaşi: Junimea, 2001) and of recent poems in *Foothill, Euphony, Scrisul Romanesc,*

Apostrof, and *Alpha*. Carla is currently preparing a translation and critical edition of Ion Budai-Deleanu's *Țiganiada*, Romania's earliest known epic. One book that she would never burn is Thomas Mann's *Der Zauberberg*.

Greg Alan Brownderville, a native of Pumpkin Bend, Arkansas, is the author of *Gust: Poems* (Northwestern University Press/TriQuarterly, 2011) and *Deep Down in the Delta: Folktales and Poems* (Butler Center Books, 2012). His literary honors include awards from the Sewanee Writers' Conference, the *Missouri Review*, the University of Nebraska, the Porter Fund, and *New Millennium Writings*. Brownderville holds an MFA from Ole Miss, and is currently an associate professor in the creative writing program at Southern Methodist University in Dallas, Texas. The book he would not burn is the King James Bible.

William Coker is an Assistant Professor in the Program in Cultures, Civilizations and Ideas at Bilkent University in Ankara, Turkey, where he has taught courses in literature and intellectual history since 2008. Having received his PhD in Comparative Literature from Yale in 2010 for a thesis on the theory and practice of mimesis in romantic poetics, he has published articles on Keats, Hegel, Jean Paul and Rousseau in *Comparative Literature* and *Eighteenth-Century Fiction*, and chaired the organizing committee for an international conference on "Alternative Enlightenments," held at Bilkent in April 2013. An avid observer of the Turkish and Middle Eastern scene, he has published political commentary on several web-based platforms including *Open Democracy* and *Solidarity*, as well as *LeftEast*, on whose editorial board he serves.

Andrew Crabtree lives in Winnipeg, Canada, in a small apartment where it's always summer. When not teaching living languages (or studying dead ones), he is often found with his nose in a book, and would sooner succumb to the ravages of Canadian winter than burn any of them.

Cara De Silva is a writer, award-winning journalist, scholar (member of the National Coalition of Independent Scholars), lecturer on the topics of food, food history, culture, ethnicity, New York, and Venice. For over a decade, she wrote for *Newsday/New York Newsday*, where her specialty was ethnic New York. She edited *In Memory's Kitchen: A Legacy from the Women of Terezín*, which became one of the *New York Times's* noteworthy books of the year and a *New York Times* and *Publishers Weekly* bestseller. Her recent essays can be found in *Savoring Gotham* (Oxford, 2015), *Words: A Norton Anthology of Food Writing* (Norton, 2015), and the *Oxford Companion to Sugar and Sweets* (Oxford, 2015). Other articles have appeared in the *New York Times*, the *Washington Post, Gastronomica*, and *Saveur*. Her current project is a book on sixteenth century Venice, and she continues to research and lecture on "War and the Food of Dreams." There are hundreds of books she would want to save for humanity (and herself) if the last copies were to be burned. But among the dearest and most precious to her are Sir Thomas Malory's *Le Morte D'Arthur*; *The Collected Works of W.B. Yeats*; and P.L. Travers' *Mary Poppins*, a book that has dazzling meaning, breadth, purpose, and value far beyond what the Disney film has reduced it to in the popular mind.

Irina Dumitrescu teaches medieval literature at the University of Bonn, and writes on literature, food, immigration, and dance. Her scholarly essays have appeared in *PMLA, Anglia, Exemplaria, Forum for Modern Language Studies*, and in various collections. Her belletristic writing has appeared in *The Yale Review, The Southwest Review*, and *Petits Propos Culinaires*. She blogs about dance at atisheh.com and about culinary disasters at foodgonewrong.com. The two books she needs to live are *The Poetical Works of Byron* and *Penguin Modern Poets 10: The Mersey Sound*.

Denis Ferhatović currently works as an Assistant Professor of English at Connecticut College in New London, CT. He has published scholarly articles in *Neophilologus*, *Studies in Philology*, and *Forum for Modern Language Study*, and delivered talks in the US, Western Europe, Turkey, and the Balkans. He would never burn Световом, мојом брат ("The World My Brother"), a collection of poems by Liljana Dirjan.

Susannah Hollister recently returned to the Hudson Valley after teaching as Lecturer and ACLS New Faculty Fellow in the University of Texas system. Her work on poetics, geography, and social feeling has appeared in *Twentieth-Century Literature*, *Contemporary Literature*, *Chicago Review*, *Bat City Review*, and elsewhere. With Emily Setina, she edited Gertrude Stein's *Stanzas in Meditation: The Corrected Edition* (Yale, 2012). Her first literary love was W.B. Yeats, whose poems she could never burn.

Prashant Keshavmurthy is Assistant Professor of Persian Studies in the Institute of Islamic Studies, McGill University. He is the author of *Persian Authorship and Canonicity in Late Mughal Delhi: Building an Ark* (Routledge, 2016). He spends his days looking for real toads in his imaginary rose garden of Classical Persian and Urdu literature. If abandoned on a deserted island with the choice of only one book, he would choose to bring Abdul Qadir Bedil's three-volume Divan or collection of poems whose heft would ensure enough dense poetry would be left over to read after culling it for fire-fuel.

Sharon Portnoff is Associate Professor of Religious Studies at Connecticut College. She holds degrees from St. John's College (Annapolis), Harvard University, and the Jewish Theological Seminary. She is the author of *Reason and Revelation*

Before Historicism: Strauss and Fackenheim (University of Toronto Press, 2011) and co-editor of *The Companionship of Books: Essays in Honor of Laurence Berns* (Lexington Books, 2012) and *Emil L. Fackenheim: Philosopher, Theologian, Jew* (Brill, 2007). Her most recent articles are "'Not in Our Stars': Primo Levi's 'Reveille' and Dante's *Purgatorio*" (*Idealistic Studies*) and "Reenacted Humanism: *If This is a Man* and Primo Levi's 'New Bible'" (*The Value of the Particular: Lessons from Judaism and the Modern Jewish Experience*). Her poems have appeared in *Midstream* and *The Poetry Porch* (www.poetryporch.com).

Anand Vivek Taneja is Assistant Professor in the Department of Religious Studies at Vanderbilt University. He received his PhD in Anthropology from Columbia University in 2013. His research and teaching interests include the anthropology of religion, historical and contemporary Islam and inter-faith relations in South Asia, everyday life and postcolonial urbanism, Urdu literature, and Bombay cinema. His peer-reviewed articles have been published in the *Indian Economic and Social History Review*, *HAU: Journal of Ethnographic Theory* and *Comparative Studies of South Asia, Africa and the Middle East*. His other writings have appeared in *Seminar*, *The Sarai Reader*, *Economic and Political Weekly*, *The Indian Quarterly*, and on the blogs *Chapati Mystery* and *Kafila*. He is currently working on a book on time, Islam, and enchantment in the medieval ruins of Delhi. One book he would never burn is Walter Benjamin's *Illuminations*.

Judith Verweijen is a researcher at the Nordic Africa Institute, Sweden, and the Conflict Research Group at Ghent University, Belgium. She specializes in the study of civilian-military interactions, processes of militarization, and the internal workings of state and non-state armed forces in the Kivu provinces of the eastern DR Congo. She has conducted extensive field research in this area since 2010, including among various army units and rebel groups. Recent publications include articles on rebel-military integration (*African Affairs*, 2013), military economic involvement (*Review of African Political Economy*, 2013), and military interference in disputes between civilians (*Third World Quarterly*, 2014). Due to her drift for exploration, she would always save from being burnt the one book she has not yet read.